Debt, the IMF, and the World Bank

Debt, the IMF, and the World Bank

Sixty Questions, Sixty Answers

By Éric Toussaint and Damien Millet

Translated by Judith Abdel Gadir, Elizabeth Anne, Vicki Briault,
Judith Harris, Brian Hunt, Christine Pagnoulle and Diren Valayden,
with the collaboration of Francesca Denley, Virginie de Romanet
and Stephanie Jacquemont

MONTHLY REVIEW PRESS

New York

Library of Congress Cataloging-in-Publication Data
available from the publisher

ISBN: 978-1-58367-222-8 paper
ISBN: 978-1-58367-223-5 cloth

Monthly Review Press
146 West 29th Street, Suite 6W
New York, NY 10001
www.monthlyreview.org

5 4 3 2 1

Contents

Abbreviations 10

Introduction 11

1. HUMAN RIGHTS, DEVELOPMENT, AND DEBT. 13
   1. What is meant by "developing countries"? 15
   2. Why is the term "development" ambiguous? 19
   3. What is the link between debt and poverty? 22
   4. What are the "Millennium Development Goals" (MDG)? . . . 27
   5. What are the different kinds of debt
      for developing countries? 44

2. THE ORIGIN OF THE DEBT IN DEVELOPING COUNTRIES 47
   6. What part did private banks play in the
      development of developing countries'
      external debts in the 1960s & 1970s? 49
   7. What part did the World Bank play in the
      development of the developing countries'
      external debts in the 1960s and 1970s? 51
   8. How does the World Bank function? 54
   9. What part did the governments of countries
      of the North play in the evolution of the developing
      countries' external debt in the 1960s and 1970s? 61
   10. How was the borrowed money used in the
       developing countries? 63

3. THE DEBT CRISIS 71
11. How did the price of commodities evolve during
    the last quarter of the twentieth century? 73
12. What role did the evolution of interest rates play
    in the 1982 debt crisis? 75
13. Are the World Bank, the IMF, and private banks
    somehow responsible for the debt crisis? 79
14. How did creditors respond to the debt crisis? 82
15. Are there any similarities with the 2007 subprime crisis? ... 88

4. THE IMF, THE WORLD BANK,
   AND THE LOGIC OF STRUCTURAL ADJUSTMENT 93
16. How does the IMF function? 95
17. What are the short-term or shock measures imposed by
    structural adjustment, and what are their consequences? ... 106
18. What are the long-term or structural measures imposed by
    structural adjustment, and what are their consequences? ... 109
19. What is the impact of the IMF/World Bank logic
    on the world food crisis of 2007? 119

5. OTHER INTERNATIONAL PLAYERS:
   THE PARIS CLUB AND THE WTO 125
20. What is the Paris Club? 127
21. Are all the developing countries treated in
    the same way by the Paris Club? 131
22. What is undermining the Paris Club? 135
23. What is the role of the World Trade Organization (WTO)?. 138

6. THE STRUCTURE OF DEVELOPING COUNTRIES' DEBT . . 143
24. Of what does the external debt of
    developing countries consist? 145
25. How has the debt changed since 1970? 150
26. Do developing countries repay debts? 152
27. What about the external public debt of
    developing countries? 155
28. How are the debt-related financial flows directed? 161
29. What about the domestic debt of developing countries? ... 164

7. DECIPHERING THE OFFICIAL DISCOURSE
    ON DEBT RELIEF 171
    30. How did the debt relief initiative come about? 173
    31. What is the Heavily Indebted Poor Countries
        (HIPC) initiative? 175
    32. Has the HIPC initiative achieved its goal?.............. 178
    33. What was contained in the latest debt relief
        announced by the G8 in 2005? 188

8. THE SHAM OF THE DOMINANT MODEL 195
    34. Does Official Development Assistance (ODA)
        help to mitigate the effects of the debt?................ 197
    35. Is micro-credit a solution to the excessive debt
        of developing countries? 204
    36. Have the policies promoted by the World Bank and
        the IMF contributed to the fight against climate change?... 206
    37. What is NEPAD?................................. 211

9. DEBT CANCELLATIONS AND SUSPENSIONS
    OF PAYMENT IN THE PAST............................ 215
    38. Is it impossible to cancel debt?....................... 217
    39. Why do the governments of the South
        continue to repay the debt? 228
    40. What are vulture funds?............................ 230

10. THE CASE FOR CANCELING THE DEBT
    OF DEVELOPING COUNTRIES 237
    41. What are the moral arguments in favor of canceling
        the debt of developing countries?.................... 239
    42. What are the political arguments in favor of canceling
        the debt of developing countries?.................... 241
    43. What are the economic arguments in favor of canceling
        the debt of developing countries?.................... 244
    44. What are the legal arguments in favor of canceling
        the debt of developing countries? 246
    45. What are the environmental arguments in favor of
        canceling the debt of developing countries? 254

46. What are the religious arguments in favor of canceling
    the debt of developing countries?. 257
47. Who owes what to whom?. 261
48. Who has the right to impose conditions
    on debt cancellation?. 262
49. Can the development of emerging countries
    be ensured simply by repudiating their debt?. 264

11. ISSUES RAISED BY CANCELING THE DEBT
    OF THE DEVELOPING COUNTRIES 267
50. Would canceling the debt of developing countries
    cause a global financial crisis ?. 269
51. If developing countries' debts were canceled,
    would the citizens of the North end up paying the bill?. . . . 273
52. Will canceling the debt help reinforce
    existing dictatorial regimes?. 276
53. Should borrowing be avoided at all cost?. 281

12. CONSTRUCTING RADICAL ALTERNATIVES 285
54. What are the alternatives for human development in
    the developing countries?. 287
55. If and when the debt is canceled, how can a new round
    of indebtedness be avoided?. 302
56. What is debt auditing?. 304
57. Are China, sovereign funds, or the Bank
    of the South valid alternatives?. 307
58. Can the developing countries' external public debt
    be compared to the public debt of the North?. 315

13. INTERNATIONAL CAMPAIGN FOR
    DEBT CANCELLATION. 319
59. How did the international campaign
    for debt cancellation start?. 321
60. What is CADTM and how was it born?. 324

Appendix 1: The 145 Developing Countries in 2008. 329
Appendix 2: Glossary 333
Notes 347

A Denise Comanne (1949-2010),
ma compagne d'amour et de lutte
—Éric Toussaint

ABBREVIATIONS

ATTAC	Association for the Taxation of Financial Transactions for the Aid of Citizens
BIS	Bank of International Settlements
CADTM	Committee for the Abolition of the Third World Debt (initials are for the French name)
FAO	Food and Agriculture Organization
G7	Group of the seven most industrialized countries (Canada, France, Germany, Great Britain, Italy, Japan, and United States)
G8	G7 + Russia
GATS	General Agreement in Trade on Services
GDP	Gross Domestic Product
GMO	Genetically Modified Organisms
HIPC	Heavily Indebted Poor Countries
IBRD	International Bank for Reconstruction and Development (World Bank group)
IDA	International Development Association (World Bank group)
IFIs	International Financial Institutions
IMF	International Monetary Fund
MDRI	Multilateral Debt Relief Initiative
NEPAD	New Partnership for Africa's Development
OAU	Organization of African Unity replaced in 2002 by African Union
ODA	Official Development Aid
OECD	Organization for Economic Cooperation and Development
OPEC	Organization of the Petroleum Exporting Countries
PSRP	Poverty Reduction Strategy Paper
SAP	Structural Adjustment Program
TRIPS	Trade Related Aspects of Intellectual Property Rights
UN	United Nations
UNCTAD	United Nations Conference for Trade and Development
UNDP	United Nations Development Program
USSR	Union of Soviet Socialist Republics
WHO	World Health Organization
WTO	World Trade Organization

Introduction

Many countries in the South possess vast natural and human resources, yet since the debt crisis in 1982 they have been bled dry. Repaying an ever-increasing debt makes it impossible to meet even the most basic human needs. The debt has become a subtle instrument of domination, casting the net of a new form of colonization. Policies implemented by debtor countries are too often decided by the creditors rather than by the elected representatives of the countries concerned. The latest debt relief initiative, announced with much fanfare at the Gleneagles G8 meeting in 2005, does not alter the situation. A radically different approach must be considered: the cancellation—no more and no less—of an immoral and often odious debt.

This book counters a number of objections. Won't these countries run the risk of relapsing into unsustainable indebtedness after their external debt is canceled? Won't corrupted and dictatorial regimes get a boost from debt cancellation? Won't taxpayers in the North have to bear the cost of cancellation? What part will be played by new protagonists, such as China, Latin America, sovereign funds, and vulture funds? Is it really a solution to replace external public debt by internal public debt? What's the connection between the debt and the global food crisis that started in 2007? The present book shows that cancellation of the debt is a necessary but not a sufficient condition, that it must go hand-in-hand with other measures such as the recovery of ill-acquired goods, fair distribution of wealth on a global level, and alternative financing approaches. It raises the question: Who owes whom? It supports the claim for reparations put forward by social movements in the South.

These sixty answers to sixty questions explain in clear, precise terms how and why we have ended up in the dead end of debt. Tables and graphs further point to the responsibility of the proponents of neoliberalism, of international financial institutions, of industrialized countries, but also of complicit leaders in the South.

Six years after the publication of *Who Owes Who? 50 Questions about World Debt,* originally written in French and translated into eight languages (English, Arabic, Korean, Spanish, Italian, Japanese, Portuguese, and Turkish), Damien Millet and Éric Toussaint have produced an updated version that decodes the official discourse on the debt and considers possible alternatives for getting out of the present impasse. They develop the moral, political, economic, legal, and environmental arguments that underpin the demand for cancellation of the public debt in developing countries.

CHAPTER ONE

Human Rights, Development, and Debt

What is meant by "developing countries" (DCs)?

First we need to define the vocabulary. The terms *North, rich countries, industrialized countries*, or *Triad* all refer to the countries of Western Europe, North America, Japan, South Korea,[1] Australia, New Zealand, and a number of other high-income countries (see list in Appendix).

However debatable it may seem to group such diverse countries as Thailand, Haiti, Brazil, Niger, Russia, or Bangladesh in one category, we have chosen to adopt the terminology found in the statistics provided by the World Bank and the IMF, as well as the OECD, the UNDP and other UN agencies. Thus we refer to all the countries outside the Triad as *developing countries (DCs)*. In 2008 there were 145 of these according to our figures. Within this category we make the distinction, for historical reasons, between the group of countries designated as Central and Eastern Europe, Turkey, and Central Asia, and the others—Latin America and the Caribbean, Middle East and North Africa, Sub-Saharan Africa, South Asia, East Asia, and the Pacific—classified as the *Third World* or *South* (see list in Appendix).

In 1951, I spoke in a Brazilian journal of three worlds, although I did not actually use the term "Third World." I invented and used that expression for the first time when writing in the French weekly *l'Observateur*, on 14 August 1952. The article ended: "Because finally this Third World—ignored, exploited and despised as was the Third

Estate— also wants to be something." I thus transposed Sieyes'
famous words about the Third Estate during the French Revolution.
—ALFRED SAUVY, French economist and demographer

Distribution of developing countries is as follows:

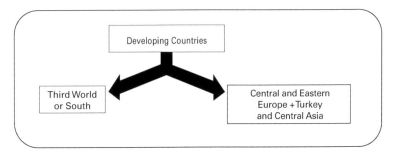

Out of a world population of approximately 6.5 billion people, about 84
percent live in the developing countries:

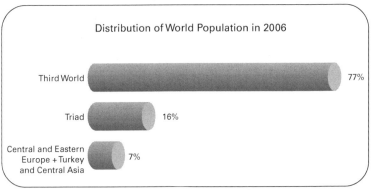

Source: World Bank, *World Development Indicators 2008*[2]

The Gross Domestic Product (GDP) is the conventionally accepted indicator used by many economists to evaluate the production of output
(goods and services; see Glossary) in the world. However, the information
it gives is incomplete, biased, and questionable, for at least four reasons:

1. It does not take into account unpaid work, provided mainly by
   women;

2. Damage to the environment is not treated as a debit;
3. The unit on which the calculation is based is the price of a commodity or a service, and not the amount of work it requires;
4. Inequalities within a country do not enter into the calculation.

Despite these inadequacies, GDP is an indicator of economic imbalances between North and South. GDP and all other monetary figures appearing in this book are expressed in U.S. dollars, since 60 percent of exchange reserves, international loans, and exchanges are still transacted in this currency.

The production of wealth is largely concentrated in the North, and is almost inversely proportionate to the distribution of population:

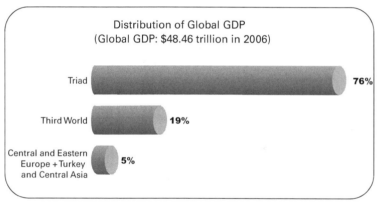

Distribution of Global GDP
(Global GDP: $48.46 trillion in 2006)

Triad — 76%
Third World — 19%
Central and Eastern Europe + Turkey and Central Asia — 5%

Source: World Bank, *World Development Indicators 2008*

Neoliberal globalization has been actively promoted by the authorities of the rich countries, which receive most of the profits, even though this can only be to the detriment of billions of inhabitants in the developing countries, as well as a large number of those in industrialized countries.

The GDP per inhabitant data reveal the economic gulf separating North and South (see below). However, this provides an incomplete overview of the world economic situation, as it ignores the often flagrant income disparities within a given category of country.

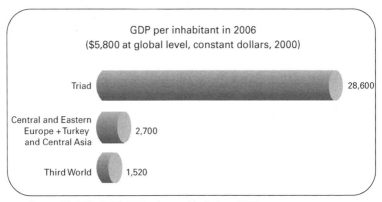

GDP per inhabitant in 2006
($5,800 at global level, constant dollars, 2000)

Triad   28,600

Central and Eastern
Europe + Turkey   2,700
and Central Asia

Third World   1,520

Source: World Bank, *World Development Indicators, 2006*

The income of the world's 500 richest people exceeds the cumulative
income of the world's 416 million poorest people.
—UNITED NATIONS DEVELOPMENT PROGRAM[3]

Consequently, it is never useful to oppose North and South in overall
terms. These words are used only to express a geographical state of
affairs: most of the decisions are made in the North and have serious consequences for the developing countries. Nevertheless, within each region,
the same mechanism of domination exists. In the final analysis—and this
is fundamental—the main problem is the oppression of one part of
humankind (not exclusively located in the South) by another part, much
smaller in number but much more powerful. In other words, very different interests separate those who are subjected to the present system (the
majority of the population in both North and South) from a relative handful of individuals who benefit from it, in both North and South. This
handful of individuals makes up the capitalist class, which is driven by the
desire for maximum profit. It is therefore crucial to make the right distinction, to avoid misunderstanding some of the underlying issues and failing
to identify interesting alternatives.

You would help the poor, whereas I want poverty abolished.
—VICTOR HUGO, *Ninety-Three*

QUESTION 2
Why is the term "development" ambiguous?

The term *developing countries* implies that these countries are making progress and "catching up" with the highly industrialized countries—as if there were only one way to "develop," as if the industrialized countries were the absolute development model, and as if some countries were further along the road than others in the race to make up for lost time. The purpose of using this pernicious term is to have the world believe there is only one possible form of development, and to legitimize the decisions of the major powers and institutions that share the same logic, while marginalizing the arguments of those who affirm that there are other possible, and even essential, alternatives.

The conventional idea of development is far from neutral: it has a strong ideological connotation and conceals choices that can legitimately be questioned. The term was used for the first time in 1948 by U.S. President Harry Truman:

> We must embark on a bold new program for making the benefits of our scientific advances and industrial progress available for the improvement and growth of underdeveloped areas. . . . Their poverty is a handicap and a threat to them and to more prosperous areas. . . . The material resources which we can afford to use for the assistance of other peoples are limited. But our imponderable resources in technical knowledge are constantly growing and are inexhaustible. . . . we should foster capital investment in areas needing development. Our aim should be to help the free peoples of the world, through their own efforts, to produce more food, more clothing, more materials for housing, and more mechanical power to lighten their burdens. . . . All countries, including our own, will greatly benefit from a constructive program for the better use of the world's human and natural resources. Experience shows that our commerce with other countries expands as they progress industrially and economically. Greater production is the key to prosperity and peace.
>
> —HARRY TRUMAN, State of the Union address, 1948

Aimé Césaire deconstructed this message clearly and concisely:

> In other words, big American finance considers the time has come
> to grab all the world's colonies.
>
> —AIMÉ CÉSAIRE, *Discourse on Colonialism*, 1950

Moreover, one should note that this kind of development overlooks two essential aspects: the living conditions of populations and the ecological constraints imposed by the finite resources of our planet. Sixty years after Harry Truman's speech, the words *growth* and *sustainable development* have replaced the term "development." The economic press is full of analyses defending a development presented as healthy and worthy of every kind of sacrifice. The world's financiers point to China and India as models—countries where companies are relocating, growth is strong, labor is dirt cheap, and working conditions deplorable. So what is behind such growth?

The economic growth of a country or region is directly related to the policies practiced there. Similar figures notwithstanding, the reality of the situation can vary widely from one case to another. Economic growth ought to reflect improved living conditions, in particular for the poorest, enabling them to take part in the country's economic activity and thereby encouraging the development of local businesses that will produce goods and services primarily for the domestic market. This is not the case today. Growth today is an unfair process by which the global economy is in the hands of huge transnational corporations whose turnover often exceeds the gross domestic product of certain countries, or even whole continents. These corporations operate all over the planet but are careful to maintain powerful roots back home, where they generally rely on the state to protect their interests (ExxonMobil and Boeing are supported by Washington, Total by the French government). Along with the transnationals of the highly industrialized countries, we now see the emergence of powerful transnationals based in developing countries (Lenovo in China, Petronas in Malaysia, Petrobras in Brazil, Celtel in Africa, Techint in Argentina, Anglo-American in South Africa, Tata in India, and so forth). The capitalists and traditional political elite of the South profit comfortably from this situation, while the economies of their countries are forcibly tied to the global marketplace. In the prevailing model, their growth is largely reliant on exports. This means that commodity prices and outlets for their manufactured goods are essentially dictated by the most industrialized countries. An economic downturn in the United States, Europe, or Japan can have dramatic consequences for the economies of the developing countries because they depend so heavily on exports to these powers. To make matters worse, the export-driven growth model in no way seeks to satisfy basic human rights or emancipate peoples in the South. Indeed, the proponents of unfettered economic growth are careful to conceal its impoverishing potential. In reality, this growth model invariably leads to destruction of the environment, widening inequalities, and unlimited accumulation of wealth to the exclusive benefit of a tiny minority, while an overwhelming majority of the population lives in increasingly precarious conditions.

> What development are we talking about? Are we talking about the neoliberal development model which means that 17 people die of hunger every minute? Is it sustainable or unsustainable? Neoliberalism is to blame for the disasters of our world. We do not put out the fire and we leave the arsonists in peace.
> —HUGO CHÁVEZ, president of Venezuela, World Summit on Sustainable Development, in *Le Monde*, September 4, 2002

Unrestrained growth as advocated by the present system is not self-perpetuating. To last, it must continually create new consumer needs, pollute in order to purify (water, for example), and destroy in order to rebuild (see Iraq). The tsunami of December 2004 was "positive" for Asia's growth (even if it caused the death of 200,000 people), because the industrial areas were not affected and rebuilding is proving long and costly. To sustain the pace of private automobile development, the agro-fuel sector (which we are tempted to call necro-fuel, since vast land areas are given over to its production instead of producing vital food) is booming, thus causing steep price hikes for certain food products and increased undernourishment in many developing countries.

If nothing is changing, as we stand at the threshold of an ecological crisis of historic gravity, it is because the powerful ones of this world don't want it to. . . . The pursuit of material growth is for the oligarchs the only way of making societies accept extreme inequalities without questioning them. Growth creates a surplus of apparent wealth which oils the system without changing the structure.
—HERVÉ KEMPF, *How the Rich Are Destroying the Earth*, 2008

However, all peoples have the right to decide their own future and to possess the means to do so. This will not be possible as long as growth remains the absolute indicator of the world's state of health.

Not simply to develop but to develop oneself.
—JOSEPH KI-ZERBO, *A quand l'Afrique?*, 2003

Although we are aware of all the inadequacies and semantic manipulations, we will be using the notion of developing countries throughout this work to allow us to refer to the statistics of the international institutions and place them under scrutiny. Thus the reader can check the data we ourselves provide with the data presented on these institutions' websites and in their printed publications.

QUESTION 3
What is the link between debt and poverty?

The living conditions of the most deprived have deteriorated almost everywhere over the last twenty-five years, though at different times, to different degrees, and at different rates from one country to another. Several developing countries were hit very early in the 1980s (Latin America, Africa, and some countries of the former Soviet bloc), and others were struck only in the second half of the 1990s (Southeast Asia). International institutions have persisted in demanding repayment of the external debt. They make it a priority in their pursuit of dialogue with the governments of indebted countries. Yet we shall see that there have been many reasons why governments of the South could refuse what is often an immoral and illegitimate debt. Political, economic, social, moral, legal, ecological, and religious arguments have their place in this debate. But the pressures exerted by the great moneylenders of the world and the collusion between the ruling classes of North and South are such that most leaders of developing countries have no qualms about seeing their populations crushed by the burden of debt.

> In government, you can only spend what you can earn. I inherited a very big debt that we are trying to reduce, while respecting a primary surplus of 4.25 percent, because it is important to show my creditors that I am responsible, that I pay my debts.
> —LUIS INÁCIO LULA DA SILVA, president of Brazil, in *Le Monde*, May 25, 2006

The debt in the developing countries has become far too heavy for their fragile economies and has crushed all attempts at development. According to Kofi Annan, UN secretary general in 2000, debt servicing (see Glossary) represented that year an average 38 percent of the budget of the Sub-Saharan African states. In 2006, the government of Ecuador devoted 38 percent of the budget to debt repayment while allocating 22 percent to total social spending (health, education, and so on). For some countries, debt servicing accounts for more than half the budget.

If the developing countries follow the directives of the IMF (see Q16), the World Bank (see Q8), and the other creditors, they have no choice but to instigate strict budgetary austerity measures. That means reducing public spending to a minimum in areas such as education, health, maintenance of infrastructures, public investment in projects—which generate employment—and housing, not to mention research and culture. The only areas where spending is not reduced are those related to defense, security, and, to a lesser degree, the law.

In order to pay these colossal sums, governments have to procure hard currencies (mainly dollars, but also euros, yen, sterling, Swiss francs, among others) in which repayments must be made. To do this, priority is given to export programs: accelerated exploitation of natural resources (such as minerals, oil, and gas) and the unchecked development of cash crops (such as coffee, cocoa, cotton, tea, ground nuts, and sugar).

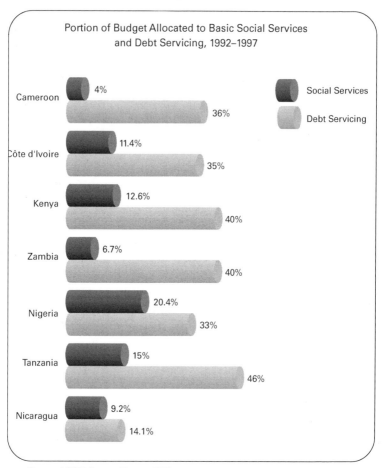

Source: UNDP, *Poverty Report, 2000*

Monocultures, which are particularly dangerous because they create a state of dependency on a number of transnational corporations that control the market, are becoming the rule. Subsistence crops are abandoned, which often means that countries that export agricultural produce have to import the foodstuffs they need. Thus Madagascar exports luxury-grade rice and is forced to import poor-grade rice to feed its people.

With the dramatic rise in prices for basic food products (wheat, rice, maize) that started in 2006, countries that abandoned their food sovereignty under pressure from the World Bank and the export-based agribusiness sector have suddenly become destitute. This has been the case for the majority of African countries, but also for the Philippines, Bangladesh, and several Latin American countries, including Mexico.

In the battle to produce export goods as cheaply as possible, no attention is paid to how people will manage to live or survive. Existing social benefits—meager as they are—are often placed at risk, and working conditions are deplorable.

In addition, the often abundant and varied natural resources of the developing countries are overexploited—a cause of serious environmental problems. According to some forecasts, the main natural resources of certain countries will run out in a few decades, for example, oil in Gabon, Colombia, and Ecuador, where production is decreasing. Many countries in the South are alarmed at the ravages of deforestation from intensive logging of tropical hardwoods or the increased size of areas sown for crops.

According to many scientists specializing in biodiversity, our planet is today facing the sixth major crisis to threaten the extinction of species since the beginning of life on Earth. But though the five previous crises were spread over very long periods of time, the present crisis seems to be unfolding in a much shorter time span because of the decisive role played by human activity. The red list published by the International Union for Conservation of Nature and Natural Resources (IUCN) named over 16,000 species threatened with extinction in 2006: one mammal out of four, one bird out of eight, one amphibian out of three.[4]

In an attempt to address these dire threats, the United Nations organized in the summer of 2002 the World Summit for Sustainable Development in Johannesburg, South Africa. The then president of France, Jacques Chirac, spoke with emotion, in his inimitable manner: "Our house is burning and we are taking no notice. Nature, mutilated and overexploited, can no longer reconstitute itself and we refuse to admit it."[5] Yet at the same time he was one of the most fervent defenders of the neoliberal economic model and intensive farming.

The relationship between debt and human development needs to be made clear. The debt mechanism enables the international financial institutions, the states of the North, and the multinationals to exert control over the economies of the developing countries and, for a derisory sum, lay hands on their resources and wealth, to the detriment of the local population. It is a new form of colonialism regulated by the implementation of Structural Adjustment Programs (see Q17 and Q18). Decisions concerning the South are not made by the South but in Washington (in the U.S. Treasury or at the head office of the World Bank or the IMF), in Paris (at the head office of the Paris Club—the group of creditor states of the North (see Q20) or in the London Club (which represents the big banks of the North—and does not always hold its meetings in London). This is why the fulfillment of basic human rights is not given priority. The priority is to satisfy economic, financial, and geopolitical criteria, such as debt repayment, opening up borders to capital and merchandise, and privileged treatment for countries allied to the great powers.

The latest figures published showed that the amount repaid by developing countries to service the external public and private debt totaled $520 billion in 2006. If we take only the servicing of the external public debt, which falls under DC state budgets, the figures were approximately $190 billion in 2007.[6] If we now add servicing of the internal public debt, also paid for out of state budgets and at least three times more than the servicing of the external public debt according to the World Bank, we arrive at the astronomical sum of $800 billion repaid each year by public authorities for their external and internal debt.[7]

Comparatively, official development aid from rich countries (a problematic issue in itself; see Q34) barely reached $104 billion in 2007. These very costly repayments deprive the developing countries of precious resources to combat poverty efficiently.

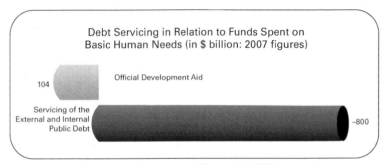

Debt Servicing in Relation to Funds Spent on
Basic Human Needs (in $ billion: 2007 figures)

104   Official Development Aid

Servicing of the
External and Internal   –800
Public Debt

Source: World Bank; *Global Development Finance 2008*; OECD

We see, therefore, that debt repayment is bleeding the economies of developing countries and that new loans are insufficient to make up for the outflow. For example, in 2007 the public authorities of developing countries repaid $19 billion more than they received in loans that year. The net transfer[8] was negative and reached $760 billion for the period 1985–2007, whereas for the same period the external public debt more than doubled, growing from $600 billion to $1.35 trillion!

If we now take as our period of reference the years 1970–2007, we realize that the external public debt of developing countries has increased from $46 billion to $1.35 trillion, and that during this time, their public authorities have repaid $460 billion more than they have received in the form of loans.

Today, it is clear that debt is one of the main obstacles to the fulfill-ment of basic human needs, at the heart of a system of domination by the rich countries of all the developing countries.

> Just as cultivated and well-informed Frenchmen knew what their troops were doing in Vietnam and Algeria, cultivated and well-informed Russians knew what their troops were doing in Afghanistan, and cultivated and well-informed South Africans and Americans knew what their "auxiliaries" were doing in Mozambique and Central America, so today, cultivated and well-informed Europeans know how children die when the whip of the debt cracks over the poor countries.
> —SVEN LINDQVIST, *Exterminate All the Brutes*, 1997

QUESTION 4
What are the "Millennium Development Goals" (MDG)?

In 2000, on the occasion of the United Nations Millennium Summit, the world's leaders pledged their commitment to a number of goals (see below), complete with figures, called "Millennium Development Goals," with a view to finding solutions to the problem of poverty by 2015. What happened next?

Halfway through the allotted time span, it was clear that the project was bound to fail. Why? First, because the wrong principles were used to address the problem. How can the central goal be to reduce poverty and not eradicate it when humanity has more than enough resources to free the poor from deprivation? Moreover, these patently ill-adapted and inadequate goals will very likely never be achieved, since some of them concern areas where the situation has in fact deteriorated in many countries. Despite all the statistical manipulations designed to conceal this reality,[9] the present poverty reduction policies are proving to be a lamentable failure.

In its *Global Monitoring Report 2007*, the World Bank provides a precisely documented account.[10] Although it is pleased to report on slight progress in this region or that, the World Bank figures show without a doubt that basic human rights throughout the developing countries are largely ignored.

> The unprecedented combination of resources and technology at our disposal today makes the argument that the 2015 targets are beyond our reach both intellectually and morally indefensible. We should not be satisfied with progress that falls short of the goals set—or with half measures that leave whole sections of humanity behind.
>
> —UNITED NATIONS DEVELOPMENT PROGRAM, 2006[11]

OBJECTIVE 1—ERADICATE EXTREME POVERTY AND HUNGER
• *Halve, between 1990 and 2015, the proportion of people whose income is less than $1 a day*

An emblematic measure—but the choice of an arbitrary threshold ($1 a day) poses a problem. Can one really claim to have eradicated poverty when a person's revenue reaches this threshold? What precise standard of living does this reflect? Also, the goal is not to halve the number of poor people but the proportion of poor people. Given the demographic growth factor, the number of poor people "authorized" by this objective will increase as time goes by and the goal will be easier to reach than it would seem at first glance.

According to the World Bank, in 1990 there were 1.245 billion people living on less than $1 a day. In 2004, there were 986 million and forecasts for 2015—very optimistic, especially in view of the international crisis that started in 2007—quote a figure of 721 million. So where's the failure? The World Bank proclaims a victory, with the famous proportion dropping from 28.7 percent to 11.7 percent.

On a global level, if the published goal can still be achieved, it is primarily thanks to China, where one person out of five currently lives. The irony of the situation is that China has not strictly respected the World Bank's requirements. According to the Chinese authorities and the World Bank, poverty is declining a little but the inequality gap is widening dramatically. The World Bank acknowledges that the poorest Chinese have seen their situation deteriorate over the last ten years. This is partially due to reduced state intervention and the introduction of paying health and education schemes. In other parts of the world, countries that have more readily accepted the recommendations of international institutions and their dubious medicines have often seen poverty increase: Sub-Saharan Africa, Latin America, and South Asia are still very far from the target.

It must also be remembered that these figures do not reflect the precarity factor. For example, the number of people living on less than $2 a day would evolve far more slowly: 2.647 billion in 1990, 2.556 billion in 2004, a forecasted 2.095 billion in 2015. It comes down to this: a few hundred million have seen their revenue creep just over the threshold of $1 a day while hundreds of millions of others have seen their situation worsen.

Finally, the method of calculation used by the World Bank to arrive at these figures is questionable. First, the World Bank defines poverty in terms of the purchasing power of a person earning $1 a day during a given year. Then it converts this poverty threshold into other currencies and for

Number of People with Income of Less than $1 per Day (in million)

REGION	1981	1990	2004	2015 est.
Sub-Saharan Africa	168	240	298	326
Latin America and the Caribbean	39	45	47	38
South Asia	473	479	462	304

Source: World Bank

the other years. According to several specialists, including Thomas
Pogge, currently professor of philosophy at Yale University, "Its method
of carrying out this double conversion is extremely problematic."[12]

In September 2008, the World Bank acknowledged that there were
major errors in its calculations concerning the poverty situation worldwide.[13] In fact, though "World Bank poverty estimates [are] strengthened
by better cost-of-living data," the result is in itself a brutal challenge to the
statistics produced by an institution that has been going through a serious
legitimacy crisis for several years. Suddenly the World Bank has discov-
ered that "400 million more people live in poverty than earlier thought."
That's more than half the population of Sub-Saharan Africa!

According to a World Bank information release, "1.4 billion people in
the developing world (1 in 4) were living on less than $1.25 a day in
2005," whereas previous estimates were around one billion people. With
errors like this in World Bank poverty calculations, the whole edifice of
current international anti-poverty policies falls apart. Structural
Adjustment Programs (cuts in social spending, cost recovery in health
and education sectors, export-driven agricultural policies and reduction
of basic food crops, loss of food sovereignty, and so forth) imposed by the
IMF and the World Bank since the start of the 1980s have worsened living conditions for hundreds of millions of people.

> The World Bank's methods of calculation are extremely dubious. It
> seems probable that with a more plausible method, we would see
> a more negative trend and much more widespread poverty. . . .
> Determination of a plausible concept of poverty must start from a
> conception of human beings' basic needs, and then go on to see
> what are the different products that would help us meet those
> needs. We must therefore consider as poor those people who can-
> not afford an adequate set of these products. . . . Such a concept of
> poverty corresponds to the usual meaning of the term "poverty"
> and moreover ensures that the poverty thresholds calculated on
> this basis for different years and different places have a uniform
> meaning. It is only by developing such an alternative method that
> we can reliably study the quantitative dimensions of the problem
> of world poverty. As long as the World Bank's present method and

the resultant data hold their monopoly in international organizations and in academic research on poverty, we cannot claim to be
dealing with the problem seriously.

—THOMAS POGGE, Yale University, 2006

The World Bank's optimism about poverty reduction is ill-founded,
to say the least.

> • *Halve, between 1990 and 2015, the proportion*
> *of people who suffer from hunger*

According to the United Nations Food and Agriculture Organization,
848 million people were suffering from hunger between 2003 and 2005,
a figure comparable to that of 842 million between 1990 and 1992.[14] But
the situation has deteriorated seriously due to the explosion in food
prices (see Q19), and in September 2008 the FAO revised its estimate
upward, judging the trends to be "worrisome": 923 million people were
undernourished in 2007, including 907 million in the developing world.
Of these, 583 million were living in Asia, 273 million in Africa and the
Middle East, and 51 million in Latin America.[15]

The dramatic world food situation reminds us of the fragile balance
between world food supplies and the needs of the world's inhabitants, and the fact that the previous commitments to hasten
progress toward the eradication of hunger have not been fulfilled.

—JACQUES DIOUF, FAO director-general, May 2008

According to the World Bank, "Nearly one-third of all children in
developing countries are estimated to be underweight or stunted, and an
estimated 30 percent of the total population in the developing world suf-
fers from micronutrient deficiencies. Undernutrition is not only a threat
to progress with poverty reduction; it is the underlying cause of over 55
percent of all child deaths."

In this context, the sharp rise in the price of cereals on world markets
since 2006 is especially alarming. The FAO has established "a list of 22

countries that are particularly vulnerable due to the high levels of chronic undernourishment (over 30 percent), combined with a high dependency on grain and oil product imports." Certain countries show alarming percentages: the proportion of people suffering from hunger is 73 percent in Eritrea, 72 percent in the Democratic Republic of the Congo, and 67 percent in Burundi.[16]

OBJECTIVE 2—ACHIEVE UNIVERSAL PRIMARY EDUCATION
• *Ensure that, by 2015, children everywhere, boys and girls like,*
will be able to complete a full cycle of primary schooling

The United Nations Educational, Scientific and Cultural Organization (UNESCO) reports with some severity on the meager progress made toward education for all: "Steady progress has been made since 1998 . . . but the pace is insufficient for the goals to be met in the remaining ten years to 2015."[17] In point of fact, some 100 million children are still not receiving primary education: 55 percent of them are girls. Schooling rates are even dropping in twenty-three countries.

Beyond these figures, the United Nations Millennium Project Overview Report 2005 declares that "most poor children who attend primary school in the developing world learn shockingly little."[18] UNESCO writes that "fewer than two-thirds of primary school pupils reach the last grade in 41 countries (out of 133 with data)." Thus there is a gap between the fact of attending school and the lasting acquisition of basic skills.

The World Bank has managed to become an obligatory partner in educational policymaking, edging out UNESCO by exploiting its status as creditor and sponsor.[19] This fact is significant. The World Bank is basically against the notion of free essential public services. It would like to see education privatized: low-cost public schools for the poor and quality private schools for the upper middle class and the wealthy.

The path to program failure is thus charted in advance. According to the World Bank, "38 percent of developing countries are unlikely to reach 100 percent primary completion by 2015 and another 22 percent of countries, which lack adequate data to track progress, are also likely to be

off track." Yet a free, high-quality education system is vital if a country is
to make the structural changes required to leave poverty behind.

OBJECTIVE 3—PROMOTE GENDER EQUALITY
AND EMPOWER WOMEN
• *Eliminate gender disparity in primary and secondary education,
preferably by 2005, and in all levels of education no later than 2015*

For UNESCO, "The 2005 gender parity target has been missed by 94
countries out of 149 with data: 86 countries are at risk of not achieving
gender parity even by 2015; 76 out of 180 countries have not reached
gender parity at primary level, and the disparities are nearly always at the
expense of girls."

UNESCO goes on to say: "Women are less literate than men: worldwide, only 88 adult women are considered literate for every 100 adult
men, with much lower numbers in low-income countries such as
Bangladesh (62 per 100 men) and Pakistan (57 per 100 men)."

Yet education for girls would have a positive impact on many areas of
daily life. Gender inequalities are still flagrant at various levels of human
development. The fight for gender parity must be a priority, first of all on
principle, but also because women play a leading role in improving family
well-being and in the general development of communities and countries.

OBJECTIVE 4—REDUCE CHILD MORTALITY
• *Reduce by two-thirds, between 1990 and 2015,
the under-five mortality rate*

For the World Bank, "Progress on child mortality lags other MDGs,
despite the availability of simple, low-cost interventions that could prevent
millions of deaths each year. Oral rehydration therapy, insecticide-treated
bednets, breastfeeding, and common antibiotics for respiratory diseases
could prevent an estimated 63 percent of child deaths. Yet in 2005 only 32
of 147 countries were on track to achieve the child mortality MDG.
Moreover, 23 countries reveal stagnant or worsening mortality rates."

The World Bank refrains from mentioning that with the debt crisis and structural adjustment policies (see Q17–18), it has indiscriminately imposed privatization of the health system, recovery of costs, reduction of health personnel, and employee precarity. All these measures have helped worsen a situation that had seen major advances over the period 1950–70.

Thus each day more than 30,000 children die of diseases that are easily curable. For the UNDP, these children are the "invisible victims of poverty."[20] In reality, it would often take only "simple and easily provided improvements in nutrition, sanitation and maternal health and education" to prevent these deaths.

OBJECTIVE 5—IMPROVE MATERNAL HEALTH
• *Reduce by three-quarters, between 1990 and 2015,*
the maternal mortality ratio

Each year more than 500,000 women die of pregnancy- or childbirth-related complications. In Sub-Saharan Africa, one woman out of sixteen dies of complications arising from pregnancy or childbirth, as opposed to one woman out of 3,800 in the developed countries. According to the World Bank, there is little reliable data available, but where progress has been noted, it is "highly concentrated among richer households. *"*

By enforcing the application of cost recovery policies in the area of health care, and especially prenatal care and delivery, the IMF and the World Bank contribute significantly to continuously high mortality rates. Many poor women no longer have access to prenatal care and delivery assisted by trained medical staff, simply because they cannot pay for it. Governments that agree to adopt such policies are guilty of non-assistance to persons in danger.

OBJECTIVE 6—COMBAT HIV/AIDS, MALARIA,
AND OTHER DISEASES

• *Have halted by 2015 and begun to reverse the spread of HIV/AIDS*

By the end of 2006, 39.5 million people had been infected with the AIDS virus (two-thirds of them in Sub-Saharan Africa), which is 2.6 million more than in 2004 and 6.1 million more than in 2001. The epidemic is spreading fast in Asia and in the ex-Soviet bloc, while the number of AIDS sufferers in Sub-Saharan Africa is presently stationary. Nearly three million people died of AIDS in 2003, an increase of more than a third compared with the 2.2 million in 2001.

The situation is worsening, and yet the world has the financial means, the technical know-how, and the therapies to eradicate the disease. Too few sufferers have access to anti-viral medicines: only 700,000 were able to take advantage of them for the first time in 2006, as against 4.3 million new cases.

If so few have benefited, it is largely because the pharmaceutical laboratories jealously guard the patents that ensure juicy profits at the expense of the sick, and refuse to allow replication of the molecules their research-and-development departments have developed. This replication would allow Third World patients to benefit from treatment at a more reasonable price. To block initiatives by governments in the South to produce generic treatments, the pharmaceutical multinationals first took the legal route. In 1997, the South African government adopted health laws authorizing local companies to produce anti-AIDS treatments, or to import them, thus bypassing the patents of the big pharmaceutical companies. The same year, thirty-nine big companies lodged a complaint against South Africa.[21] Former U.S. vice president Al Gore, at the time head of the commission for bilateral relations between the United States and South Africa, took the matter in hand so as to defend the interests of the U.S. pharmaceutical industry.[22] Finally, under pressure from international public opinion and protests organized on U.S. university campuses, these multinationals withdrew their complaint. But far from admitting defeat, they took their cause to the World Trade Organization (WTO; see Q23). On November 14, 2001, during the Doha summit in Qatar, the WTO authorized a country to grant a national company a "compulsory license" allowing it to copy a treatment in the case of an emergency health situation. But only a few countries (India, Brazil, and Thailand, for example) had a pharmaceutical industry with the capacity to produce such treatments, a fact that very much reduced the scope of the measure. A few days before the next WTO summit in Cancún, Mexico, in 2003, another agreement was signed allowing the countries of the South, after having met drastic conditions, to bypass patent law and import generic treatments for AIDS. However, importing AIDS medicines proved to be neither easy nor effective: it was only four years later, in July 2007, that Rwanda, and Rwanda alone, managed to do so. In other words, the WTO fulfilled its mission at the behest of the multinational drug companies: ensure their mega-profits by slowing down access to generic medicines for patients in the South. Is it surprising then that the Millennium Goal concerning AIDS cannot be achieved?

> I don't see why the pharmaceutical industry should be expected to make special efforts. No one asks Renault to give cars to those who don't have one.
>
> —BERNARD LEMOINE, director general,
> French Pharmaceutical Industry Union, 2000

- *Halt by 2015 and begin to reverse the incidence of malaria and other major diseases*

In 1970, the annual number of malaria-related deaths had dropped to 500,000. A major reverse trend followed: according to the World Bank, malaria now affects between 300 million and 500 million people per year and causes some 1.2 million deaths, mainly children, most of them in Africa. Malaria has even reemerged in regions where it had completely disappeared, such as the Middle East and Turkey.[23] The World Health Organization (WHO) reports that a child dies of malaria every thirty seconds.[24] The economic consequences are easy to imagine.

Yet solutions do exist. The use of insecticide-treated mosquito nets[25] and artimisine-based combination therapy (ACT) have been a real step forward, because in an "aggressive" environment this combination of measures is the most effective way to avoid contracting malaria. But it is never enough, and must be accompanied by public policies designed to sanitize the environment, in particular by reducing areas of stagnant water, which are an ideal breeding place for mosquitoes. The problems of housing and drainage are therefore closely related to the problem of malaria.

Tuberculosis is another major cause of mortality, with at least 1.6 million deaths per year, mainly among the most deprived, who have no access to treatment (195,000 of them HIV-seropositive). For the United Nations, the total number of cases continues to rise: 8.8 million in 2005, including 7.3 million in Sub-Saharan Africa and Asia.[26]

It is vital that we learn from the failure of recent international health policies. It is vital that we question new institutional structures in the health care sector (public-private partnerships, the emergence of "global health governance" in which partnerships and private foundations take the lion's share). But above all, it is vital to understand that health is mainly determined by social factors, and to attack the structural causes of the present failures: the spread of malaria and tuberculosis is closely related to undernourishment, insufficient income, absence of health equipment and trained staff, together with the neoliberal policies dictated by the World Bank and the IMF and meekly implemented by the overwhelming majority of governments. In consequence, improved public health must go hand-in-hand with increased spending on health care (increased services, improved quality, more staff, higher wages, better training), investment in sanitation services (waste water drainage and purification), and thorough reform of the neoliberal model that has brought about the collapse of health systems. The damage inflicted on people's health is just a fraction of the overall social damage inflicted by this model.

It is an indication of the topsy-turvy world in which we live that the doctor, the schoolteacher or the nurse feel more threatened by financial conservatism than does the general and the air marshall.
—AMARTYA SEN, Nobel Laureate in Economics,
"Health and Development," keynote address to the 52nd World
Health Assembly, Geneva, May 1999

OBJECTIVE 7—ENSURE ENVIRONMENTAL SUSTAINABILITY
  • *Integrate the principles of sustainable development into*
    country policies and programs and reverse the loss of
    environmental resources

The issue of fishing is crucial because fish provides at least 20 percent of the required daily animal proteins to 2.6 billion people. But the situation has become critical. From the FAO: "Overall, more than 75 percent of world fish stocks for which assessment information is available are reported as already fully exploited or overexploited (or depleted and recovering from depletion), reinforcing earlier observations that the maximum wild capture fisheries potential from the world's oceans has probably been reached."[27]

In addition, still according to the FAO, "the world lost about 3 percent of its forest area from 1990 to 2005," which means that 105 million hectares (one hectare equals about 2.47 acres) of forest have disappeared in fifteen years.[28] Regional disparities are considerable: deforestation almost exclusively affects countries that are characterized "*by developing economies and tropical ecosystems,*" and some very vulnerable populations depend on forests for their very existence.

Deforestation not only leads to loss of biodiversity and food sources for many people, but it is also a major factor in the current climate change process. According to the United Nations, "Between 18 and 25 percent of greenhouse gas emissions is caused every year by deforestation." In this regard, CO_2 emissions are the main threat: they are still on the rise, and even doubled in Southeast Asia and North Africa between 1990 and 2004. In 2006, China for the first time became the world's leading source of CO2 emissions in absolute figures. But let's not be misled by this fact. Carbon dioxide emissions, which in 2004 amounted on a global scale to 29 billion tons, are principally the consequence of the activities of rich countries if correlated to the number of inhabitants.

In 2004, the rate in developed regions was an average 12 tons per person. West Asia, which among developing regions had the highest emissions per inhabitant, produced less than half this amount. The rate per inhabitant in Sub-Saharan Africa amounted to less

than a tenth of CO_2 emissions produced by one person in the
developed world.

—UNITED NATIONS

According to the UNDP, we need to devote 1.6 percent of global
GDP (some $720 billion in 2008) simply to stop accelerating climate
change, but the United States regularly opposes any restrictive and quan-
tifiable commitment. The responsibility of the prevailing economic
model is insufficiently emphasized. As the UNDP stated in its 2007
World Report on Human Development, "One of the hardest lessons
taught by climate change is that the economic model which drives
growth, and the profligate consumption in rich nations that goes with it,
is ecologically unsustainable."

• Halve, by 2015, the proportion of people without sustainable
   access to safe drinking water and basic sanitation.

Access to water has high symbolic significance in the context of the
Millennium Goals. The UNDP made it the theme of its 2006 World
Report on Human Development. Behind this vital issue one senses the
failures and cowardice of the world's big moneylenders.

The present situation is nothing short of disastrous. According to the
UNDP: "Today, some 1.1 billion people in developing countries have
inadequate access to water, and 2.6 billion lack basic sanitation." The
human consequences are, of course, intolerable. The UNDP report states
that absence of hygiene and lack of drinking water "together contribute to
about 88 percent of diarrhea-related deaths—more than 1.5 million—
among children under five. Infestation by intestinal worms caused by
defecating in the open affects hundreds of millions of mainly school-age
children, resulting in reduced growth, physical debilitation and cognitive
impairment." Everything, in other words, is interrelated.

Most of the 1.1 billion people categorized as lacking access to clean
water use about 5 litres a day—one-tenth of the average daily
amount used in rich countries to flush toilets. . . . Dripping taps in

rich countries lose more water than is available each day to more
than 1 billion people.

—UNITED NATIONS DEVELOPMENT PROGRAM

The scale of inequalities in the matter of access to water is enormous. Yet the problem is far from insoluble, since it is rooted *"in institutions and political choices, and not in water availability."* To ensure universal access to drinking water and basic sanitation (waste water drainage is fundamental to radically reduce the number of malaria-carrying mosquitoes) decisive opposition must be mounted against privatization of water distribution services as imposed by the World Bank to the huge benefit of the transnationals that control the sector (in particular Suez Ondéo, Véolia Water, and Saur). And protests must also be made against the inclusion of water in the WTO's General Agreement on Trade in Services (GATS). Fortunately, several successful grassroots protests have taken place (for example in Bolivia in Cochabamba in 2000 and in El Alto in 2003–4) demanding that water be returned to, or remain under, public control.[29] The right to drinking water must be made tangible by ensuring that every person has fifty liters of drinking water per day. Water is one of the world's public goods, and an important part of our world heritage.

- *Achieve by 2020 a significant improvement
in the lives of at least 100 million slum dwellers*

By definition, a slum is a dwelling in which at least one of the three basic housing conditions is lacking: adequate hygiene, an adequate water supply, a lasting structure, or sufficient living area. Increased urban migration and demographic growth have severely aggravated the problem. In 2005, according to the United Nations, 37 percent of town dwellers lived in a slum, but the figure is 62 percent for Sub-Saharan Africa and even 80 percent for Chad, the Central African Republic, and Ethiopia.

As of 2008, more than half the world's inhabitants live in an urban environment, and in the developing countries the majority live in underprivileged urban communities. For Mike Davis, this situation reflects the violence of capitalistic plunder organized on a planetary level: the shantytown is the only possible horizon for the impoverished masses because "with a veritable great wall of high-tech border controls preventing any migration to rich countries, shantytowns remain the only really accessible solution to the problem of storing this century's human surplus."[30]

OBJECTIVE 8—DEVELOP A GLOBAL PARTNERSHIP
FOR DEVELOPMENT

This last goal is a departure from the previous ones and gives a precious insight into the logic behind the Millennium Development Goals. It outlines the methods necessary for trying to achieve the first seven goals. The deception becomes evident: the developing countries are to have no say in the measures to be applied and no right to question the macroeconomic choices decided on by the major powers.

Let us look more closely. The targets set out are of two kinds:

1. They are declarations of good intent such as "Address the special needs of landlocked developing countries and small island developing states"; "In cooperation with developing countries, develop and implement strategies for decent and productive work for youth"; or "Deal comprehensively with the debt problems of developing countries through national and international measures in order to make debt sustainable in the long term."

2. They carry strong restrictions that go counter to an improvement of the human situation in developing countries: "Develop further an open, rule-based, predictable, non-discriminatory trading and financial system." This implies giving up all forms of protection for the economies of the South and is strangely reminiscent of the famous "free and undistorted competition" that caused a majority of French and Dutch citizens to vote no to the referendum on the European constitutional treaty in the spring of 2005.

The text states: "Address the special needs of the Least Developed Countries (includes tariff- and quota-free access for Least Developed Countries' exports, enhanced program of debt relief for heavily indebted poor countries and cancellation of official bilateral debt, and more generous official development assistance for countries committed to poverty reduction)." This text proposes waiving quotas and tariffs for the poorest countries, a charitable measure, but does not question the commercial rules that are unfavorable to poor countries, nor the history behind the debt, nor what is contained in development assistance.

The sentence "In cooperation with pharmaceutical companies, provide access to affordable essential drugs in developing countries" means finding a solution to health issues, including the AIDS problem, based on the requirements of the pharmaceutical multinationals, which rules out any acceptable solution!

Finally, "In cooperation with the private sector, make available the benefits of new technologies, especially information and communications technologies." This also means not displeasing the private companies in the sector, whereas this target concerns public policies on which everything depends.

So not only do the Millennium Development Goals lack the necessary vigor to achieve the objective of basic rights for all, but worse, they dis-

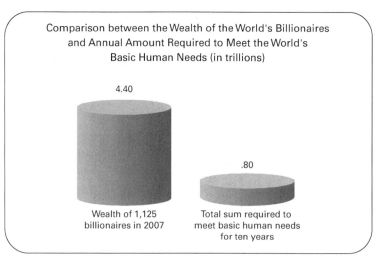

Comparison between the Wealth of the World's Billionaires and Annual Amount Required to Meet the World's Basic Human Needs (in trillions)

4.40

.80

Wealth of 1,125 billionaires in 2007

Total sum required to meet basic human needs for ten years

Source: *Forbes*, 2008

creetly impose economic measures that have already proven powerless to reduce poverty wherever they have been scrupulously applied. Beyond the obvious failure is the subtle deception: the MDG has no chance of succeeding since they refuse to question the current economic context that has made them necessary.

MORE INTERESTING FINDINGS ON HUMAN DEVELOPMENT

According to figures published by *Forbes* magazine in March 2008, the number of the world's billionaires in 2007 was estimated at 1,125 (as opposed to only 946 the previous year and 497 in 2001). The cumulative wealth of these billionaires amounts to $4.4 trillion, while it was "only" $1.5 trillion six years earlier.

Now it would take $80 billion over ten years, or a total of $800 billion, to provide the world's people with essential social services, such as access to basic health care, drinking water, sanitation, and primary education.[31] This would be a fundamental step forward for a large majority of the world's inhabitants.

An exceptional 20 percent tax on the fortunes of this handful of billionaires would provide the amount needed to ensure, in ten years, the fulfilment of elementary needs for all.

This example is simply to show that solutions exist. To identify the others, we must understand the mechanisms in play.

> When I give food to the poor, I am called a saint. But when I ask why the poor have nothing to eat, I am called a troublemaker.
>
> —DOM HELDER CAMARA, Brazilian prelate,
> archbishop of Recife from 1964 to 1985

What are the different kinds of debt for developing countries?

Before examining the impact of debt, the vocabulary of debt needs to be clarified. The total debt of a country is composed of *internal debt* (contracted with a creditor within the country) and *external debt* (contracted with a foreign creditor). A country's internal debt is in principle expressed in terms of the local currency.[32] This debt has risen sharply since the second half of the 1990s with the impetus of the World Bank and the IMF. In 2007, the internal public debt was three times the amount of the external public debt. This is why we will be returning to the subject later (see Q29). For the time being, we will give our attention to the external debt.

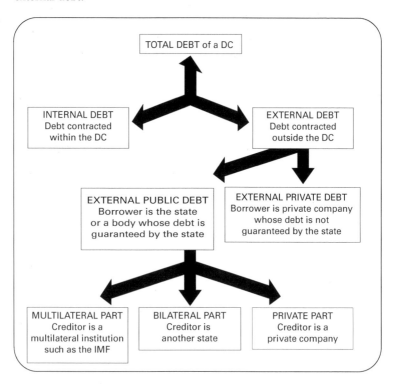

TOTAL DEBT of a DC

INTERNAL DEBT
Debt contracted
within the DC

EXTERNAL DEBT
Debt contracted
outside the DC

EXTERNAL PUBLIC DEBT
Borrower is the state
or a body whose debt is
guaranteed by the state

EXTERNAL PRIVATE DEBT
Borrower is private company
whose debt is not
guaranteed by the state

MULTILATERAL PART
Creditor is a
multilateral institution
such as the IMF

BILATERAL PART
Creditor is
another state

PRIVATE PART
Creditor is a
private company

I do not say that we should isolate ourselves as we have done in the past, but we are not trying to find out how to develop our country. We are trying to sell our country to foreigners for them to develop it in our stead. We are still in a colonial relationship whereby, in our own land, we Africans own nothing, control nothing, and manage nothing. Soon we will be foreigners in our own land.

—FRED M'MEMBE, editor, *The Post* (Zambia),
in *Washington Post*, April 22, 2002

The external debt of developing countries can be broken down into external public debt and external private debt. The former is contracted by the government—the state, local authorities, or public bodies—or by private bodies whose debt is guaranteed by the state. *External private debt* is contracted by private companies—for example, the subsidiary of a Northern multinational firm, a local bank, or a local industrial company—and is not guaranteed by the state.

Moreover, the external public debt can be broken down into three parts depending on the nature of the creditors. The *multilateral part* is lent by a multilateral institution such as the IMF, the World Bank, or another international institution.[33] The *bilateral part* is lent by another state, and the *private part* is lent by a private bank or comes from debt securities issued by the country on an international financial market. Two further debt categories exist, based on the length of the loan:

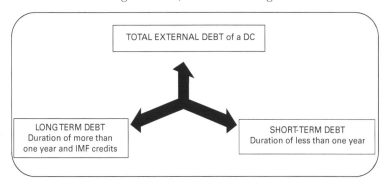

It should be noted that short-term debts are largely private debts. The great majority of developing countries' external public debts are long-term debts.

CHAPTER TWO

The Origin of the Debt in Developing Countries

QUESTION 6
What part did private banks play in the development of developing countries' external debts in the 1960s and 1970s?

After the Second World War, the United States unilaterally set up the European Recovery Program (ERP) for the reconstruction of Europe, a program better known as the Marshall Plan. Proposed by George C. Marshall, U.S. secretary of state in 1947, the plan made it possible for the United States to massively invest in the European economy, with a double objective in mind: help European countries get back to a position in which they could again be trade partners, and prevent a deteriorating economic situation that might have led to a shift by these countries to the Soviet bloc. About $13 billion (the equivalent of $100 billion today) went to Europe, including over $11 billion in the form of gifts.[34] Sixteen West European countries benefited from it (the USSR and East European countries were not eligible).

As a consequence, more and more dollars were sent out of the United States, their territory of issue, and started circulating around the world. In accordance with the agreements signed at Bretton Woods in 1944, which were valid until August 1971, these dollars could be converted into gold. But the U.S. monetary authorities had no interest in exchanging large quantities of gold present in their vaults against dollars they had issued themselves, especially since an excessive number of returning dollars might have led to an inflationary surge. From the

Countries Benefitting from the Marshall Plan (in $ million)

COUNTRY	TOTAL	GIFTS	LOANS
Austria	677.8	677.8	–
Belgium / Luxembourg	559.3	491.3	68.0
Denmark	273.0	239.7	33.3
France	2,713.6	2,488.0	225.6
Germany (FRG)	1,390.6	1,173.7	216.9
Greece	706.7	706.7	–
Iceland	29.3	24.0	5.3
Ireland	147.5	19.3	128.2
Italy (including Trieste)	1,508.8	1,413.2	95.6
Netherlands (and Indonesia)	1,083.5	916.8	166.7
Norway	255.3	216.1	39.2
Portugal	51.2	15.1	36.1
Sweden	107.3	86.9	20.4
Turkey	225.1	140.1	85.0
United Kingdom	3,189.8	2,805.0	384.8
Regional	407.0	407.0	–
TOTAL	**13,325.8**	**11,820.7**	**1,505.1**

Source: *The Marshall Plan: Fifty Years After,* 2001

second half of the 1960s they attempted to curb the demands for dollar conversion into gold and did all they could to keep the greenbacks in Europe. This is why in the 1960s Western banks were brimming with dollars—called "eurodollars." To ensure that they got profit from them, these private banks lent them at favorable conditions to countries of the South wishing to finance their development, particularly newly independent African and Asian countries and rapidly industrializing Latin American countries. They also covered—or indeed systematically encouraged—misappropriation of these loan funds, thus retaining or recovering a much appreciated control over the decisions made by the leaders of borrowing countries, whose actual motivations could be far removed from the wish to develop their countries. These banks offered leaders the opportunity to open numbered accounts where such misappropriated money could be safely stashed away. Should the countries concerned threaten to suspend repayment of the debt, the banks could counter this threat by blocking the numbered accounts. This complicity on the part of the banks allowed them to establish strong customer loyalty with these leaders.

From 1973 onward, the rise in the price of oil, commonly called the first "oil shock," ensured comfortable revenues to oil-producing countries. This money was placed in Western banks, thus increasing the problem. Again, banks offered petrodollar loans at enticingly low rates to countries of the South (including oil exporting countries such as Mexico, Algeria, and Venezuela that had no need of them and yet contracted heavy debts). All those loans from private banks made up the private part of the developing countries' external debts. While it was close to zero in the early 1960s, this private part of the debt reached $36 billion in 1970 and $380 billion in 1980.

QUESTION 7

What part did the World Bank play in the development of the developing countries' external debts in the 1960s and 1970s?

The second player contributing to the indebtedness of the developing countries during these two decades is the World Bank. An institution created at Bretton Woods in 1944, it considerably increased its loans to Third World countries from 1968 onward, when Robert McNamara was head of its board.

It is interesting to have a closer look at McNamara's background. He became the first CEO of the Ford automobile corporation who was not a member of the Ford family, but after five weeks he left this position and became U.S. defense secretary in the administration of John F. Kennedy (1961–63), a position he retained under President Lyndon Johnson (1963–68). McNamara was thus one of the main devisers of U.S. military aggression in Vietnam. He exerted repeated pressure to send more and more troops, totaling over 500,000 soldiers. Around one million

Vietnamese communist fighters and four million civilians were killed between 1961 and 1975. Years later, McNamara would recognize his errors: "We of the Kennedy and Johnson administrations who partici-pated in the decisions on Vietnam . . . were wrong, terribly wrong." He added: "I had never been to Indochina and did not understand its his-tory, its language, its culture, its values. I wasn't sensitive to it at all. . . . When deciding about Vietnam we were facing a terra incognita."[35] In 1968, when the situation had become inextricable for the United States, McNamara was appointed head of the World Bank.[36] In this position he acted like a missionary in an anticommunist campaign.[37] He experienced this period in his life as a resurrection.[38]

McNamara's arrival in 1968 marked a change in World Bank policies. It started using debts as a geopolitical weapon. From 1968 to 1973 (five years), the World Bank granted more loans than from 1945 to 1968 (twenty-three years). It also invited countries of the South to contract massive loans to finance the modernization of their exporting industry and be more closely connected to the world market. Indeed, McNamara pushed countries of the South to accept the conditions of these loans, pointless infrastructures, insufficient social budgets, expensive dams erected in destroyed landscapes, and crushing debts. The bait was sim-ple: cash made available to established governments without any attempt at curbing corruption and embezzlement. In exchange, leaders accepted more recommendations from the World Bank.

The support the World Bank brought to countries of the South was related to the geopolitical interests of the Western bloc. After 1945, in the Cold War period, the two superpowers, the United States and Soviet Union, accumulated weapons and indirectly confronted each other through the extension of their respective influence zones.

In the 1950s and 1960s, numerous countries initiated their own par-ticular political experiments. After a relentless struggle, first Asian then African countries managed to bring about their decolonization. Some of those countries wanted to move away from the former colonial powers. They convened for the first time in 1955 in Bandung (Indonesia). The conference marked the emergence of the Third World on the interna-tional scene and was the prelude to the nonaligned movement that was launched officially in 1961 in Belgrade (Yugoslavia).

The World Bank took action to counter Soviet influence and various nationalist and anti-imperialist initiatives. This action was in the financial sphere. As French MP Yves Tavernier put it in the *French National Assembly Finance Commission's Report on the Activities and Control of the IMF and the World Bank*, the World Bank's role "was to win over Third World custom, to the advantage of the Western world."[39] It was a two-edged strategy: the loans would be used both to support allies and to bring recalcitrant countries under control.

On the one hand, the World Bank supported the United States' strategic allies in different regions of the world (Joseph Mobutu in Zaire from 1965 to 1997, Mohamed Suharto in Indonesia from 1965 to 1998, Ferdinand Marcos in the Philippines from 1965 to 1986, the Brazilian dictatorship from 1965 to 1980, Augusto Pinochet in Chile from 1973 to 1990, the generals Videla and Viola in Argentina from 1976 to 1983, and many others) to strengthen the zone of U.S. influence.

I cannot see why we should allow a country to become Marxist just because its people are irresponsible.

—HENRY KISSINGER, as Salvador Allende was overthrown
by Pinochet's coup in Chile, 1973

On the other hand, the World Bank granted conditional loans to the countries that were trying to implement policies that did not comply with the dominant capitalist model. It would offer them the capital needed, telling the countries that the export of the raw materials they produced would be enough to cover both repayments and the modernization of their industrial base. By this means the World Bank acquired the right of inspection over the economic policies practiced by these countries, and strove to halt the development of independent policies and to bring a number of leaders who were moving away (for example, Gamal Abdel Nasser in Egypt from 1954 to 1970 and Kwame N'Krumah in Ghana from 1960 to 1966) back under the aegis of the great industrial powers. When any leaders of the South refused to comply, the Northern powers did not hesitate to overthrow and replace them with dictators (the assassinations of Patrice Lumumba in the former Belgian Congo in 1961, Sylvanus Olympio in Togo in 1963, and Salvador Allende in Chile in 1973—and later, Thomas

Sankara in Burkina Faso in 1987) or to organize military intervention (U.S. interventions in Santo Domingo in 1965, in Vietnam, in Cuba through the intermediary of mercenaries in 1961; French interventions in Gabon in 1964 to restore Léon M'ba to power, in Cameroon several times during the 1960s in support of the government of Ahmadou Ahidjo, in Chad several times since 1960, in the Central African Republic in 1979 to install David Dacko after a putsch, as well as many others). When such actions fall through, as was the case with Fidel Castro, who has been in power in Cuba since 1959, the country is ostracized from the community of nations, which is once again a high price to pay.

Geopolitical data are thus part of the backdrop to the process through which countries of the South contract debts. Those loans, added to those from other multilateral institutions,[40] functioning along the same kind of logic, and to the IMF loans, made up the multilateral part of the public external debt. From a low in the early 1960s, this multilateral part increased to $8 billion in 1970, then $58 billion in 1980, including $32 billion to the World Bank and $12 billion to the IMF.

> In many cases, the loans were used to corrupt governments during the Cold War. The issue was not whether the money was improving a country's welfare, but whether it was leading to a stable situation, given the geopolitical realities of the world.
>
> —JOSEPH STIGLITZ, chief economist of the World Bank from 1997 to 1999, Nobel Laureate in Economics in 2001, appearing on French televison's *L'Autre mondialisation* (The Other Globalization), on Arte, March 7, 2000

QUESTION 8
How does the World Bank function?

The International Bank for Reconstruction and Development (IBRD) was established at Bretton Woods in July 1944, at the initiative of forty-five countries that had come together for the first monetary and financial conference of the United Nations. In 2010, it had 186 member countries, with Kosovo its latest addition (it joined in June 2009).[41]

The IBRD's initial objective was to supply public capital for the reconstruction of Western Europe after the Second World War so that it remained a stable ally and provided a market for the goods manufactured in the United States. It later shifted to financing the development of countries of the South, becoming, to use its own words, "a vital source of financial and technical assistance to developing countries around the world."[42] The strategy behind this assistance is hardly neutral and most controversial.

Four other bodies were later formed, to make what is known as the World Bank Group. These are the International Finance Corporation set up in 1956 to finance the private sector in developing countries; the International Development Association (IDA), in 1960, for loans to the poorest countries; the International Center for Settlement of Investment Disputes in 1966 (a court to which private companies can turn if they consider that their interests were slighted by a public decision, even if democratically taken by a government that cares for people's living conditions); and the Multilateral Investment Guarantee Agency in 1988 to encourage investment in the developing countries.

The World Bank includes the IBRD and the IDA. In 2008, it had about 7,000 employees in Washington, D.C., and 3,000 in some thirty country offices worldwide. From 1945 to 2007, the IBRD lent $433 billion to its various borrowers while the IDA committed itself for $181 billion. At the end of 2005, the World Bank had $200 billion in outstanding credit.[43]

Each member country appoints a governor as its representative, generally its finance minister, and in some cases the minister for development. They come together within the Council of Governors (CG), which is the World Bank's executive committee. The CG sits once a year (in the fall, two years out of three in Washington) and decides on general objectives. It is in charge of major decisions, such as accepting new member countries or preparing the annual budget. The spring meeting (held jointly with the IMF in Washington) evaluates the impact of the World Bank's and IMF's actions. These two meetings are the occasion of protest demonstrations and increasingly visible counter-summits.

For the daily running of the World Bank's missions, the Council of Governors delegates its power to a Board of Executive Directors that consists of twenty-four members. Each of the following eight countries has the privilege of appointing a director: United States, Japan, Germany, France, United Kingdom, Saudi Arabia, China, and Russia. The other sixteen are appointed by groups of countries with often surprising boundaries: a rich country is usually associated with a group of developing countries, and of course it is the rich country that holds a seat on the Board of Executive Directors and votes for all countries in the group. For instance, an Austrian director represents the group that consists of Austria, Belarus, Belgium, Hungary, Kazakhstan, Luxembourg, Slovakia, Czech Republic, Slovenia, and Turkey.[44] Similarly, Switzerland is head of the group that is ironically called Switzistan since it consists of Azerbaijan, Kyrgyzstan, Poland, Serbia, Switzerland, Tajikistan, Turkmenistan, and Uzbekistan.

The Board of Executive Directors, which meets at least three times a week, elects a president for five years. Against all democratic principles, a tacit rule determines that the position must go to a U.S. representative who has been selected by the U.S. president. The Board of Executive Directors merely sanctions the choice. From 1995 to 2005, the ninth president of the World Bank was James D. Wolfensohn. Formerly director of the Business Bank sector of Salomon Brothers in New York and Australian-born, he had to become a U.S. citizen to be appointed to this strategic post.

In March 2005, U.S. President George W. Bush appointed Paul Wolfowitz president of the World Bank. As a former Pentagon top gun, Wolfowitz was one of the instigators of the invasion of Iraq in March 2003 by an armed coalition led by the United States. In April 2007, while he posed as a leader of the struggle against corruption, Wolfowitz was strongly criticized for having granted a substantial rise in salary to his partner, Shaha Riza, who also worked at the World Bank. Wolfowitz, who had been caught in the act, had no option but to resign, despite the continued support of George W. Bush. According to the same tacit rule, he was replaced by a Bush appointee, namely Robert Zoellick, who had been successively head of the first President Bush's cabinet in the early 1990s, trade secretary in the early 2000s, and number two at the State Department next to Condoleezza Rice from January 2005 to June 2006. After that, he worked for Goldman Sachs, one of the world's biggest investment banks.

Still, there is considerable room for making global institutions more democratic. Many proposals have been made to remove such patently undemocratic practices as the veto on the UN Security Council and the way the leaders of the IMF and World Bank are selected.

—UNDP, *Global Human Development Report*, 2002

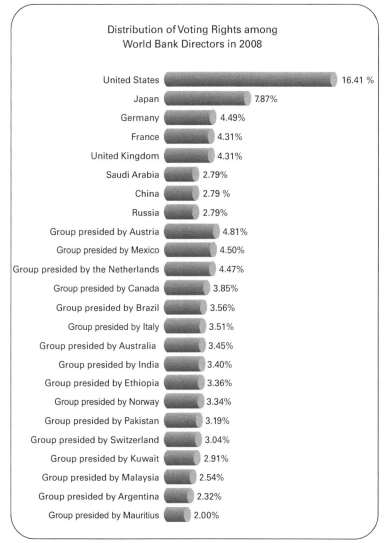

Distribution of Voting Rights among
World Bank Directors in 2008

United States	16.41 %
Japan	7.87%
Germany	4.49%
France	4.31%
United Kingdom	4.31%
Saudi Arabia	2.79%
China	2.79 %
Russia	2.79%
Group presided by Austria	4.81%
Group presided by Mexico	4.50%
Group presided by the Netherlands	4.47%
Group presided by Canada	3.85%
Group presided by Brazil	3.56%
Group presided by Italy	3.51%
Group presided by Australia	3.45%
Group presided by India	3.40%
Group presided by Ethiopia	3.36%
Group presided by Norway	3.34%
Group presided by Pakistan	3.19%
Group presided by Switzerland	3.04%
Group presided by Kuwait	2.91%
Group presided by Malaysia	2.54%
Group presided by Argentina	2.32%
Group presided by Mauritius	2.00%

Source: World Bank

Each member country in the World Bank is granted a quota that determines what influence it can (or cannot) have within the bank. From this quota (established in relation to its economic situation), a complicated reckoning determines the country's voting power: a fixed part of 250 votes and a part that is proportional to its quota. Contrary to what happens at the UN General Assembly, where each country has one vote (with the major exception of the Security Council where five countries hold a right of veto), the World Bank system amounts to $1 = one vote. But contrary to a company's shareholders, a country cannot decide to increase its World Bank quota in order to have more weight. The system is completely locked.

As can clearly be seen, the developing countries cannot counter countries of the Triad, which have a lion's share and thus can ensure the ways and means of systematically imposing their policies.

The scandal is not limited to the unfair distribution of voting rights. The United States fashioned this institution to its requirements and managed to enforce the rule that all major decisions can be made only with a majority of 85 percent of votes. As it is the only country with more than 15 percent of voting rights, it can, de facto, block any major change in the World Bank. The E.U. countries that could also reach 15 percent are generally content with ratifying the U.S. position. On the few occasions when

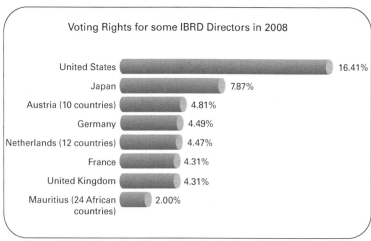

Voting Rights for some IBRD Directors in 2008

United States — 16.41%
Japan — 7.87%
Austria (10 countries) — 4.81%
Germany — 4.49%
Netherlands (12 countries) — 4.47%
France — 4.31%
United Kingdom — 4.31%
Mauritius (24 African countries) — 2.00%

Source: World Bank

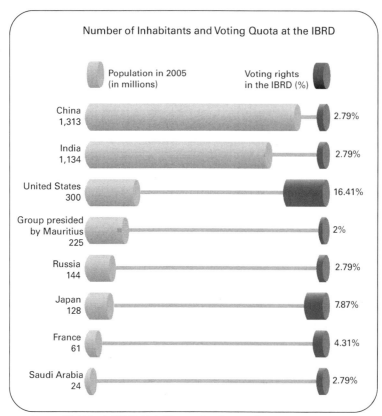

Number of Inhabitants and Voting Quota at the IBRD

Population in 2005 (in millions)

Voting rights in the IBRD (%)

China 1,313 — 2.79%
India 1,134 — 2.79%
United States 300 — 16.41%
Group presided by Mauritius 225 — 2%
Russia 144 — 2.79%
Japan 128 — 7.87%
France 61 — 4.31%
Saudi Arabia 24 — 2.79%

Source: World Bank; UNDP, *Global Human Development Report, 2007*

European countries joined forces and threatened to use the blocking minority, it was in defense of their own selfish interests.[45] In the future, we could imagine a coalition of developing countries reaching a blocking minority to oppose the election of the next U.S. candidate as president of the World Bank. In any case, so far the U.S. Treasury is the undisputed skipper and can freeze any change that would not fit its views. The physical location of the institution's headquarters in Washington, a stone's throw from the White House, is significant. Over the years, readjustments in the voting rights led to the emergence of new nations. But though the United States agreed to reduce its share, it made sure it would still be over the 15 percent threshold.[46]

Some blame the Bank's dispersion on its main shareholder (the United States), which, in view of the reduction of its bilateral aid program, considers the institution as a particularly useful instrument for exerting its influence in the developing countries. It can then be used as a source of funding to be granted to its friends and denied to its enemies.

—YVES TAVERNIER, French MP, French National Assembly
Finance Commission's Report on the Activities and Control
of the IMF and the World Bank, 2001

The International Development Association (IDA) is officially just an association, but it is tied up with the IBRD, which runs it. In 2008, it numbered 167 member states, of which 78 (and 39 of those in Africa) met the conditions to benefit from its loans, that is, an annual income per inhabitant of less than $1,095 (figure updated each year). These countries borrow over long periods (usually between thirty-five and forty years, with an initial deferral of ten years) and at very low interest rates (of around 0.75 percent). The money comes either from the richest countries, which reconstitute the IDA fund every three years, or from the benefits the IBRD derives from repayments by middle-income countries. Notice the IDA's principles are apt to change when it suits the World Bank: China can borrow both from the IBRD and from IDA even though the income per capita is well over $1,095.

The other developing countries borrow from the IBRD at rates close to going market rates. The IBRD is careful to select profitable projects, just like a normal bank. The World Bank gets the money it needs for these loans by borrowing on the money markets. Indeed, the World Bank, guaranteed by the rich countries that are its biggest shareholders, is solid enough to get money at very good rates. Then the IBRD lends it out to the member countries, which repay the loans over a period of fifteen to twenty years.

Such a privileged position for borrowing from the markets enables the IBRD to set money aside for running costs and even to make profits: between $1 billion and $3 billion a year. Of the $24.7 billion of World Bank loans in 2007, more than half were made through the IBRD: $12.8 billion, in comparison with $11.9 billion for the IDA.[47]

As indebtedness has grown, the World Bank, in conjunction with the IMF, has increasingly turned to actions aimed at producing macroeconomic effects and imposed more and more structural adjustment policies (see Q17 and Q18). The Bank does not hesitate to "advise" the countries subjected to IMF therapy on the best ways to promote a most controversial kind of growth—through reducing budget deficits, attracting foreign investors, liberalizing their economies, and opening markets (and doing away with all protection of their local economy). It even directly participates in the financing of such reforms through specific loans.

Is it reasonable that the World Bank should be giving its support to private small-scale business projects for access to water and electricity, instead of contributing to the construction of public systems? Should the World Bank be financing private systems of health and education?
—YVES TAVERNIER, French MP, French National Assembly Finance Commission's Report on the Activities and Control of the IMF and the World Bank, 2001

QUESTION 9

What part did the governments of countries of the North play in the evolution of the developing countries' external debt in the 1960s and 1970s?

Though not the direct cause of the global economic crisis in 1973–75, the 1973 oil shock marked for countries of the North the end of the period of sustained growth that came after the Second World War. Between 1973 and 1975, these countries were hit by a major recession, with massive unemployment. The rich countries then decided to distribute purchasing power to countries of the South, so as to entice them to buy goods from the North. This led to loans from state to state, often in the guise of export credits— what is called tied aid. For instance, France might have loaned ten million francs at a low interest rate to an African country on condition that it bought ten million francs' worth of French goods. This amounted to a subsidy to companies in the creditor country, while the population of the debtor country paid interest! This is how the bilateral part of the developing countries' external debt came into being. Although it was very low in the early 1960s, it reached $26 billion in 1970, then $103 billion in 1980.

Until the end of the 1970s, indebtedness remained tolerable for countries of the South because interest rates were low and those loans enabled them to produce and thus export more, which meant getting strong currency (from the export sales) in order to repay the loans and invest the remainder. But the rise in the developing countries' external debt was exponential: though very low in the early 1960s, it reached $70 billion in 1970, and $540 billion in 1980. It rose eightfold in ten years.

[TESTIMONY]
John Perkins in Ecuador

In his book, *Confessions of an Economic Hit-Man*, John Perkins tells of the part he played in the 1970s when he was head of a U.S. electrical engineering company that had covert connections with the CIA and the Pentagon.[48] His mission was "to encourage world leaders to become part of a vast network that promotes U.S. commercial interests. In the end, those leaders become ensnared in a web of debt that ensures their loyalty. We can draw on them whenever we desire—to satisfy our political, economic, or military needs. In turn, they bolster their political position by bringing industrial parks, power plants, and airports to their people. The owners of U.S. engineering/construction companies become fabulously wealthy."

But he also worked with progressive people such as President Jaime Roldós in Ecuador: "Jaime Roldós was moving forward. He took his campaign promises seriously and he was launching an all-out attack on the oil companies. . . . The oil companies reacted predictably—they pulled out all the stops. . . . [They] tried to paint the first democratically elected president of Ecuador in modern times as another Castro. But Roldós would not cave in to intimidation. . . . He delivered a major speech at the Atahualpa Olympic Stadium in Quito and then headed off to a small community in southern Ecuador. He died there in a fiery helicopter crash, on May 24, 1981." As indeed the president of Panama, Omar Torrijos, who at about the same time wanted to renegotiate the treaty that ceded to the United States the area along the Panama Canal, also fell victim to an accident. Perkins is convinced that there was nothing accidental about these untimely deaths. "They were assassinated because they opposed that fraternity of corporate, government, and banking heads whose goal is global empire. We EHMs failed to bring Roldós and Torrijos around, and the other type of hit men, the CIA-sanctioned jackals who were always right behind us, stepped in."

The balance is all too clear: "Ecuador is awash in foreign debt and must devote an inordinate share of its national budget to paying this off. . . . The only way Ecuador can buy down its foreign obligations is by selling its rain forests to the oil companies." In short, by trampling Ecuador's sovereignty which is supposed to be inalienable, "the global empire demands its pound of flesh in the form of oil concessions."

John Perkins was back in Ecuador on May 22, 2007, to apologize to the Ecuadorian people. Other people equally responsible for illegitimate debts ought to follow suit.

QUESTION 10
How was the borrowed money used in the developing countries?

The populations hardly benefited from the loans contracted by the leaders of the countries of the South. Most were contracted by dictators who were the strategic allies of the great powers of the North. One only has to study the list of the most heavily indebted countries in 1980 to find a high proportion of regimes with close political ties to the Triad, often authoritarian to boot.

A sizable proportion of the sums borrowed was embezzled by corrupt regimes. They were all the more ready to lead their countries into debt since they were able to skim off commissions for themselves with the complicity of the other instigators of indebtedness.   How could Mobutu Sese Seko, who had ruled Zaire for over thirty years, leave a fortune when he died estimated at $8 billion, equivalent to two-thirds of his country's debt? Not to mention the accumulated wealth of those close to him. And how is it that in Haiti, in 1986, the external debt came to $750 million when the Duvallier family, which had ruled for thirty years (first François—known as Papa Doc, then Jean-Claude—known as Baby Doc) fled to the French Riviera with a fortune estimated at more than $900 million? How else can we explain the newly acquired wealth of the Suharto family in Indonesia, whose fortune, when they were routed in 1998 after reigning for thirty-two years, was estimated at $40 billion, at a time when the country was in utter depression?

Sometimes, as in the case of the Argentine dictatorship (1976–83), the situation was ludicrous. During that period, the debt rose more than five-fold, reaching a total of $45 billion in 1983, mainly contracted with private banks with the agreement of the U.S. government. As of 1976, an IMF loan gave a clear signal to the banks of the North: the Argentine dictatorship was to be supported. The junta in power undertook to force public companies into debt, such as the oil company YPF, whose external debt was multiplied by sixteen in seven years, rising from $372 million to $6 billion. But hardly any of the hard currency borrowed ever reached the coffers of the public companies. The sums borrowed from U.S. banks were largely deposited in these same banks in the form of deposits, at a lower rate of interest than that of the loan. Large commissions then contributed to the personal enrichment of those close to the dictatorship. For example, between July and November 1976, the Chase Manhattan Bank received monthly deposits of $22 million, on which it paid interest at 5.5 percent. At the same time, Argentina's Central Bank was borrowing $30 million each month from the same bank at a rate of 8.75 percent. All this took place with the active support of the IMF and the United States, maintaining the regime of terror, while Argentina and the United States drew closer after the nationalist experiment of Perón and his successors.[49]

From 1976 to 1983, the policy of indebtedness and loans was totally arbitrary. This implicates the staff and Executive Boards of public and private institutions. The existence of an explicit link between the external debt, the flow of foreign capital in the short term, the high interest rates on the internal market, and the corresponding sacrifice of the national budget after 1976 cannot have escaped the notice of the IMF authorities who were supervising economic negotiations at that time.
—FEDERAL COURT OF ARGENTINA decision, July 14, 2000

So the debt increased very fast, as did the personal wealth of those close to the dictators. It was also profitable for the banks of the North. Part of the money came back into their vaults and could be loaned again to others, in an endless cycle. Moreover, the wealth of the dictators was very useful to the banks because it served as a guarantee. If leaders were suddenly less compliant and challenged the repayment of debts contracted in the name of the state, the Bank could threaten to freeze their secret personal assets, or even confiscate them. Corruption and embezzlement thus played a major role.

> In the poorer countries a caste developed in the higher spheres of the state in collusion with that in Western countries: local ruling classes negotiated their participation in the spoliation of the earth through their capacity to make natural resources available to multinational corporations or to insure social order.
>
> —HERVÉ KEMPF, *How the Rich Are Destroying the Earth*, 2008

The money that eventually did reach the borrowing country was used in such a way that the population hardly reaped any benefit. Priority was given to financing huge energy or infrastructure projects (big dams, power plants, pipelines, deepwater harbors, railways, and the like) that were very often inappropriate or megalomaniac, and nicknamed "white elephants." The aim was not to improve the daily life of the local populations, but rather to extract the natural resources of the South and transport them easily and at the cheapest cost to the world markets. For example, the Inga Dam in Zaire made it possible, from 1972, to install a 1,900-km high-voltage power line to the mineral-rich province of Katanga, with a view to its exploitation. Yet no transformers were installed along the way to supply electricity to villages where people still use oil lamps. Other, often overreaching dam projects have been made possible by finance from the North: Kariba between Zambia and Zimbabwe, Katse and Mohale in Lesotho, Sardar Sardovar in India, Tarbela in Pakistan, Arun in Nepal, Yaceryta on the river between Argentina and Paraguay, Chixoy in Guatemala, Nam Theun in Laos, and so many more.

In many countries debt strangles the public purse—and is often for
money spent unproductively long ago by authoritarian regimes.
—UNDP, *Global Human Development Report 2002*

The same logic still prevails regularly, as is borne out by the construction of the Chad-Cameroon pipeline begun in the 1990s, to bring oil from
the Doba region, an enclave in Chad, to the maritime terminal of Kribi
(Cameroon), 1,000 km away. The consortium, consisting of ExxonMobil,
ChevronTexaco (United States), and Petronas (Malaysia), succeeded in
completing this $3.7 billion project thanks to the powerful strategic and
financial backing of the World Bank.

The construction of the pipeline, completed in 2004, was carried
out with a total disregard for the populations concerned. For example,
the indemnities initially offered to those living in the path of the projected pipeline amounted to a mere 3,000 CFA francs (4.6 euros) per
mango tree destroyed, whereas according to the Chad MP Ngarléjy
Yorongar, the first crop of this tree alone yields 1,000 mangoes, each
tradable at around 100 CFA francs (15 euro cents), or 150 euros per
mango tree.[50] It was only after much protest and pressure that these
amounts were slightly raised.

A French-trained officer, Chad's president Idriss Déby Itno seized
power in 1990 after toppling Hissene Habre. He enjoys the long-stand-
ing support of France and French-African networks. His record so far:
fixed elections with ballot stuffing and vote-rigging; repression of any
form of democratic opposition and free press; and revision of the constitution to allow the president to stand for a third term. The resounding
failure of the lawsuit brought by Déby against François-Xavier Verschave,
author of *Noir silence,* the book that recounted it all, was widely reported.

The World Bank could not openly approve such a regime. It therefore
sought to justify itself by promoting a pilot scheme that would allow
Chad's populations to benefit from profits made. Having invested more in
Chad than anywhere else in Sub-Saharan Africa, it required Déby to
deposit 10 percent of the money earned from oil sales in a blocked account
at Citibank, London, under the control of the World Bank, and to reserve
this money for future generations. To manage this account, the World
Bank put forward the idea of a Committee for the Control and Supervision

of Oil Resources (CCSRP) composed of nine members.[51] But five of these members were nominated by Déby himself. The remaining 90 percent of oil revenues was to be distributed as follows: 80 percent for social projects that the World Bank had approved, 10 percent for the state's operating expenses, and 5 percent for investments in the Doba area.

The big winner in the Chadian oil project is the consortium, but government and its cronies are not complaining either. The distribution of revenues between the Chadian state and the oil consortium seems extremely unfavorable to the state, which should get only 12.5 percent of royalties on direct oil sales. To this should be added various taxes and bonuses, which are paid directly into Chad's public treasury. The first bonus, paid as an advance, was not a shining example of probity: $7.4 million was embezzled on this occasion. The president's son misappropriated another $4.5 million for the purchase of helicopters.[52] The World Bank, deeply involved in the project, generously closed its eyes so as not to prejudice its credibility.

That was not enough for Déby, who contested the figures provided by ExxonMobil and the consortium which were used to calculate how oil revenue would be distributed. This is why on October 7, 2004, the Chad president's office published a very unusual release titled "Consortium Swindle, Concealment and Fraud," denouncing the fact that the multinational corporations claim all these oil revenues and that Chad cannot control the consortium's dubious declarations. The mechanism set up by the World Bank was blown to pieces: by the end of 2005, Déby had embezzled $27 million of the funds that had been intended for future generations. Moreover, he had changed the rules of the game in that he included security expenditure in the definition of priority sectors to be financed with oil revenues. While weakened by deep social tensions, attempted coups, and desertions in the army, Déby tried to build up his repressive military power. The World Bank reacted by freezing disimbursements of $124 million intended for Chad. A few months later, under pressure from Washington in support of Déby, an agreement was reached between Chad and the World Bank. Made official in July 2006 and publicized as a victory, it confirms the World Bank's step backward. Déby committed himself to dedicate 70 percent of oil revenues to poverty reduction programs; that is less than the 80 percent that had been initially announced.

All this shows that the discourse of World Bank experts on good governance, corruption, and poverty reduction is nothing but a grim farce. It was clear from the start that this project would make a notorious dictator even richer. In fact, each party did what was expected of it. The World Bank made it possible to build a pipeline, thanks to which oil corporations can get their oil cheap and so provide high dividends to their shareholders. Chad's president sells the wealth of his people, who suffer and pay.

Here is another example. In 1994, China started to build the huge Three Gorges dam, whose surface exceeds 1,000 square kilometers—about twice the size of Lake Geneva! This dam led to 1.9 million people being displaced and irretrievably upset the local ecosystem. Encroachments on human rights and on the environment did not at all deter corporations of the North such as Alstom, Hydro-Québec, or BNP Paribas from participating in the project.

The purchase of weapons and military equipment to oppress people is another cause of indebtedness. Many dictatorships maintained their hold on the populations thanks to weapons they had bought on credit with the active or passive complicity of their creditors. So today, people in poor countries repay a debt that was used to buy the weapons that killed friends and relatives, whether it be the 30,000 disappeared in Argentina under the dictatorship (1976–83), the violent repression in Chile under Pinochet (1973–90), the victims of the Apartheid regime in South Africa (1948–94), or the genocide in Rwanda (1994). The borrowed money was also used to feed government slush funds, to compromise opposition parties, sometimes even to create fake opposition parties or to finance costly election campaigns and vote-catching policies.

Loans were also used for tied aid, that is, the money was then used to buy goods manufactured in the creditor country, even when these goods were neither adequate nor cheaper. The real needs of the populations in developing countries were not taken into account; all that mattered were trading outlets. There have been instances in which goods were not even unwrapped after they had been taken to the debtor country. But of course the loans had to be repaid.

White elephants, tied aid, purchase of weapons used for massive repression, embezzlement, and corruption—this is what the money borrowed over decades was used for. Today, populations are bleeding themselves dry to pay back debts from which they did not benefit.

> Which bankers batted an eyelid when they saw that a loan destined for a Mexican or Philippine state company was in fact paid straight into the account in Boston or Geneva of a high-ranking state official?
>
> —PHILIPPE NOREL and ÉRIC SAINT-ALARY, *L'endettement du Tiers-Monde* (*Third World Indebtedness*), 1988

CHAPTER THREE

The Debt Crisis

QUESTION 11
How did the price of commodities evolve during the last quarter of the twentieth century?

From the end of the 1970s to the beginning of the year 2000, the countries of the South were confronted with a major change: exports of raw materials and agricultural goods, which had been continually on the rise, started to abate.

The majority of loans were based on strong currencies like the U.S. dollar. Moreover, and this is an essential point, repayments needed to be made in the same currency as the loan, because lenders who, for example, lent dollars expect dollars in return—they are not at all interested in Congolese francs from the DRC or currency from any other developing country. Throughout the 1970s, with their debt spiraling out of control, indebted countries had to obtain more and more strong currencies to repay their lenders. In order to do this they had no choice but to sell to whomever possessed this hard money. Developing countries thus had to resort to structuring their economic policies around the expectations of foreign economic actors, most notably in industrialized countries.

Produce what we need and consume what we produce, instead of importing.
    —THOMAS SANKARA, president of Burkina Faso, 1983–1987

Conditioned to make the payments at all costs, developing countries had to export more of their "tropical" products or mining resources. They strengthened their specialization in certain commodities, on which they had become dependent, like copper for Zambia and Chile, or bauxite for Guinea and Jamaica. At the same time, these countries injected an increased quantity of raw materials into the market, while the demand in the North, which was dealing with its own crisis, didn't rise in proportion to this new supply. Developing countries thus competed among themselves and saw the price of all raw materials, including oil, the price of which had been increasing since 1973, crumble. The fundamental turning point took place in 1981, when the price of oil fell sharply, provoking the debt crisis in Mexico, a major oil exporter. The price of certain raw materials had already dropped years earlier, as was the case with copper, which collapsed in 1976, provoking a payment crisis for Mobutu's Zaire.[53]

From a global point of view, it was an irregular drop, with periods of collapse followed by short-lived peaks. However, the overall movement between 1977 and 2001 was a net drop in all raw materials, falling about 2.8 percent annually.[54] This fall also affected minerals and metals, dropping 1.9 percent yearly, with most notably silver, tin, and tungsten falling more than 5 percent. Between 1997, the year when Southeast Asia experienced a large-scale collapse, and 2001, prices were sliced in half; "53 percent in real terms. . . . That is, commodities lost more than half their purchasing power in terms of manufactured goods."[55] In addition, a study of the structure of exports worldwide demonstrates that, in terms of value, rich countries export more than two-thirds of all manufactured goods, and developing countries export more than half of the commodities. Despite everything, developing countries continue to be areas of harvest and extraction, providing the indispensable raw materials to an industrialized economy, yet receiving only a small portion of the benefits in return.

With the reversal of price trends in the early 1980s, the financial situation of indebted countries has become much more difficult. Not only is increasing production no longer sufficient; it aggravates the already present phenomenon of an overabundance of supply on the world market. The structural adjustment policies that followed (see Q17 and

Q18) have since deprived these countries of any form of protection they previously had.

> The free play of market forces via price liberalization and deregula-
> tion was held up as promising the most efficient allocation of
> resources and welfare gains. The concept of international commod-
> ity price stabilization thus suffered a major setback.
>
> —UNCTAD, 2003[56]

QUESTION 12
What role did the evolution of interest rates play in the 1982 debt crisis?

At the end of 1979, to get out of the financial crisis that hit the United States (as well as most other industrialized countries) and reassert their world leadership after a string of humiliating failures in Vietnam in 1975, in Iran (the Shah's overthrow in February 1979), and Nicaragua (the removal of the dictator Anastasio Somoza in July 1979), the government began a sharp turn away from liberal Keynesianism, greatly accentuated when Ronald Reagan took over the presidency in January 1981. For several months, the United Kingdom, ruled with a rod of iron by Margaret Thatcher's government, had already initiated a harshly neoliberal change of direction. Paul Volcker, the chairman of the Board of Governors of the U.S. Federal Reserve System, decided on a steep rise in U.S. interest rates. For someone holding capital, this meant that it suddenly became very worthwhile to invest in the United States, as it would bring in higher profits. That was indeed one of Volcker's objectives: to attract investment and revive the U.S. economy (in particular, by launching a huge military-industrial program). Investors rushed in from all over the planet. One after another, European governments followed by raising interest rates in order to keep the capital from going abroad.

In the U.S. the Prime Rate is the interest rate which banks charge each other for overnight loans made to fulfil reserve requirements. The Prime Rate is usually some 3 percentage points higher than the Federal Funds Rate, that is, the interest rate set by the Federal Reserve.

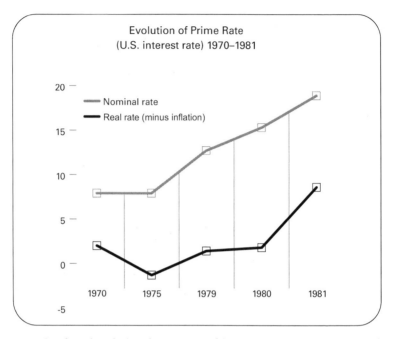

It is clear that during the 1970s, real interest rates were very low, and even negative at one point. It was thus a perfect opportunity to borrow: when the real rate is negative, inflation is higher than the nominal interest rate, and thus the cost of borrowing is extremely low, or nothing at all in some cases.

During this period, the expense represented by debt repayment by the developing country was sustainable, especially if export revenues were high—and rising.

At the beginning of the 1980s, the situation changed drastically. Bank loan interest rates accorded to countries of the South were clearly very

Evolution of the U.S. Prime Rate, 1970–1981

YEAR	NOMINAL RATE	REAL RATE (minus inflation)
1970	7.9%	2.0%
1975	7.9%	−1.3%
1979	12.7%	1.4%
1980	15.3%	1.8%
1981	18.9%	8.6%

low during the previous two decades, but variable and linked to the Anglo-Saxon rates (the prime rate and the LIBOR, determined in New York and London respectively, are basically the lowest lending rates, those charged by the largest banks to their largest customers). From around 4 to 5 percent in the 1970s, the interest rates climbed to 16–18 percent and higher at the peak of the crisis, as the risk premium had become enormous. Thus practically overnight, countries of the South saw a threefold increase in interest, while export revenue was falling (see Q11). Lending countries had thus unilaterally modified the rules. On the one hand, it was the central banks of most of the industrialized countries, starting with the Federal Reserve, that unilaterally decided to raise interest rates. Moreover, these same countries also forced the price of raw materials to fall, in particular by weakening OPEC thanks to their ally, Saudi Arabia, and by putting an end to the coffee cartel. The "trap" was set for the indebted countries. The effect of this was clear: indebted Third World countries found themselves under the heel of lenders.

The consequences were terrible. The South had to repay more with less income. In the vise-like grip of the debt, it was impossible to meet payments as they fell due. Countries had to get even deeper into debt in order to pay, but this time at high rates. The situation rapidly deteriorated.

In August 1982, Mexico was the first country to announce that it was no longer able to repay. Other heavily indebted countries, such as Argentina and Brazil, followed. This was the debt crisis that rocked all the countries of the South, one after the other. Even countries of Eastern Europe were hit, especially Poland, and a little later Yugoslavia and Romania.

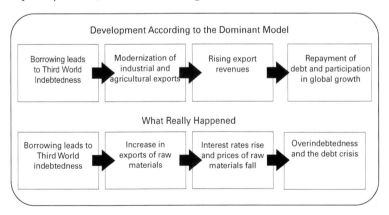

The debt crisis resounded like a great clap of thunder. The international institutions, whose job it is to regulate the system and prevent crises, didn't sound the alarm and acted as if everything was fine.

It will be more difficult for developing countries to manage their debts, however, [current tendencies] do not indicate a general problem.
—WORLD BANK, *Global Development Report*, 1981

Although the World Bank and the IMF knew that clouds were gathering and a typhoon was forming, they didn't want to advertise the real economic forecast. They wanted to give the major banks some time to pull out without harm.[57] This was done with good reason, as the World Bank's new president was none other than a former top man at one of the most important U.S. private banks, Bank of America, which had lent an arm and a leg to Mexico and Latin America.

In short, the debt crisis had been caused by two phenomena, which occurred in quick succession:

• an enormous increase in the amounts to be repaid, due to the sudden rise in interest rates decided in Washington;
• an enormous price drop for products exported on the world market by the indebted countries, the proceeds of which were to repay their loans, and a halt in bank loans.[58]

All the indebted countries in Africa and Latin America and several Asian countries (such as South Korea), regardless of the type of government, the degree of corruption or of democracy, were confronted with the debt crisis.

The basic responsibilities are largely on the side of the industrialized countries, their central banks, their private banks, and their stock exchange (Chicago, London) that fix the prices of the raw materials. Corruption, megalomania, and the lack of democracy in the South (see Q10) certainly made matters *worse* but were not responsible for *triggering* the crisis.

The Latin American debt crisis in the 1980s was brought about by a huge increase in interest rates, a result of the Federal Reserve chairman Paul Volcker's tight money policy in the United States.
—JOSEPH STIGLITZ, *Globalization and Its Discontents*, 2002

QUESTION 13
Are the World Bank, the IMF, and private banks somehow responsible for the debt crisis?

Yes, definitely. In 1960, the World Bank was cognizant that a possible debt crisis could transpire with the principal indebted countries' incapacity to keep up with increasing repayments. The warning signs that multiplied throughout the 1960s were eventually topped off with the energy crisis of 1973. Many leaders of the World Bank, private banks, and the General Accounting Office (GAO) published reports highlighting the risks of the crisis. However, the tone changed radically when the price of oil increased in 1973, and, at the same time, major banks in industrialized countries performed a massive recycling of petrodollars. The World Bank stopped talking about the crisis. Yet the debt was quickly flying out of control. It became a competition between the World Bank and private banks to see which could allocate the most loans in the shortest time. Up until the explosion of the crisis in 1982, the World Bank maintained a double discourse: one, official, reassuring the public and indebted countries that there was no cause for alarm and that any potential problems would only be temporary; the other, much more unsettling, restricted to private discussions behind closed doors.

Let's consider some examples demonstrating that the debt crisis didn't just appear out of the blue.

In 1969, Nelson Rockefeller, brother of the president of Chase Manhattan Bank, explained in a report to the U.S. president the problems Latin America had to face: "Heavy borrowing by some Western Hemisphere countries to support development has reached the point where annual repayments of interest and amortization absorb a large share of foreign exchange earnings.... Many of the countries are, in effect, having to make new loans to get the foreign exchange to pay interest and amortization on old loans, and at higher interest rates."[59]

Many poor nations have already incurred debts past the possibility of repayment.

— GENERAL ACCOUNTING OFFICE, 1969[60]

Some time later, in 1970, in a report to the U.S. president, Rudolph Peterson, president of Bank of America, sounded the alarm: "The debt burden of many developing countries is now an urgent problem. It was foreseen, but not faced, a decade ago. It stems from a combination of causes [but] whatever the causes, future export earnings of some countries are so heavily mortgaged as to endanger continuing imports, investment, and development."[61]

In short, from the late 1960s, diverse influential and interrelated sources in the United States considered that a debt crisis could break out in the ensuing years.

For his part, Robert McNamara also considered the rate at which Third World indebtedness was growing as a problem. He declared: "At the end of 1972, the debt represented 75 billion dollars and the annual service of the debt exceeded 7 billion dollars. The amount paid in debt servicing had increased by 18 percent in 1970 and 20 percent in 1971. The average rate of increase of the debt since the decade of the 1960s represented almost double the growth rate of the export revenues with which the indebted countries had to service the debt. This situation could not go on indefinitely."[62]

Yet the World Bank under McNamara's direction kept up the pressure on the countries of the periphery to get them even more into debt.

The rise in prices of petroleum products and other raw materials in 1973 led countries to rush blindly into even greater debt. Pessimistic forecasts appeared to be thinning out.

The investment of the surpluses of oil-exporting countries in national and international financial markets together with the expansion of international financing (through both bilateral arrangements and multilateral facilities) has resulted in a satisfactory channeling of funds into the current account deficits of the oil-importing countries.

—IMF, *Annual Report*, 1975

Robert McNamara made a great show of confidence in the 1970s. In 1977 he declared in his annual address that "the major lending banks and major borrowing countries are operating on assumptions which are broadly consistent with one another" and he concluded, "We are even more confident today than we were a year ago that the debt problem is indeed manageable." [63]

In October 1978, one of the vice presidents of the World Bank, Peter Cargill, in charge of finance, addressed a memorandum to the president, Robert McNamara, titled "Riskiness in IBRD's Loans Portfolio." In it, Cargill urged McNamara and the whole of the World Bank to pay a lot more attention to the solvency of indebted countries.[64] Cargill claimed that the number of indebted countries in arrears regarding payments to the World Bank or were seeking to renegotiate their multilateral debt had risen from three to eighteen between 1974 and 1978! McNamara himself vented his concern, albeit internally, on several occasions, particularly in a memorandum dated September 1979. One internal memorandum reads that if banks see risks rising, they will cut down on loans and "we may see a larger number of countries in extremely difficult situations."[65]

The *World Development Report* published by the World Bank in 1980 gives an optimistic view of the future, predicting that interest rates would stabilize at the very low level of 1 percent. This was completely unrealistic, as was proved by events. It is edifying to learn through World Bank historians that in the first, unpublished version of the report, there was a second hypothesis based on a real interest rate of 3 percent. That projection showed that the situation would eventually be unsustainable for the indebted countries. Robert McNamara managed to get that gloomy scenario out of the final version![66]

The World Bank's *World Development Report* of 1981 mentions that it seemed very likely that borrowers and lenders would adapt to the changing conditions without starting a general crisis of confidence.[67]

On March 19, 1982, six months before the crisis, the new president of the World Bank, Alden W. Clausen, who replaced McNamara, sent the following letter to the Mexican president, José López Portillo:[68] "Our meeting in Mexico City with your top aides reinforced my confidence in the economic leaders of your country. You, Mr. President, can be rightfully proud of the achievements of the last five years. Few countries can claim to have achieved such high growth rates, or have created so many jobs. . . . I wish to congratulate you on the many successes already achieved. As I stated during our meeting, *the recent setback for the Mexican economy is bound to be transient*, and we will be happy to be of assistance during the consolidation process" (authors' emphasis).[69]Less than a year earlier, Alden W. Clausen still chaired the Bank of America, which was busy providing loan upon loan to Mexico.

On August 20, 1982, Mexico, which had paid back considerable amounts over the first seven months of the year, stated it could not pay any more. The crisis spread like wildfire.

In conclusion, the lenders knew perfectly well that the debt crisis was lurking, but they feigned ignorance. Once the crisis was under way, they profited by having the upper hand over those countries that had expressed a desire to be independent, increasing their degree of exploitation over all developing countries and their inhabitants.

QUESTION 14
How did creditors respond to the debt crisis?

When the debt crisis broke out in Mexico in 1982, then in the other Latin American countries, creditors realized they were at an impasse and the world's financial system wobbled. The banks of the North were in danger because of the numerous loans they had made. For example, in 1982 the money owed by Brazil, Argentina, Venezuela, and Chile represented 141 percent of Morgan Guaranty Bank's own capital, 154 percent of Chase Manhattan Bank, 158 percent of Bank of America, 170 percent of Chemical Bank, 175 percent of Citibank, and 263 percent of Manufacturers Hanover. The bankers were in a critical situation.

As soon as a country found itself incapable of repayment (which was the case in the 1980s for the majority of Latin American and African countries, and for emerging Asian countries at the end of the 1990s), the first on the scene was always the IMF, coming to the rescue like a financial fireman—but a peculiar fireman, exacerbating the pyromaniac's evildoing, extinguishing lenders' fires often caused by hazardous investments, and at the same time igniting others.

Following the exigencies of the governments of the richest companies, the IMF permitted countries in crisis to borrow in order to avoid default on their repayments. Caught in the debt's downward spiral, developing countries soon had no other recourse than to take on new debt in order to repay the old debt. Before providing them with new loans, at higher interest rates, future lenders asked the IMF to intervene with the guarantee of ulterior reimbursement, asking for a signed agreement with the said countries. The IMF thus agreed to restart the flow of the "finance pump" on condition that the concerned countries first use this money to reimburse banks and other private lenders, while restructuring their economy at the IMF's discretion: these were the famous conditionalities, detailed in the Structural Adjustment Programs (SAP: see Q17 and Q18). The IMF and its ultra-liberal experts took control of the borrowing countries' economic policies. A new form of colonization was thus instituted. It was not even necessary to establish an administrative or military presence; the debt alone maintained this new form of submission.

In August 1982 the Mexican government announced that it could not service its external debts. The IMF organized and supervised the administration of a plan to reschedule the private commercial debts that the Mexican government had incurred over the previous decade. IMF lending did not channel net new funding to Mexico. Rather it lent the money to enable Mexico to service the debt. Mexico's debt increased, but it avoided default. The IMF made its loans conditional on the implementation of a package of long-term economic reforms. Many of the conditions required sacrifices by the local population, loss of jobs and deep reductions in living standards. Other developing countries, particularly in Latin America, found that net private capital inflows declined or became negative.

—IFI ADVISORY COMMISSION, also known as
the Meltzer Commission, 2000[70]

What was the rich countries' desired goal in placing the IMF in such an important position? It was simply to impose a strict financial discipline on the indebted countries. Reestablishing financial equilibrium was of the utmost importance for the international financial institutions. The goal established in the countries in the South was clear: export more and spend less. The IMF and World Bank's Structural Adjustment Programs have also been known since 1990 as the "Washington Consensus." Privileging the statistical over the human aspect, they had terrible effects on the populations and economies in the countries of the South. For decades, the people made huge sacrifices in order to pay off a debt that brought them no profit. At the same time, the macroeconomic criteria favored by the IMF and the World Bank led to a great deterioration of the living conditions of hundreds of millions of people worldwide. From a human development standpoint, it was a complete failure for both institutions, as both saw their position considerably weaken over time.

Modern high-tech warfare is designed to remove physical contact: dropping bombs from 50,000 feet ensures that one does not "feel" what one does. Modern economic management is similar: from one's luxury hotel, one can callously impose policies about which one would think twice if one knew the people whose lives one was destroying.

—JOSEPH STIGLITZ, *Globalization and Its Discontents*, 2002

When an acute crisis arose (such as those of Mexico in 1982 and 1994, Southeast Asia in 1997, Russia in 1998, Brazil in 1999, Ecuador in 1999–2000, Turkey in 2000, Argentina in 2001–2, Brazil again in 2002), the IMF then made available considerable amounts of money. Not in order to help the population of a country that could not make ends meet at the end of the month but to keep the rich creditors, often responsible for speculative investments that triggered or worsened the crisis, out of bankruptcy. For example, the IMF and the G7 lent $105 billion to the Asian and Southeast Asian countries in 1997 (where the crisis, aggravated by the measures imposed by the IMF, led to twenty million people losing their jobs); the IMF lent $31 billion to Turkey between the end of 1999 and 2002 (Turkey, a geo-strategic ally of the United States, is near

the oil and gas of Central Asia, and next to Iraq and Iran); over $21 bil-
lion lent to Argentina in 2001 before it sank in the crisis and defaulted on
its private creditors; and $30 billion promised to Brazil for 2002–3 (to
avoid contamination by the Argentine crisis and to tie down President
Lula, elected in October 2002). However, these injected billions are never
used to provide subsidies for basic necessities to help the poorest populations, nor to create jobs and protect local producers. The IMF insists
that creditors must be repaid as a matter of urgency. Moreover, these creditors are often the same private lenders that made speculative investments
in the countries concerned and then suddenly withdrew them, causing an
aggravation of the crisis. Worse still, when private bodies suspend payments, the IMF and the World Bank often oblige the state to take on the
debt, which amounts to getting the taxpayer to pay it off.

Thus, the amounts lent increase the debt of the borrower country,
only to leave it immediately in the form of repayments to the creditors in
the North. Since the IMF is in the habit of playing this role, creditors are
prepared to take even greater risks in their financial operations, knowing
that in case of default by the borrower country, the IMF is there to bail
them out, as a last-resort lender. This will be set off against a considerable
increase in the external debt of the developing country concerned. The
IMF works against the interests of numerous member countries it is supposed to help. This betrayal of its principles appears not to raise the
slightest doubt: when the crisis comes, it never questions its prescrip-
tions, never wonders whether its choices are perhaps misguided, but
always accuses the indebted states of not having applied its excellent recommendations rigorously enough.

> All obstacles to free trade will be removed, leaving companies free
> to produce and export their products as they wish and as the market
> decides.
> —Michel Camdessus, managing director of the IMF, 1987–2000,
> L'Autre mondialisation (The Other Globalization),
> on Arte, March 7, 2000

The IMF was clever enough to hold the governments of the South
responsible for these decisions. Regularly, each state has to sign a letter of

intent, actually dictated by the IMF, where an economic plan is addressed that considers future economic actions. Loans and rescheduled payments are only granted when these discussions, personally verified by experts of the World Bank and the IMF, advance "in the right direction." If a problem arises, it is henceforth the indebted countries' governments that are at fault since they proposed these policies, whereas the IMF simply agreed to accompany them along the way.[71]

> We were created after the events of 1929 with the intent of rebuild-
> ing confidence by installing reformatory policies and by engender-
> ing cooperation among the international community. We must do
> whatever we can to avoid the irresponsible behavior of governments
> and/or lenders. The International Monetary Fund's programs are
> negotiated with sovereign countries that execute them and thus
> have the final word. The adopted measures have the fewest costs
> from a humanitarian perspective, and represent the shortest path to
> resolve what has become a catastrophic situation, of which the poor
> are the first victims.
> —MICHEL CAMDESSUS, IMF managing director, 1987–2000

The IMF's failure in terms of human development is not the result of misfortune or of incomprehension but the deliberate result of the measures it imposed. But why were such measures recommended so vigorously? It would be absurd to believe that the goal of the IMF and major economic powers is to fight against poverty and provide the populations of the South with the necessary means to construct their own destiny. Quite the contrary: the IMF favored above all else international finance in order to assure lenders that all repayments would be carried out as expected.

> Simplistic free market ideology provided the curtain behind which
> the real business of the "new" mandate could be transacted. The
> change in mandate and objectives, while it may have been quiet,
> was hardly subtle: from serving global economic interests to serving
> the interests of global finance. Capital market liberalization may not
> have contributed to global economic stability, but it did open up vast
> new markets for Wall Street. . . . Looking at the IMF as if it were pur-

suing the interests of the financial community provides a way of
making sense of what might otherwise seem to be contradictory and
intellectually incoherent behavior.

—JOSEPH STIGLITZ, *Globalization and Its Discontents*, 2002

The rich countries, led by the United States, took a series of initiatives
to prevent the indebted countries from forming a united front, which is
the last thing the rich countries wanted. Before any discussions could
begin, they insisted that negotiations with indebted countries take place
on a case-by-case basis, thus isolating each debtor country from the rest
and keeping the upper hand.

As for the creditors, nothing could come between them.

- At the World Bank and the IMF, the quota system gives the rich
  countries a comfortable majority to impose their views.
- Furthermore, the creditor states all belong to the Paris Club
  through which they reschedule the bilateral part of the external
  debt of the states with repayment problems.
- The banks of the most industrialized countries belong to the
  London Club, which serves the same purpose regarding sovereign
  debt of the indebted states.

Thus a disproportionate balance of power was set up from the beginning of the debt crisis. For the last twenty years, the IMF, the World Bank,
the Paris Club, and the London Club have seen to it that the same policies would be maintained in favor of the rich countries.

Give me control of a nation's money and I do not care who makes
the laws.

—AMSCHEL ROTHSCHILD, German banker, 1743–1812

But since the year 2000, their power has met with increased resistance.
Numerous countries that were at one point subjected to contracts with the
IMF have since taken measures to rid themselves of this cumbersome
guardianship. Several among them have expedited their payments in order
to sever all ties with the IMF: Brazil, Argentina, Uruguay, Indonesia, the

Philippines, and Turkey being the most recent. The IMF (whose pocket-book was pretty much cleared out in recent years, falling from $107 billion in 2003 to $16 billion in 2007) was incapable of attracting new customers and quietly awaited another large crisis to shake the developing countries in order to take control of the wheel and become the major actor once again. The financial and economic crisis affecting the world has dramatically changed the picture and, alas, given the IMF a new start.

QUESTION 15

Are there any similarities with the 2007 subprime crisis?

Since August 2007, U.S. and European banks have constantly made headline news concerning the deep crisis they are going through and its negative effect on the neoliberal economic system as a whole. According to the IMF's estimates, the total write-downs borne by banks and other financial institutions for 2007–10, "including about $1 trillion already taken, could be nearly $4.1 trillion on . . . assets originated in the United States, Europe, and Japan."[72]

How did the banks manage to build such an irrational lending system? Eager for profit, mortgage companies made loans to a sector of the population that was already heavily indebted. The conditions attached to these mortgages—highly profitable for the lender—amounted to daylight robbery for the borrower: the interest rate was fixed and reasonable for the first two years but thereafter rose sharply. Lenders assured borrowers that the property they were buying and that served as collateral for the loan would quickly appreciate thanks to the boom in the real estate sector. The problem was that this was a speculator's argument, whereas the people that were buying in these conditions intended to live on their property. The real estate bubble burst in 2007, and house prices started to go steadily down. The number of defaults on payment soared, and mortgage brokers had trouble repaying their own loans. To protect themselves, the big banks either refused extra credit to the mortgage lenders or agreed to new loans at far higher interest rates. But the spiral did not stop there, since the big banks had bought up a large number of the original loans as off-balance-sheet operations by creating specific companies called Structured Investment Vehicles (SIV), which finance the purchase of high-yield mortgages converted into bonds (CDOs, or Collateralized Debt Obligations).

As of August 2007, investors stopped buying the unguaranteed commercial papers issued by SIVs, which no longer looked like a safe or credible option. Consequently, the SIVs lacked the liquidity needed to buy up mortgages and the crisis worsened. The big banks that had created the SIVs therefore had to bail them out to stop them going bankrupt. Up to then, SIV operations had not appeared in the banks' accounts (thus allowing them to conceal the risks involved), but now the SIV debts had to come out of the closet and onto the books.

The result was general panic. Several segments of the debt market collapsed, taking down with them the powerful banks, hedge funds, and the investment funds that had created them. Private financial groups were rescued only through massive public intervention. Privatization of benefits, socialization of losses was once again the order of the day.

Which brings us to a key question: How is it that banks can readily waive bad debts to the tune of tens of billions of dollars yet constantly refuse to cancel the debts of developing countries? The proof exists that the latter option is perfectly feasible and extremely necessary. In 2007, the long-term debt owed by the authorities of developing countries to international banks reached $201.4 billion.[73] Since August 2007, the banks have already erased a much higher amount.

It is clear that the big private banks have failed in three ways:

1. They have built up catastrophic private lending structures that have led to the present disaster.
2. They have made loans to despotic regimes and forced the democratic governments that replaced them to repay this odious debt down to the last cent.
3. They refuse to cancel the debts of developing countries, for whom repayment means ever-worsening living conditions for their people.

Instead of admitting their mistakes and accepting the consequences, large banks solicited help from the one organization whose actions they had denigrated since the beginning of time: the state. They didn't hesitate to beg for strong public action from the state, previously considered to be too interventionist. For the banks, public administrations must submit to the laws of the markets, the only laws that allow for the efficient allocation of resources and fix prices at the correct levels.

Like faithful dogs, U.S. and European public administrations obeyed: nothing can be refused to the leaders of major banks who support the leading presidential candidates and who are raised in the same elite spheres. Governments thus hastened to the aid of the private sphere. The solution: nationalization of struggling banks, purchasing depreciated titles at face value (accounting for more than $200 billion in the United States), cash injections, bailout plans, lowering of interest rates, and more.

In the United States, eighty-four mortgage companies either went bankrupt or partially stopped doing business between January 1 and August 17, 2007, as opposed to only seventeen similar cases for the whole of 2006. In Germany, the IKB BANK and SachsenLB were saved by the skin of their teeth. Recently, in England, the bankrupt Northern Rock has had to be nationalized. On March 13, 2008, the Carlyle Capital Corporation (CCC) fund, known to be close to the Bush clan, collapsed with debts thirty-two times its capital. The following day, the prestigious U.S. bank Bear Stearns (fifth-largest U.S. investment bank) called on the U.S. Federal Reserve to provide an emergency credit line. Bear Stearns was snapped up by JPMorgan Chase for a mere pittance.

Subjecting the management of the global economy to the logic of maximum profit results in enormous costs to society. Banks played with the savings and cash deposits of hundreds of millions of individuals. Their financial missteps led to enormous losses and human tragedy.

The market is always right.
—MICHEL CAMDESSUS, IMF managing director, 1987–2000

The similarities between the North and the South are striking. In the South, the debt crisis at the beginning of the 1980s was provoked by the United States' decision to unilaterally increase interest rates. As a result, Third World countries, which the banks had convinced to borrow at variable rates, were flooded with calls for repayment (see Q12). At the same time, the collapse of the price of raw materials made these countries incapable of facing the demands for repayment, thus viciously throwing them into the crisis. The IMF, controlled by the United States and other powerful countries, then imposed drastic reforms on the developing countries: reduction of social budgets, immediate and total liberalization of the economy, an end to control of capital movements, full opening up of markets, and massive privatizations (see Q17 and Q18). Contrary to what happened in the North in 2008, the states of the South were not allowed to lower interest rates or provide banks with cash, which provoked a torrent of bankruptcies and detrimental recessions. Finally, just like the North in 2008, developing countries were forced to bail out struggling banks before privatizing them, much to the benefit of large North American or European banks. In Mexico, the cost of rescuing banks in the second half of the 1990s represented 15 percent of GDP. In Ecuador, an identical operation in 2000 cost 25 percent of GDP. In every case, internal public debt rose significantly because it was the state that handled the cost of the bailouts (see Q29).

The international crisis resulting from the subprime crisis will have an enormous cost. In a report published April 2008, the IMF estimated this cost at $945 billion for the international financial system, $565 billion of which affects the subprime mortgage lending sector. Financial ministers of the North quickly reacted, as if it were dangerous to display the extent of the damages.[74] In April 2009, the IMF reevaluated the cost at $4.1 trillion. However, in the countries of the North, be they conservative or social democrat, the governments introduced neoliberal policies that are extremely rough on the majority of their fellow citizens. Unable to come to the rescue of their populations in need, these same governments didn't hesitate when private companies called for help.

Economic deregulation over the past few decades has proven to be a total flop. The only feasible solution is a complete reversal of the current priorities: strict constraints on private companies, massive public investments in those sectors that will assure fundamental rights and protect the environment, and reinstallation of public authorities at the reins in order to promote the general interest. We must begin to move in the right direction, so that finance can reestablish its disregarded role as a tool at the service of human beings—of all human beings.

CHAPTER FOUR

The IMF, the World Bank, and the Logic of Structural Adjustment

How does the IMF function?

The IMF, like its twin institution, the World Bank, was founded in 1944 at Bretton Woods. Its aim was to stabilize the international finance system by regulating the flow of capital. In 2010, it had 186 member countries (the same as for the World Bank). The organization is similar to the World Bank: each country appoints a governor to represent it, usually the Minister of Finance or the governor of its central bank. The Board of Governors, the sovereign body of the IMF, meets once a year in October. It deliberates over important decisions such as the admission of new countries or the preparation of the budget.

For the daily administration of IMF missions, the Board of Governors delegates its powers to the Executive Board, composed of twenty-four members. Each of the following eight countries enjoys the privilege of appointing a director: United States, Japan, Germany, France, United Kingdom, Saudi Arabia, China, and Russia. The remaining sixteen are appointed by groups of countries that can differ slightly from the ones in the World Bank, and they can decide to elect a representative of a different nationality. It is noteworthy that France and the United Kingdom have succeeded in realizing the amazing feat of nominating the same representative on the Executive Board of both the IMF and the World Bank, which shows the proximity and complementarity of these institutions.

The third governing body is the International Monetary and Financial Committee (IMFC) which is composed of the twenty-four governors of the countries on the Board of Governors. It meets twice a year (in spring and autumn), and in its consultative role, advises the IMF on the running of the international monetary system.

The Board of Governors elects a Managing Director for five years. The same tacit rule that exists in the World Bank reserves this post for a European. The French Michel Camdessus occupied the post from 1987 to 2000, and resigned following the Asian crisis. The role of the IMF, in helping creditors who had engaged in risky investments and in imposing economic measures that lead to the unemployment of more than twenty million people, had caused massive popular protests and destabilized several governments. The German Horst Köhler replaced Camdessus at the head of the organization, until his resignation in March 2004 to become president of the German Republic. He was succeeded by Rodrigo Rato, who was the Spanish finance minister in the conservative government of José Maria Aznar, until his electoral defeat in March 2005. Rato surprisingly resigned in June 2007, and has since worked for several giants of international banking. In November 2007, he was succeeded by the French liberal socialist Dominique Strauss-Kahn, former finance minister who received the backing of the conservative French president Nicolas Sarkozy.

In July 2008, the Managing Director managed a team of 2,596 higher officials from 146 countries, though mainly based in Washington. The "Number Two" of the IMF is always a representative of the United States, whose influence is significant. During the Asian crisis of 1997–98, Stanley Fischer, who held the post at the time, upstaged Michel Camdessus on several occasions, and this was one of the reasons for Camdessus's resignation. In the Argentinean crisis of 2001–2002, Anne Krueger, a George W. Bush appointee, played a more active role than Horst Köhler. Since September 2006, this post has been held by John Lipsky, ex-chief economist of JPMorgan, one of the main U.S. commercial banks.

Since 1969, the IMF has its own accounting unit, which regulates its financial activities with its member states, called Special Drawing Rights (SDR). It was created at a time when the Bretton Woods system, based on fixed exchange rates, was wavering, so as to safeguard the credit reserve, namely gold and the dollar. But this did not prevent the Bretton Woods system from collapsing, following President Nixon's decision to stop the direct convertibility of the dollar to gold in 1971. With a floating rate, the SDR has effectively become another credit reserve. According to the IMF: "The SDR is neither a currency, nor a claim on the IMF. Rather, it is a possible claim on the freely usable currencies of IMF members." Originally equal to $1, it is now reevaluated on a daily basis from a selection of strong currencies (dollar, yen, euro, and the pound sterling). On 12 April 2010, 1 SDR was worth about $1.53.

Unlike democratic institutions, the IMF has been endowed with a mode of operation similar to that of a corporation. Any country that joins the IMF has to pay an entry fee which is a *pro rata* share. Thus the country becomes a shareholder in the IMF, since it contributes to its capital. This share is not freely chosen by the country but calculated according to its economic and geopolitical importance. Theoretically, 25 percent must be paid in SDR or one of the component strong currencies (or in gold, until 1978), and the remaining 75 percent in the country's local currency. This has given the IMF a large stock of gold (the third largest gold holder in March 2008 after the United States and Germany), as countries paid their IMF subscription in the precious metal. Furthermore, in 1970–71 South Africa, considered perfectly respectable by the IMF despite its continual violations of human rights under the Apartheid regime, sold it huge quantities of gold. At the end of March 2008, the IMF's gold reserves amounted to 103 million ounces (3,217 tons), with a market value of $103 billion. Surprisingly, this amount appears on IMF accounts based on its 1970s valuation, that is, it is estimated at less than $9 billion. This has allowed the IMF to play down its gold holdings, at least until this booty raised an internal debate, resolved in April 2008, as we will see later, to reduce a worrying deficit. Although these reserves do not enter into the IMF's loans, they confer upon the institution a stability and stature that are essential in the eyes of the players of international finance.

In February 2008, the IMF's total resources represented the equivalent of $362 billion, of which $95 billon were not to be used for loans (gold, weak currencies) and $267 billion which were usable (mainly currencies of the Triad countries).[75] However, the outstanding credit of the IMF to the member states considerably decreased in the last few years and the IMF was desperately waiting for new borrowers to knock on its

IMF Outstanding Credit
(in $billion)

YEAR	AMOUNT
31 December 1998	94.0
31 December 1999	78.9
31 December 2000	64.2
31 December 2001	75.3
31 December 2002	95.8
31 December 2003	106.9
31 December 2004	96.5
31 December 2005	49.6
31 December 2006	20.5
31 December 2007	15.5
31 December 2008	33.1
31 December 2009	66.3
31 December 2010	70.2

Source: IMF. http://www.imf.org/external/ np/fin/tad/extcred1.aspx (conversions from SDR to US$ were made using the exchange rate prevailing at the end of each period).

doors. The economic and financial crisis that erupted in 2008 brought the IMF to the forefront again. Its lending capacity increased considerably and loans began a strong upward swing starting in 2008.

After the 2010 spring meeting of the IMF and the World Bank, the lending capacity of the IMF was tripled to $750 billion. The main contributors were: Japan ($100 billion); EU ($178 billion); United States ($100 billion); Brazil ($10 billion); Russia ($10 billion); China ($50 billion); India ($10 billion).[76] Its outstanding credit (see table below) amounted to $33.1 billion at the end of 2008, $66.3 billion at the end of 2009, and $70.2 billion on 31 March 2010.

Unlike the World Bank, which borrows on the financial markets, it is member states' contributions that enable the IMF to build loan reserves, to countries with a temporary deficit. Such loans are conditional upon the signing of an agreement stipulating the measures the country must take in order to get the money. These are the notorious Structural Adjustment Programs. The money is released in instalments, after verification that the stipulated measures have indeed been implemented.

As a rule of thumb, a country in difficulty may undertake yearly borrowings of up to 100 percent of its share value from the IMF and up to a maximum of 300 percent in total, except in the case of emergencies. These are short-term loans that the country is expected to repay as soon as its financial situation improves. The greater the share value, the greater the amount that can be borrowed.

The interest rates on funding granted by the IMF to member states can be calculated from the SDR's interest rate (valued at 0.26 percent on 12 April 2010). At the time, the interest rate at which stranded countries could borrow from the IMF was 1.27 percent. At the same time, the IMF was remunerating rich countries for the sums they loaned it at a rate of 0.25 percent.[77] The difference allows the IMF to finance its day-to-day running costs.

As in the World Bank, a country's share determines its number of votes in the IMF, which corresponds to 250 votes plus one vote per 100,000 SDRs portion of the share. That's how IMF's Executive Board allocates a prominent place to the United States (over 16 percent of voting rights), followed by Japan, Germany, the group led by Belgium, then France and the United Kingdom. By way of comparison, the group led by Rwanda, including twenty-four Sub-Saharan African countries (French- and Portuguese-speaking) and representing 225 million people, has only 1.39 percent of voting rights.

Such blatant inequalities have been the cause of much anger among developing countries, which are demanding a review of voting rights. In 2006, the increasingly precarious position of the IMF led the managing director to propose a reform. Instead of a thorough reform of a shaky organization, it was decided that a revamp in multiple stages and over several years would take place. The first phase concerned only four developing countries, close to the United States and big buyers of U.S. Treasury bonds: China, South Korea, Mexico, and Turkey. The chosen ones have had to make do with a few tenths of percentages more on their respective allocations, not adequate to loosen the stranglehold of the big powers, but just enough to massage the ego of the leaders of these countries, which the United States and Wall Street consider strategically important. Dominique Strauss Kahn has made democratization of the IMF his main warhorse. The next phase of this project is moving at pedestrian speed, but one thing remains certain: the division of powers at the IMF is a subterfuge, and it will remain so.

With such a system, it is clear that the Triad countries easily manage to get the majority of voting rights and are thus in the driving seat at the IMF. Their power is utterly disproportionate if compared to that of the developing countries, whose voting rights are ridiculously small in relation to the size of the populations they represent.

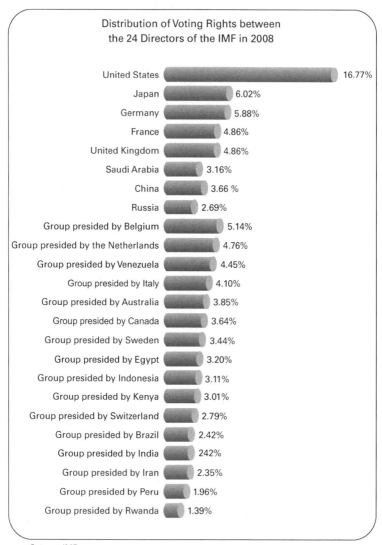

Distribution of Voting Rights between
the 24 Directors of the IMF in 2008

United States	16.77%
Japan	6.02%
Germany	5.88%
France	4.86%
United Kingdom	4.86%
Saudi Arabia	3.16%
China	3.66 %
Russia	2.69%
Group presided by Belgium	5.14%
Group presided by the Netherlands	4.76%
Group presided by Venezuela	4.45%
Group presided by Italy	4.10%
Group presided by Australia	3.85%
Group presided by Canada	3.64%
Group presided by Sweden	3.44%
Group presided by Egypt	3.20%
Group presided by Indonesia	3.11%
Group presided by Kenya	3.01%
Group presided by Switzerland	2.79%
Group presided by Brazil	2.42%
Group presided by India	242%
Group presided by Iran	2.35%
Group presided by Peru	1.96%
Group presided by Rwanda	1.39%

Source: IMF

As in the World Bank, the 85 percent threshold allows the United States to rule the IMF. Indeed, this majority of 85 percent is required for all important decisions over the future of the IMF, such as the allocation and the annulment of SDR, the increase or decrease in the number of elected directors, decisions affecting certain operations or transactions

Source: IMF

concerning gold, evaluation of SDR, the modification of shares, the temporary suspension of certain measures or various operations and transactions with SDR, and others. As in the World Bank, the United States is the only country with more than 15 percent of voting rights, which automatically gives it a blocking minority for any far-reaching change in the IMF. Initially, this threshold was 80 percent, but with the increase in independent countries, the United States saw the erosion of its voting rights. The United States only agreed to hold less than 20 percent of the votes if the threshold was raised to 85 percent.

The missions of the IMF are carefully defined in its statutes:

(i)   To promote international monetary cooperation through a permanent institution that provides the machinery for consultation and collaboration on international monetary problems.

(ii) To facilitate the expansion and balanced growth of international trade, and to contribute thereby to the promotion and maintenance of high levels of employment and real income and to the development of the productive resources of all members as primary objectives of economic policy.[78]

(iii) To promote exchange stability, to maintain orderly exchange arrangements among members, and to avoid competitive exchange depreciation.

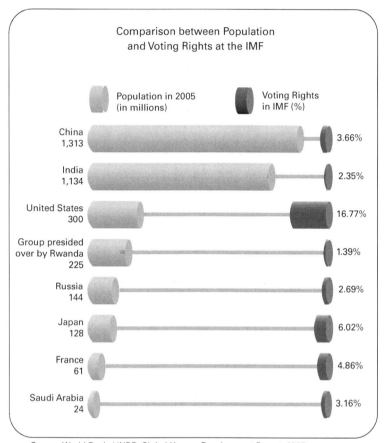

Source: World Bank; UNDP, *Global Human Development Report, 2007*

(iv)   To assist in the establishment of a multilateral system of pay-
       ments with respect to current transactions between members
       and in the elimination of foreign exchange restrictions that
       hamper the growth of world trade.

(v)   To give confidence to members by making the general
       resources of the Fund temporarily available to them under
       adequate safeguards, thus providing them with opportunity to
       correct maladjustments in their balance of payments without
       resorting to measures destructive of national or international
       prosperity.

Voting Rights in the IMF, 1945–2000 (in percent)

COUNTRY	1945	1981	2000
Industrialized Countries :	67.5	60.0	63.7
United States	32.0	20.0	17.7
Japan	–	4.0	6.3
Germany	–	5.1	6.2
France	5.9	4.6	5.1
United Kingdom	15.3	7.0	5.1
Oil Producing Countries:	1.4	9.3	7.0
Saudi Arabia	–	3.5	3.3
DC:	31.1	30.7	29.3
Russia	–	–	2.8
China	7.2	3.0	2.2
India	5.0	2.8	2.0
Brazil	2.0	1.6	1.4

Source: Yves Tavernier, *French National Assembly Finance Commission Report on the Activities and Control of the IMF and the World Bank, 2000*

(vi)   In accordance with the above, to shorten the duration and lessen the degree of disequilibrium in the international balances of payments of members.

In reality, the IMF's policies contradict its statutes. Contrary to the second point, the IMF does not give priority to full employment, whether in the highly industrialized countries or in the developing countries. The IMF, under the influence of the U.S. Treasury and with the support of the other highly industrialized countries of the North, has taken the initiative to become a major actor that has greatly influenced the political and economic orientations of its member states. To achieve this, it was not unwilling to act beyond its rights.

The IMF has thus favored the complete liberalization of capital flows. This freedom of capital is one of the major causes of the financial crises that have violently hit the developing countries. The removal of all restrictions on capital flows promotes speculation and contradicts what is stipulated in Section 3 of Article 6 of the statutes of the IMF, titled "Control of Capital Transfers," which states: "Members may exercise such controls as are necessary to regulate international capital movements." Blinded by its neoliberal will, the IMF management tried in April 1997 to change this part of the statutes to give a legal framework to its deregulatory activities. This project failed due to bad timing: the meeting held in Hong Kong and the South Asian crisis was just starting. The opposition of the governments of some developing countries buried the project. Consequently, the continued abolition of all controls on capital flows enacted by the IMF constituted a clear violation of the spirit of the institution's statutes.

The IMF sees the end of the Asian recession as proof that its policies are right. That is stupid. All recessions come to an end. All the IMF managed to do was to make the Asian recession deeper, longer and more painful.
—JOSEPH STIGLITZ, in *The New Republic*, April 2000

Surveillance, financial aid, and technical assistance are the IMF's three areas of intervention. Yet clearly, when one takes stock of the situation, it verges on total failure. The annual consultations with member countries and the recommendations of its experts did not enable the IMF to foresee nor avoid any of the major crises after 1994. Some critics maintain that its policies even worsened the crises.

The G7 governments, particularly the United States, use the IMF as a vehicle to achieve their political ends. Numerous studies of the effects of IMF lending have failed to find any significant link between IMF involvement and increases in wealth or income. IMF-assisted bailouts of creditors in recent crises have had especially harmful and harsh effects on developing countries. People who have worked hard to struggle out of poverty have seen their achievements destroyed, their wealth and savings lost, and their small businesses bankrupted.

Workers lost their jobs, often without any safety net to cushion the loss. Domestic and foreign owners of real assets suffered large losses, while foreign creditor banks were protected. These banks received compensation for bearing risk, in the form of high interest rates, but did not have to bear the full (and at times any) losses associated with high-risk lending. The assistance that helped foreign bankers also protected politically influential domestic debtors, encouraged large borrowing and extraordinary ratios of debt to equity.

—INTERNATIONAL FINANCIAL INSTITUTION
ADVISORY COMMISSION (US Congress),
known as the Meltzer Commission, 2000

At the beginning of the twenty-first century, the IMF was in bad shape. Its managing directors had resigned before the end of their term, as soon as a less risky job had become available. The challenges to its authority kept growing, both from global justice movements and many governments of developing countries. All its major borrowers had paid their debts or stopped asking for its help. This was not without consequence on the finances of the IMF, as an early reimbursement implies a major shortfall. That is why in April 2008 the Executive Board approved the sale of 403 tons of gold, for a value of $11 billion. The investment of this transfer allowed the IMF to refill its coffers.

During the 1970s, following Nixon's decision to effectively end the Bretton Woods agreements by suspending the convertibility of the dollar into gold, the IMF was profoundly destabilized and only recovered thanks to the debt crisis that hit the countries of the South in the 1980s. In a different context, the international crisis of 2007 has again given the IMF a prominent role.

QUESTION 17

What are the short-term or shock measures imposed by structural adjustment, and what are their consequences?

- *The end of subsidies on products and services of primary necessity: bread, milk, rice, sugar, fuel, electricity*

In the developing countries, to compensate for the absence of a guaranteed minimum income, governments traditionally intervene to allow the poorest sector to get basic foods and other vital goods and to have access to fundamental services such as electricity. The IMF and the World Bank demand that such subsidies be ended. The effects are felt immediately. The cost of basic foodstuffs rises suddenly, and fuel, used among other things to prepare food, goes through the roof. People then have enormous difficulty in cooking food on the one hand and in boiling water to make it safe to drink on the other, which can lead, among other consequences, to outbreaks of cholera and dysentery. Furthermore, public transport costs shoot up with immediate repercussions for market-gardening activity. Small farmers who have to bring their produce to markets shift the increase to their sales prices. In several cases they don't even go to the market anymore, because they lack money to pay for transport. Fewer available daily calories, inflation of prices, and anemic local economies are the major consequences.

The populations often react violently to these cutbacks, as their very survival is threatened. Numerous examples of rioting have followed these measures, often referred to as "hunger riots" or "anti-IMF riots." Two examples: in 1989 in Venezuela, after the SAP implementation, three days of rioting (*el Caracazo*) caused hundreds of deaths (officially 300 deaths, but unofficial sources give over 4,000); in 1991 in Peru, the price of petrol increased by a factor of thirty-one and bread by twelve overnight, and the minimum wage fell by over 90 percent in fifteen years.

In 2008, various hunger riots hit the four corners of the planet: Haiti, Côte d'Ivoire, Cameroon, Egypt, Bangladesh, Morocco, the Philippines (see Q19). The rioters demanded a reduction in the price of foodstuffs by the governments. Faced with massive popular protests, several governments renounced the IMF dogma and adopted interventionist policies, and even banned the export of foodstuffs that the population needed. However, in many countries, the governments chose the option of reducing import tariffs, which will have disastrous consequences on future national budgets (salaries of civil servants, health and education budgets) and local producers.

• A drastic reduction in social expenditure

To balance the budget, nations respond to IMF and World Bank conditions by imposing drastic cuts in public expenditures, namely in the so-called non-productive budget (education, health, housing, infrastructure). Furthermore, they demand the freezing of civil servant salaries and redundancies in the public sector. All these measures severely impact the people and account for the worrying social indicators of the developing countries.

> The Fund has repeatedly opposed the adoption of a minimum wage and has made itself the lawyer of market flexibility, ignoring international conventions on basic social norms or, at least, the application of national norms.
> —FELISA MICELI, Finance Minister, Argentina, April 13, 2007

• Devaluation of the local currency

The main purpose of devaluation is to make local export products cheaper and thus more competitive on the global market. Theoretically, they are then easier to sell. To earn the same amount of foreign currency, much larger quantities need to be sold. Reciprocally, in the domestic currency, products imported from abroad become more expensive. The cost of living rises, since in many countries, a major part of what is consumed is imported.

For example, in January 1994, the IMF and France made the African governments of the CFA franc zone (the CFA franc is used in France's former West African colonies) devalue that currency by 50 percent against the French franc. This measure was designed to benefit exports: for foreign buyers outside the CFA zone, a CFA zone product, in general a raw material yet to be transformed, cost FCFA 100, that is, FF 2. However, within a short time, its value in French francs (or any strong currency) was reduced by half, to FF 1.

However, in these countries, the effects were disastrous: overnight, a manufactured product imported from France that had cost FCFA 100 before the devaluation saw its cost jumping to FCFA 200. To earn 100 French francs, you needed to sell twice the merchandise. The purchasing power of the populations of the CFA franc zone fell dramatically, all the more so since salaries had been frozen. At the same time, the debts of these countries, in foreign currencies, doubled. Effectively, twice as much (in local money) was required to buy the foreign currency needed for debt repayments.

The effect of devaluation was not the same for all citizens of the affected countries. Poor people saw their purchasing power halved overnight, and the rich ones who had placed money abroad in the form of hard currencies were able, after the devaluation, to repatriate their money and obtain double the amount in CFA francs for the same amount of foreign currency. The local ruling classes knew that devaluation lay ahead and had taken the precaution of changing their CFA francs into foreign currency beforehand.

• *High interest rates*

This is the policy initiated by the United States in 1979; high interest rates attract foreign capital. The trouble is that when the country is in crisis, either the foreign capital does not come in or it comes in as short-term speculation. This is of no use to the local economy and can even be very harmful, because it can destabilize the currency in case of hasty departure or it can lead to an increase in the prices of land and housing.

Moreover, small producers borrow on the local market to buy seed, pesticides, and tools, and the rise in interest rates radically diminishes their capacity to borrow. Consequently, they sow less and production drops. Firms already in debt have to find extra money for the heavier repayments just when the market is depressed.

Lastly, the rise in interest rates increases the burden of internal public debt for the state, leading to a higher public budget, when the proclaimed objective was precisely to reduce it. The state then feels obliged to ax social spending even more brutally.

These drastic measures cause many bankruptcies of small and medium-size firms, as well as local banks. The state finds itself obliged to nationalize them and take over their debts. It reacts by freezing the meager savings of small savers. A private debt thus becomes a public one, and it is passed on to the taxpayer. The popular and middle classes are hit the hardest.

QUESTION 18
What are the long-term or structural measures imposed by structural adjustment, and what are their consequences?

- *The development of exports*

To procure the foreign currency needed to repay the debt, the developing countries need to increase their exports. This leads them to reduce food crops for the local population (such as manioc or millet, for example).

Very often, the countries specialize in one or several export crops, one or several raw materials to be mined, or primary activities such as fishing. They then become highly dependent on this resource or monoculture, as the below table shows.

The economies are all the more unstable because prices on the global market can suddenly vary. The great majority of raw materials are exported as such and transformed in the rich countries, which then get most of the added value. To simplify, cocoa is produced in Côte d'Ivoire but chocolate is made in France, Belgium, and Switzerland.

On a global scale, there are already 1.3 billion people living on fragile land—arid zones, marshy land and forest—from which they cannot get their subsistence.

—JAMES WOLFENSOHN, president, World Bank,
"Une chance pour le développement durable" (A chance
for sustainable development), *Le Monde*, August 23, 2002

Structural Adjustments to Exports

COUNTRY	PRINCIPAL EXPORT PRODUCT	SHARE OF PRINCIPAL PRODUCT IN EXPORT REVENUES, 2000 (%)
Benin	cotton	84%
Mali	cotton	47%
Burkina Faso	cotton	39%
Chad	cotton	38%
Uganda	coffee	56%
Rwanda	coffee	43%
Ethiopia	coffee	40%
Nicaragua	coffee	25%
Honduras	coffee	22%
Tanzania	coffee	20%
Sao Tomé & Principe	cacoa	78%
Guyana	sugar	25%
Malawi	tobacco	61%
Mauritania	fishing	54%
Senegal	fishing	25%
Guinea	bauxite	37%
Zambia	copper	48%
Niger	uranium	51%
Bolivia	natural gas	18%
Cameroon	oil	27%

Source: IMF, *The Enhanced HIPC Initiative and the Achievement of Long-term External Debt Sustainability*, April 15, 2002

- *The complete opening up of markets through the elimination of customs barriers*

The official reason for opening up markets is to allow consumers to enjoy lower prices on local markets. However, above all, it allows foreign multi-nationals to conquer considerable market shares in numerous economic sectors, to bring down local firms or producers, and, once they have the monopoly, to raise prices on imported products. Locally, inflation and rising unemployment devastate the mass of the population. What use is it to consumers to see the price of chicken or tomatoes fall if, having lost their jobs, they have no money?

Opening up the markets often leads to subsidized foreign products coming into the local market unhindered and competing freely with local producers, thus completely destabilizing the local economy. The competition is unequal. Local producers are often less highly trained, less well equipped, and unable to make even modest investments. On the other hand, the multinationals have significant financial and technological might, and the states of the North generously subsidize their production, especially agricultural. The total amount of subsidies paid by the countries of the North to their agricultural industry is estimated at $1 billion a day (or around $350 billion a year).[79] Furthermore, the countries of the South are no longer allowed to tax imported goods to protect their own products. This is why, in spite of higher production costs and considerable transport costs, products from the North are often cheaper than the same items produced locally. This is also why, in Jamaica, powdered milk imported from the United States is cheaper than the fresh milk produced on Jamaican farms.[80] This is a common occurrence with numerous products in all the developing countries.

I am determined to pursue an aggressive strategy of opening up the markets in all the regions of the world.
—BILL CLINTON, U.S. president, address to the WTO,
May 18, 1998

Is it any surprise, with such unfair competition, that the peasant farmers of the Third World cannot manage to feed their families properly and move to the slums around the big cities in hope of finding some means of subsistence to replace the living they used to get from their land? How can a local cooperative or small producer struggling to survive be placed in the same conditions as a multinational from the North? Even the most violent combat sports do not put a featherweight in the ring with a heavyweight! In the corporate-driven economy, it is "no holds barred."

Let us remember that the developed countries took great care, when it was their turn to open up their markets, to do so slowly and methodically, so that it would be carried out in the best conditions. The United States and the other Triad countries protect their industries not only with subsidies but also with protectionist measures. For example, in 2000, George W. Bush's administration decided to protect their iron and steel industry by applying taxes to steel imported from Europe and Asia. This is strictly forbidden for the developing countries.

> Most of the advanced industrial countries, including the United States and Japan, had built up their economies by wisely and selectively protecting some of their industries until they were strong enough to compete with foreign companies. . . . Forcing a developing country to open itself up to imported products that would compete with those produced by certain of its industries, industries that were dangerously vulnerable to competition from much stronger counterpart industries in other countries, can have disastrous consequences—socially and economically. Jobs have systematically been destroyed—poor farmers in developing countries simply could not compete with the highly subsidized goods from Europe and America—before the countries' agricultural and industrial sectors were able to grow strong and create new jobs. Even worse, the IMF's insistence on developing countries maintaining tight monetary policies has led to interest rates that would make job creation impossible even in the best of circumstances. And because trade liberalization occurred before safety nets were put into place, those who lost their jobs were forced into poverty. Liberalization has thus, too often, not been followed by the promised growth, but by increased misery.
>
> —JOSEPH STIGLITZ,
> *Globalization and Its Discontents*, 2002

The most flagrant example is that of cotton, where the agricultural subventions of the United States and the European Union have instigated a race to the bottom. According to UNCTAD, "The United States is the largest exporter of cotton because of the impact of the significant subsidies paid, which amounted to $3.9 billion in 2001–2002, an amount twice that of 1992 and which was larger than the whole cotton production of the United States by $1 billion." Yet, according to the International Advisory

Committee on cotton, "The cost of production of one pound of cotton is $0.21 in Burkina Faso against $0.73 in the United States."

Furthermore, the customs tariffs applied by rich countries are nearly nil for raw materials, which has discouraged Third World countries from diversifying their economy and has kept them dependent on a few basic products, and sometimes even one. On the other hand, when countries of the South want to export manufactured products to the most industrialized countries, they are faced with high tariffs. Effectively, the governments of the North practice a customs policy that aims to convince the developing countries to abandon their food sovereignty (see Q19) and to preferably export non-transformed products.

> The idea that developing countries should feed themselves is an anachronism from a bygone era. They could better ensure their food security by relying on the U.S. agricultural products, which are available in most cases at lower cost.
> —JOHN BLOCK, U.S. Secretary of Agriculture, 1986

The opening of borders to alimentary products has caused the bankruptcy of numerous local producers. Once the logic of destruction is set on course and the countries become dependent on foreign products to feed themselves, they are trapped. And yet, the development of biofuels, speculation, and the reduction of acreage since 2006 by the major cereal corporations have reduced the available quantities and caused prices to climb, up until the crisis that began in 2008.[81]

> The logic that dictates that access to markets means development is at a deadlock. Liberalization is not the key. The proof: we have greatly opened our markets, and the situation has worsened.
> —SHREE BABOO CHEKITAN SERVANSING, Ambassador and Permanent Representative of Mauritius to the UN, in Geneva[82]

- *The liberalization of the economy, especially the abolition of
  capital movement control and exchange control*

The idea is to totally open up the developing countries' economies to the investments, products, and services of the multinationals of the most industrialized countries to satisfy the multinationals: produce what they like, where they like, in conditions they lay down, at salaries they fix.

Liberalization also aims to eliminate all obstacles preventing the Northern multinationals implanted in the developing countries from repatriating their profits. As a basis for comparison, in 2006 the profits repatriated by multinationals implanted in the developing countries amounted to $238 billion, which is more than double the total amount of ODA paid by countries of the North (sometimes in the form of loans, which further increase the debt stock).[83] In other words, the North gives sparingly with one hand what it extravagantly takes back with the other. Since we are comparing various financial transfers, note that the ODA is also largely inferior to the money saved month by month by migrant workers and sent to their countries of origin, which is essential for survival there: they are estimated at $251 billion toward developing countries in 2007.[84] In fact, this figure is most probably underestimated since the amount of informal transfers, outside of specialized agencies such as Western Union, which deducts an excessive commission, is difficult to fully quantify.

Finally, the lifting of all control on capital movements enables the rich of the developing countries to delocalize "their" capital toward the countries of the North instead of investing it in the local economy. The liberalization of capital account transactions thus causes a hemorrhage of capital (see Q52).

The UNCTAD notes that far-reaching reforms undertaken by most developing countries in the 1980s and '90s, often at the behest of international financial organizations and lenders, did not deliver as promised. The reforms emphasized greater macroeconomic stability, greater reliance on market forces, and a rapid opening up to international competition. But in many cases private investment did not rise as predicted; many economies stagnated or even retracted; and many developing nations already struggling with high levels of

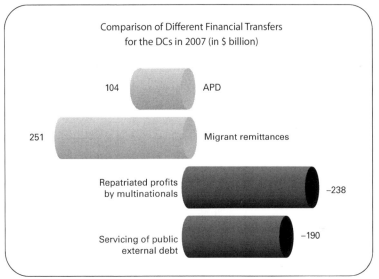

Source: OECD; World Bank

poverty found that these steps toward liberalized economies increased rather than decreased inequality.

—UNCTAD,

Trade and Development Report, 2006

In the emerging developing countries, there is another negative consequence. The capital they attract is often very volatile. As soon as there is any sign of economic difficulty, or as soon as another market offers better perspectives, the investments are withdrawn, destabilizing the country from which they flee. The arrival of such capital caused the speculative bubbles on the stock exchange and in real estate in Southeast Asia in the 1990s. In 1997–98, this volatile capital was brutally withdrawn again, causing a very severe crisis.

[T]he influx of hot money into and out of the country that so often follows after capital market liberalization leaves havoc in its wake. Small developing countries are like small boats. Rapid capital market liberalization, in the manner pushed by the IMF, amounted to setting them off on a voyage on a rough sea, before the holes in their

hulls had been repaired, before the captain had received training,
before life vests had been put on board. Even in the best of circumstances, there was a high likelihood that they would be overturned
when they were hit broadside by a big wave.

—JOSEPH STIGLITZ, *Globalization and Its Discontents*, 2002

- *A system of taxation that further aggravates inequalities,*
  with the principle of value-added tax (VAT)
  and the protection of capital revenues

The elimination of customs barriers reduces the tax revenues of the state
in question, leading to the adoption of a wider taxation system that penal-
izes first and foremost the poor. The principle of progressive taxation of
income is abandoned in favor of the VAT. And yet, VAT is the most
unjust form of taxation, since it disproportionately affects the poorest. For
example, in francophone West Africa, the VAT is 18 percent. It is applied
equally to anyone buying a kilo of rice, rich or poor. If the poor devote
their entire income to buying staple products to survive, with VAT 18
percent, it is as though they were paying 18 percent extra tax on their
entire income. On the other hand, people with high incomes, who use,
say, 10 percent for basic products and services, pay only 1.8 percent of
their total income in VAT. This is why increases in VAT or the institution
of fixed-rate deductibles are regularly promoted by those who want a
reduction of income tax.

- *Massive privatization of public companies and subsequent*
  retreat of the state from competitive sectors of production

The enforced privatization of state-owned companies often involves selling
them off for a song, from which private multinationals from the North (in
most cases) or from the South (sometimes) and a few well-placed individuals can profit. Money raised through privatization goes straight to debt
repayment. According to the IMF, the state must disengage from competitive production sectors, even if the state has strategic importance on the
national level (water, telecommunications, transport, health, education, and
the like). It has to limit its action to repression (police, justice) and defense.

For example, the Dakar-Bamako-Niger railroad, which has given rise to a significant informal economy in the regions that it crosses, was privatized in 2003 at the request of the World Bank.[85] Some critics have suggested that the railways were deliberately neglected to make the privatization inevitable. The twenty-five-year concession has been awarded to a group formed by the Canadian firm Canac (since bought by American Savage) and the French company Getma (now under the control of the group Jean Lefebvre, which has also absorbed the multinational Vinci). The group Transrail has thus been created to manage the railroad. However, the promised investments have not materialized, and since the privatization, twenty-four of the thirty-six stations have been closed: the whole informal economy around these stations, which mainly employed women, has been wiped out. More than a thousand railroad workers have been dismissed, including the most radical union officials. The redundancies have been financed thanks to a loan from the World Bank. The degradation of the rails and the matèriel has reached such proportions that it takes three days to make the 1,200 kilometers between Dakar and Bamako. The maximum speed is 30 km/h. Derailments often occur. The passenger service has been sacrificed, and raw materials have to be transported to the world market by a daily freight service. The Senegalese or Malians riders now have only the weekly express, which often arrives several days late, while the price of the ticket for a battered coach is exorbitant.

Under such conditions, the population is faced with a reduction in services to which they have had access, and unemployment increases. In Nicaragua, since it veered toward neoliberalism in 1990, the demands of the IMF have been carried out to the letter, causing 260,000 workers to be laid off in 1994 (out of a total population of less than four million inhabitants).

As a consequence of all this, the state loses control of strategic elements for development, and essential services are entrusted to the private sector. For example, in the education sector there has been a blossoming of private educational institutions, often of very mediocre quality, since the requirements in terms of teachers' training and salaries are reduced accordingly.

Transformation of the IMF into a source of long-term conditional loans has made poorer nations increasingly dependent on the IMF and has given the IMF a degree of influence over member countries' policymaking that is unprecedented for a multilateral institution. Some agreements between the IMF and its members specify scores of required policies as conditions for continued funding. These programs have not ensured economic progress. They have undermined national sovereignty and often hindered the development of responsible, democratic institutions that correct their own mistakes and respond to changes in external conditions.

—INTERNATIONAL FINANCIAL INSTITUTION
ADVISORY COMMISSION (US Congress),
known as the Meltzer Commission, 2000

The agreements signed with the IMF to obtain loans are usually valid for three years. The indebted country commits to undertake very specific economic reforms, and the promised sums are handed over in installments as these are completed. Thus, in Madagascar, the privatization of the state-owned petroleum company (Solima) fell behind the timetable planned by the IMF. Planned for 1999, it was not completed until June 2000. In July 2000, the first instalment of a new loan was paid, as a reward for a good pupil that could go to the next reform. Result: a company sold off at cut-rate price passed into private ownership and an increase in the country's indebtedness. For the population: nothing.

On any objective assessment of two and a half decades of standardized packages of "stabilization, liberalization and privatization," the right kind of growth has simply failed to materialize across most of the continent. . . . Doing so goes a long way to recognizing that the Washington institutions do not have a monopoly on technical competence.

—UNCTAD, Economic Development in Africa, 2006

All in all, structural adjustment programs (SAPs) fiercely defend the interests of the financial institutions and the multinationals of the North. But for the populations who have to bear their consequences, they are synonymous with poverty and hardship.

As economics is not an exact science, the number of counter-examples is irrelevant. If I put forward a hypothesis in physics which is proved wrong by an experiment, I must question the theory. And the theory progresses through such invalidation. In economics, you can undermine the existence of millions of people, but none of that human evidence will affect the ideology of structural adjustment.

—SUSAN GEORGE, vice president of ATTAC France,
December 6, 2000

QUESTION 19

What is the impact of the IMF/World Bank logic on the world food crisis of 2007?

Article 25 of Universal Declaration of Human Rights declares: "Everyone has the right to a standard of living adequate for the health and well-being of himself and his family, including food, clothing, housing and medical care and necessary social services." The steep rise in the price of staple food, especially in the first half of 2008, has directly threatened the survival of hundreds of millions of people. The right to food, already seriously undermined by several decades of neoliberal policies, is under even greater threat.

After a significant fall in prices during more than twenty years (see Q11), the reversal of the trend took place in the second half of 2001. First, it hit the energy and metal sectors, and later that of food. The rising trend has been violent. In one year, the prices of rice and wheat doubled, and that of maize rose by more than a third.

This explosion of prices is the direct consequence of the market liberalization imposed by international financial institutions since the 1980s. The abolition of customs barriers is responsible for the increase in the fluctuation of world prices of agricultural raw materials. Thus the FAO notes the steady increase of price instability during the last two decades, a previously absent instability, that now seems a permanent characteristic of markets.[86] According to the FAO, "The agricultural policies of developing countries have been liberalized and farmer support structures (extension, inputs, storage, marketing, price stabilization) have been gradually eliminated (better management of those structures would have protected their smallholders from the forces of an unequal international market). Was it the FAO that pressured developing countries to adopt these policies?"[87]

The rise in prices is thus mainly the consequence of speculation. In only one trading session, on March 27, 2008, the price of rice, the staple food for half of the world's population, climbed by 31 percent. The consequences for the economically most vulnerable countries are extremely worrying. Effectively, the policies imposed by the IMF and the World Bank for the majority of poor countries have created a structural dependence on food imports, since the dominant ideology imposes the development of exports over domestic food production. According to the FAO: "The total expenditure of LDCs (Least Developed Countries) and LIFDC (Low-Income Food-Deficit Countries) [will] increase by 37 to 40 percent compared to 2007, after it already increased by 30 and 37 percent last year." Hence, the bill of the LIFDC will reach $169 billion in 2008.

Oil prices reached $145 in July 2008, an ounce of gold $1,000 in March 2008, a bushel of maize $7.5 in June 2008, all record prices, which gives an indication of the rising price curve for nearly all raw materials. Cereal stocks are at their lowest levels in a quarter of a century. Some producing countries have even diminished or stopped their exports, such as Russia for cereals and Thailand for rice, so that the products will stay on the national market. The cost of a meal has greatly increased. In more than thirty countries, from the Philippines to Egypt, Burkina Faso, Haiti, Yemen, and Senegal, the population took to the streets to protest, and general strikes have multiplied.

According to some estimates, investment funds now control 50–60 percent of the wheat traded on the world's biggest commodity markets. One firm calculates that the amount of speculative money in commodities futures—markets where investors do not buy or sell a physical commodity, like rice or wheat, but merely bet on price movements—has ballooned from $5 billion in 2000 to $175 billion in 2007."

—GRAIN, "Making a Killing from Hunger," April 2008[88]

After the subprime crisis in the United States in the summer of 2007, institutional investors[89] slowly disengaged themselves from the debt market, which had been built on speculation in the U.S. real estate sector, and identified agricultural products and hydrocarbons as potential areas of high profitability. They achieve this end by buying future harvests on the stock exchanges of Chicago and Kansas City, the main exchanges for cereal speculation. Equally, they speculate on hydrocarbon raw materials on other stock exchanges. The same people who, for want of higher profits, caused the subprime crisis in the United States by exploiting the naïveté of barely solvent North American families hoping to own a property, were deeply involved in the steep increase in the prices of hydrocarbons and agricultural products. Hence the need to question the power of financial markets.

Yet the arguments are presented as facts: climate change caused a reduction in cereal production in Australia and Ukraine, a rise in petrol prices led to higher transport costs and products or the increasing demand of China and India (which explains why products in lesser demand—such as cocoa—by these two countries have not witnessed price rises). Many commentators have refused to examine the economic framework in which these phenomena were occurring. Thus, Louis Michel, the European Commissioner for Aid and Development, has above all feared "an economic and humanitarian tsunami" in Africa. The statement is ambiguous since the image of a tsunami evokes a natural catastrophe, which is beyond us and thus relieves us of responsibilities. Other explanations are equally superfluous.

Firstly, with cereal prices at a historical low until 2005, the major agribusiness corporations obtained subsidies for biofuels from the governments of the United States and the European Union. These multinationals wanted to win on two fronts: sell their cereals at a dearer price and make biofuel production profitable. They succeeded.

How did they proceed? They marketed the following hypothesis: in the coming decades oil will have to be replaced (due to declining reserves) and thus soy, beet (transformed into biodiesel), cereals, or sugar cane (as ethanol) should act as substitutes. Thus they asked public authorities to subsidize the substantial costs of biofuel to make it profitable. Washington, the European Commission in Brussels, and other

European capitals accepted this under the cover of energy security of their country or region.[90]

This policy of subsidies has turned over significant amounts of agricultural products, essential for food, toward the biofuel industry. For example, one hundred million tons of cereals were excluded from the food sector in 2007. With significant declining outputs, the prices rose. Equally, land that was geared toward the production of food was reconverted to the culture of agro-fuels. This also decreases the output of alimentary products and causes a rise in prices. In fact, in the interests of the major private companies bent on developing agro-fuels, the decision was made to steal some agricultural products that the world needs to feed itself.

Even the international institutions were alarmed by this situation. A report by the World Bank estimated that climatic phenomena and the increasing Asian demand were minor factors. On the contrary, according to this report, the development of biofuels has caused a rise of 75 percent in food prices between 2002 and February 2008 (out of the 140 percent global rise, while the rise in prices of energy and fertilizers accounted for only 15 percent).

This estimate is much higher than the 3 percent figure retained by the U.S. administration. According to the World Bank, the hike in prices has already cost consumers $324 billion in poor countries and could drive 105 million more people into poverty.[91] So as not to displease President Bush, the World Bank did not publish this report. It was a leak in the press that allowed the information to emerge.[92]

This analysis of the World Bank remains ideologically tainted by neoliberalism. The development of agro-fuels is not responsible for the "disorganization of the markets" but reveals their irrational policies and their criminal consequences. Eat, drink, or drive, the free market will not allow us to choose.

It is a crime against humanity to convert agricultural productive soil into soil . . . which will be burned into biofuel.
—JEAN ZIEGLER, UN Special Rapporteur on the Right to Food,
October 2007

A few days later, it was the turn of the OECD to publish a report, arguing for a moratorium on agro-fuels and a complete overhaul of the associated policies, criticizing the high costs of vegetable-based fuels and their dubious benefits to the environment.[93] The OECD even notes that "new policy initiatives deepen the existing problems" since agricultural prices are pushed up and the risk of famine among poor populations in developing countries increases.[94] Yet the projected figures indicate a doubling of agro-fuel production in the next ten years.

> Further development and expansion of the biofuels sector will contribute to higher food prices over the medium term and to food insecurity for the most vulnerable population groups in developing countries.
>
> —OECD, 2008

Secondly, developing countries have been particularly impoverished by the food crisis as they lack the necessary protections due to the policies imposed by the IMF and the World Bank after the debt crisis (see Q17 and Q18): reduction in land surfaces dedicated to agricultural production and specialization in a few export sectors, the end of price stability, the forsaking of cereal self-sufficiency, the reduction of cereal reserves, the weakening of economies due to an extreme reliance on market fluctuations, massive cutbacks in social budgets, an end of subsidies on basic commodities, the opening of markets, and unfair competition for small local producers from multinationals. Masters in the art of deceit, the accused institutions concede some mistakes so as to remain at the center of international affairs. Far from being worried by the increasing poverty that it causes, the World Bank seems more concerned with social troubles that put neoliberal globalization in jeopardy. In a semi-confidential report, under the guise of a *mea culpa*, it continues to promote an economic model that has deliberately denied impoverished people vital protections from the insatiable appetite of the most ferocious economic actors. From now on, the new edifice that ensures the expansion of the model of capitalist agriculture consists in making access to land subject to market forces, but also water resources, which amounts to a privatization of biological life. Finally, it promotes the concentration of agricultural resources and encourages speculation.

The "learned" experts of the IMF stated in September 2006: "Looking forward, metals prices are expected to retreat from their current highs. . . . In the baseline scenario, the real price of aluminium and copper is forecast to decline by 35 and 57 percent, respectively, by 2010."[95] On July 8, 2008, *Le Figaro* wrote: "At its highest since 2006, above the $3,310 of the time, the price of aluminum has yesterday reached a record high on the London Metal Exchange at $3,317." Four days earlier, an agency report announced: "The price of copper and aluminum exploded this week on the London Metal Exchange (LME), the red metal reaching a record high. . . . The price of copper has set a new record on Wednesday at $8,940 per ton, stimulated by the rise of the dollar and investors' fears over potential strikes in Chile and Peru. It thus surpassed the latest high of $8,880, established on April 17."[96] The high prices have not abated since. It is not difficult to be more accurate than an IMF expert.

CHAPTER FIVE

Other International Players: The Paris Club and the WTO

What is the Paris Club?

In 1955, after the military coup that overthrew the Argentinean president, Juan Domingo Perón, the new regime was eager to be recognized by the international community. Thus it quickly tried to be accepted by the IMF and the World Bank. But in order to do so, it had to sort out the problems of its debt and meet the countries to which it owed most. On May 16, 1956, the meeting took place in Paris, at the suggestion of the French Minister of the Economy. The Paris Club was born.

Fifty years later, the Paris Club, alongside the IMF and the World Bank, has become a key instrument in the strategy developed by creditor countries to maintain control of the world economy. The aim of the Paris Club—which still meets in the French Ministry of Finance, rue de Bercy, where its permanent secretary is housed—is to renegotiate the bilateral public debts of those Southern countries experiencing difficulty servicing their debt. Originally made up of eleven countries, it now has nineteen members.[97]

Between 1956 and the end of 1980, only thirty agreements were signed by the Club. Before 1976, the Club used to balk at holding meetings for countries whose debt was considered too small. Only Argentina, Brazil, Chile, Indonesia, Peru, Cambodia, Pakistan, and Zaire were summoned during this initial period. After the debt crisis at the beginning of the 1980s, the frequency of the Club's meetings greatly accelerated. Between the beginning of 1981 and September 2008, 373 agreements were signed by eighty-three debtor countries. The embarrassing record is held by Senegal (summoned to the Club fourteen times since 1982) followed by Madagascar (twelve times), then Niger and the Democratic Republic of the Congo (eleven times). The volume of debts either rescheduled or canceled by the Paris Club is more than $500 billion.

The plenary meetings, which are generally monthly, are always the same.[98] The delegation from the indebted country and its lenders sit in alphabetical order around the big conference table. Multilateral institutions (the IMF, the World Bank, UNCTAD, Regional Development Banks) are also present. The president of the Club—often the director of the French Treasury or a close colleague—opens the proceedings. The leader of the indebted country's delegation, usually the Minister of Finance or the Governor of its central bank, presents in a formal way the reasons for their presence. During the preceding months the government of their country has been in contact with the Club and has already agreed to accept two very strict conditions, one to request the meeting with the Club based on its proven impossibility of continuing repayments under the ongoing conditions, and the other to sign an economic agreement with the IMF to ensure that it will not happen again. Before meeting its creditors, the indebted country has already had to accept the conditions imposed by those creditors, which means that on the appointed day, the delegation has nothing left to negotiate.

After this opening presentation, the IMF details the reforms planned to rescue the country from its predicament and then the World Bank and UNCTAD present their conclusions, after which the question-and-answer session can begin. When the latter session—euphemistically called "negotiating"—is over, the omnipotence of the creditors is made clear when the delegation of the indebted country is requested to leave the room while the members of the Paris Club negotiate among themselves. Once they have decided what they are going to do, the president informs the delegation from the Southern country—which had to wait incommunicado while their country's future was being decided—of their conclusions. If the delegation is not satisfied with the conclusions, the discussion can be taken up again, but the potential for persuasion is small since the country is requesting a renegotiation of its debt, and the fact that it is sitting at the table is a clear indicator that it is not going to revolt against the system.

After the minutes of the meeting have been signed, all that is left for the delegation to do is to show the media of its country how enthusiastic it is about the agreement that has been reached and thank the creditor countries.

The first time a country presents itself, the Paris Club fixes a date. Officially, only loans made before that date are affected by the rescheduling. Debts contracted afterward do not normally qualify for restructuring. This is to reassure the financial markets and the funding agencies that any new loans granted will be repaid. For Madagascar, Niger, and Côte d'Ivoire, that date was July 1, 1983, which considerably reduces the volume of debt concerned by any possible reduction.

The Paris Club distinguishes between two kinds of debt: ODA loans (Official Development Aid loans) granted at lower interest rates than those of the market, which are supposed to enhance development,[99]and non-ODA loans (or commercial loans), which are the only ones that may qualify for reduction. Generally, debt reduction by the Paris Club is reserved for the poorest and the most heavily indebted countries (see Q31). For the great majority of developing countries with payment difficulties, the Paris Club responds with debt rescheduling, which merely postpones the problem to a later date.

The living conditions of the poorest populations are in no way taken into account, since the Club aims to be simply a debt-collecting institution. It is managed by a Ministry of Finance, and not by a Ministry of Foreign Affairs. Its aim is to make the indebted countries pay the most they possibly can. "The Paris Club creditors seek to maximize recoveries. They typically require immediate repayment of as much of the original claim as possible. Amounts that cannot be repaid are rescheduled on terms that balance future payments with the objective of minimizing the chance that the debtor will return to the Paris Club with additional requests for forbearance."[100] The cronyism between the Club and the large banks seems to work well. Jean-Pierre Jouyet left the presidency of the Club in July 2005 to become a non-executive president of the French subsidiary of Barclays Bank.[101] Emmanuel Moulin, general secretary of the Club, took up his new post at Citibank, the major international banking group, in January 2006.

The Club actually presents itself as an informal group, a "non-institution" with no legal basis or status. Theoretically, the conclusions of its discussions are nothing more than suggestions that only come into effect if the creditor countries—totally independently—decide to apply them in bilateral agreements. Only such bilateral agreements have the law behind them. However, it is written in the Principles of Solidarity that "creditors agree to implement the terms agreed upon in the context of the Paris Club." This is a clever way of watering down responsibility—the Paris Club is not responsible in any way since it has no legal entity, but the member states scrupulously respect its decisions. The greatest advantage of the Paris Club is that it enables creditors to act as a united front to recuperate individual bilateral loans, whereas the Southern countries are completely isolated from each other. The situation of each debtor country is examined in isolation, using data provided by the IMF, which has a strong tendency to be overly optimistic in its future projections.[102]

While requesting "good governance" from others, it does not practice what it preaches, since the agenda of its meetings is never made public before the meeting. No one outside the Club knows what the discussions are about, nor the position of the individual states. The meetings take place behind closed doors without any question of there being an observer present from either North or South social organizations. Riding roughshod over the conflict of interests of being both judge and party, the Club isolates the debtor countries from each other, making it obvious that the only concern of their meetings is the financial interests of the creditor countries.

It should also be noted that the Paris Club always capitalizes interest, that is to say, the outstanding interest due on Paris Club loans is capitalized. It is added to the initial debt—and thus generates future interest on itself![103] However, most Latin American constitutions, and even some European constitutions, such as Italy's, do not allow such a loan mechanism. The Paris Club actually manages the *tour de force* of getting the representatives of certain states to agree to decisions that are actually against their own constitution!

Furthermore, there is a very clear form of blackmail to dissuade indebted countries from forming a "front of refusal." From the Paris Club website: "Creditworthiness usually takes a long time to build, as lenders tend to assess over time the capacity of the debtor to repay its debt before entering into large lending. In contrast, failure to fulfill debt obligations can rapidly damage creditworthiness. Under circumstances where debt restructuring cannot be avoided, countries that do not accumulate arrears and take preventive steps to reach a coordinated solution with their creditors, notably in the Paris Club, can restore their creditworthiness more rapidly afterward. In contrast, debtors that declare a unilateral moratorium tend to lose access to new financing for some time."

Finally, it is important to note that after appearing before the Paris Club, the indebted state can then turn to its private bank creditors, grouped in the London Club. Here the negotiations are of a similar type but even more opaque and with an even worse stench of profit at all costs.

> Today, the emerging markets are not forced open under the threat of the use of military might, but through economic power, through the threat of sanctions or the withholding of needed assistance in a time of crisis.
> —JOSEPH STIGLITZ, *Globalization and Its Discontents*, 2002

Basically, the Paris Club is a serious institutional anomaly, where united, all-powerful creditors meet on the sly.[104] For all these reasons, it should purely and simply be disbanded.

QUESTION 21
Are all the developing countries treated in the same way by the Paris Club?

It is undeniable that the developing countries are very different, each with its own history and its specific assets. It is impossible, from an economic point of view, to put Brazil and Bangladesh, India, and the Congo, Thailand and Morocco in the same boat. Each suffered the debt crisis in its own way but all had to accept it.

Latin America became a textbook case of ultra-neoliberalism, beginning with the dictator Augusto Pinochet in Chile in September 1973. Pinochet brutally, and with bloodshed, imposed an economic model defined by the Chicago Boys (see Glossary). The World Bank and the IMF actively supported Pinochet's regime. However, the debt crisis that broke out in Mexico in 1982 and then spread to a large number of developing countries made it possible to impose this economic model without having to count on military dictatorships. Not until the beginning of the twenty-first century did alternatives start to emerge, in Venezuela, in Bolivia, in Ecuador. How long will it last? How far will they go?

The East Asian Tigers (Indonesia, Thailand, Malaysia, the Philippines) managed to attain strong economic positions that gave them a certain amount of room to maneuver until the mid-1990s. However, the 1997 crisis forced them under, later but just as brutally. Malaysia refused any agreement with the IMF in 1997–98, protected its domestic market, and, after the crisis broke out, took strict control of capital flows and exchange, and spent money on giving new impetus to production. Although the IMF announced impending disaster, Malaysia was back on its feet before the other affected countries.

For centuries, and more than other places in the world, Africa was bled dry by the slave trade, by colonialism, and by large-scale looting of its natural resources. Generations of Africans have been sacrificed, their cultural heritage stolen or scorned. Decolonization in the 1960s was most of the time limited to the simple physical withdrawal of the colonial powers (when they did in fact withdraw) and for most countries independence has never been more than an illusion. As soon as the debt crisis began, almost all the African countries came straight under the heel of the IMF, the World Bank, and the Paris Club member countries. The burden of the debt became the cornerstone of the ongoing neo-colonialism.

Some East European countries became heavily indebted toward the end of the 1970s. In the early 1990s, after the fall of the former Soviet Union and the Berlin Wall, all those countries were rapidly delivered up to the ferocious appetites of accelerated liberalization, and social conditions rapidly deteriorated. Russia was clearly in decline when the 1998 crisis occurred, with life expectancy falling by about four years during the 1990s and industrial production going down by 60 percent and GDP by 54 percent.

Just these few examples show how submission to the debt mechanism can differ from one country to the next. This submission was further facilitated by the corruption of the ruling classes of the developing countries, who soon learned how to cash in on their docility to international financial institutions, which proved to be willing accomplices.

The Paris Club responds differently to the problems encountered by the poorest countries than it does to those countries whose situation seems to be less critical. The Paris Club only reduces the debt for the poorest and most heavily indebted countries (the HIPC initiative generalized these debt reductions; see Q31), whereas the other countries have to be satisfied with a rescheduling of their debt.

Closer inspection of this seemingly logical system shows some very surprising exceptions. Some carefully selected countries receive preferential treatment. Strategic allies are simply momentarily useful for the geopolitical ambitions of countries of the North, and they have negotiated their alliance by putting the question of their debt in the balance.

Poland

In April 1991, Poland went before the Paris Club, which had decided to reschedule all debts owed to its members, almost $30 billion. Thus was Poland rewarded for opening up to liberalization, as the first East European state to join the Western camp by leaving the Warsaw Pact. Nevertheless, despite this measure, Poland was to see its bilateral public debt service increase from $183 million in 1990 to $353 million in 1991, $755 million in 1992, $779 million in 1993, and so on. This led the Polish president, Lech Walesa, to protest that his country was very poorly rewarded.

Egypt

In May 1991, $21 billion of Egypt's bilateral debt was rescheduled to reward it for its cooperation during the first Gulf war against Iraq. The service on the bilateral public debt was thus halved: from $1.14 billion in 1990 to $555 million in 1991, before climbing back to over $800 million in 1992 and 1993. But its bilateral public debt stock continued to increase.

Russia

Certain grandiloquent declarations by the Paris Club are quite simply contradicted by the facts. In 1998, Russia decreed a unilateral moratorium and has received absolutely no sanctions. On the contrary, it has greatly benefited from the unilateral suspension of payments. What is going on?

Faced with a fall in its export revenues (fall in the price of oil in 1998) and its tax revenues, Russia unilaterally suspended debt repayments for three months, starting in August 1998. This modified the balance of power in its favor, with regard to its Paris Club and London Club creditors. Thanks to the suspension of payments, it obtained the cancellation of about 30 percent of its debt to these two categories of creditors. Its status as a former nuclear superpower no doubt helped it to force the negotiations through. As for the IMF, it has continued to grant loans to Russia despite the suspension (in contradiction to its own declarations) while several billion dollars have been embezzled via Western European tax havens by top Russian officials converted to capitalism.

We have no sympathy for the Russian leaders who are conducting a ruthless war against the Chechen people and who are applying antisocial and corporate-driven policies throughout the whole of Russia. However, there is a lesson to be learned from this suspension of payments: an openly defiant attitude to the creditors can pay off.

Former Yugoslavia

In November 2001, the former Yugoslavia benefited from generous treatment for the whole of its debt from the Paris Club, which granted it the conditions normally reserved for the poorest countries. This favor came after the new Serb government handed former leader Slobodan Milosevic over to the International Criminal Tribunal in the Hague on June 29, 2001.

Pakistan

In December 2001, Pakistan was rewarded for having released the Afghan Talibans and for forming an alliance with the United States during its operations in Afghanistan after the 9/11 attacks. The Paris Club advantageously restructured almost the entire debt owed to it by Islamabad.

Your rapporteur notes that conditionality often means imposing a preestablished line of conduct upon the country benefiting from the IMF's intervention. This conduct is rarely adapted to the reality of their economic and social structures, but is modeled on the devel-

oped economies which, it should be remembered, have only
reached their present stage of development after decades, even centuries, of economic evolution.

—YVES TAVERNIER, Member of Parliament, French National
Assembly Finance Commission's Report on the Activities
and Control of the IMF and the World Bank, 2001

These few cases show the extent to which decisions on debt are
linked to the geopolitical imperatives at the time. The states of the North
meeting in the Paris Club use the debt as a means of domination over the
developing countries. As soon as it is in their interests, as soon as they
have the political will to win over a temporary ally, they know how to
manipulate debt reduction or cancellation as a means of reaching their
ends. The increase in the numbers of these types of cases over the last few
years has brought the Paris Club into the spotlight.

QUESTION 22
What is undermining the Paris Club?

Having always cultivated an ethos of secrecy, the Paris Club carefully
avoids media coverage. Yet in recent years it has hit the headlines on three
occasions.

In November 2004, Iraq's debt was the subject of unusually long
discussions between its creditors. It was the first time a session of the
Club ended on a Sunday. During the military invasion of March 2003,
the United States and its allies called for the cancellation of 95 percent
of the debt owed by Iraq to member countries. France, Russia, and
Germany, opposed to the war, did not want to go beyond 50 percent.
Agreement was reached on a three-phase debt relief of 80 percent, that
is, $31 billion out of the $39 billion held by the Club.[105] Note that to
justify the proposed reduction of the Iraqi debt, on April 7, 2003,
Washington put forward the doctrine of odious debt. However, the
U.S.government quickly put aside this important argument, for fear that
other developing countries might demand that the same doctrine be
applied to their debts (see Q44).

In January 2005, after the tsunami off Indonesia that killed more than 220,000 people, numerous associations mobilized to demand debt relief for the countries affected.[106] The media impact of this demand, coupled with the first-ever attendance of a French finance minister at one of its meetings, incited the Paris Club to announce a one-year moratorium on the debts of Indonesia and Sri Lanka. The result was that those two countries had to repay between 2007 and 2010 the amount they were due to repay in 2005. But once the public attention had fallen, the Club's true face was revealed: no generosity, no more pretense of compassion. Not only was there no cancellation, but since these countries were not paying on the due date, the creditor countries that wished to could add interest over the moratorium period.

> In accordance with the principle of a non-concessional debt moratorium, when rescheduling the due dates, some creditors invoiced the moratorium interest at the appropriate market rate. Other creditors, France included, decided not to invoice these moratorium interests at all.
> —RAMÓN FERNÁNDEZ, while vice president of the Paris Club[107]

No further details were made public.

In October 2005, the Paris Club agreed to cancel two-thirds of the debt Nigeria—Africa's biggest oil producer—owed to member countries: $18 billion out of $30 billion. This is a textbook example of the Club's phony good news. First of all, Nigeria had to repay all its outstanding arrears within six months for one-third of the sum to be canceled, and then, for the other third to be erased, Nigeria had to obtain IMF approval of its economic policy and also make further repayments. Nigeria then submitted even further to the IMF's demands by paying out $12.4 billion in a few months, even though the arrears dated from the military dictatorship of the 1990s and constituted odious debt. Not all Nigerian politicians agreed to this: a motion adopted in March 2005 by the Chamber of Representatives demanded that repayment of the external debt be stopped. Farouk Lawan, president of the Finance Commission of the Chamber, stated, "It is unconscionable that Nigeria has paid £3.5 billion in debt service over the past two years but our debt burden has risen by

£3.9 billion—without any new borrowing. We cannot continue. We must repudiate this debt."[108]

That was only the tip of the iceberg. As with the IMF, demands for early repayments to the Paris Club came thick and fast.

In summer 2005, Russia signed a check for $15 billion, out of a total of $40 billion of debt toward member countries and then, in 2006, another for $22.6 billion, which settled the balance with the Club. This allowed Russia to become a creditor country once and for all, after having had a very special status, since it was both a recent member of the Club and indebted toward other members. Russia even dared to suggest that this money be used by its creditors for the development of poor countries, incurring the wrath of several countries that did not want to be told how to spend these funds.

Many other countries followed suit. In June 2005, Peru negotiated the early repayment of $2 billion, out of a total debt of $4.2 billion. In December 2005, Brazil announced early repayment of its total debt to the Club—$2.6 billion. In March 2006, Algeria also repaid its entire debt to the Club—$8 billion, and in January 2007 Macedonia—$104 million, in May 2007 Peru—2.5 billion, in July 2007 Gabon—$2.2 billion.

The case of Gabon is worth looking at in detail. The country has been run for forty years by Omar Bongo, that "faithful friend" of France, whom Nicolas Sarkozy warmly thanked for his advice during the French president's successful electoral campaign in May 2007, and who was received at the Elysée Palace shortly afterward. Bongo, a pillar of French interests in Africa for several decades and renowned for his suspicious landslide electoral victories, is under investigation for embezzlement of public money concerning property in Paris. According to a U.S. Senate inquiry cited by the association Survie, each year he reserves about 8.5 percent of the budget of this little oil state that made Elf's fortune and filled its slush funds.[109] Elf was absorbed in 2000 by Total, the other big French oil company.

When Gabon went before the Paris Club, the country was treated with indulgence, thanks to the French. The unprecedented result was that Gabon paid off its debt at its market value, which was 15 percent less than its nominal value. A few days later, on July 27, 2007, when the French president was in Gabon, he announced an even bigger drop of 20 percent on the part held by France. The difference was converted into investments to save the forest, a major source of the wealth of rich Gabonese, whose profits are monopolized by the clan in power.

Besides wood, Gabon is rich in natural resources, notably oil, iron, and manganese. Its GNP per inhabitant is one of the highest in Africa, but the population gets nothing of this wealth, and 62 percent of the Gabonese live below the poverty line. Since the end of colonialism, French leaders have never slackened their grip on the Gabonese economy. Omar Bongo ensures it stays that way.

Other countries behaved very differently. Following Cuba in the 1980s and 1990s, Argentina stopped repaying the Paris Club at the end of 2001, and yet it was not ostracized by the great powers. However, negotiations started up again in 2007 with a view to restarting payments. The silence of the Paris Club on the subject has been deafening. As for the creditors, in 2006 Norway, despite being a member of the Paris Club, independently canceled the debts it was owed by five countries (see Q44). At the same time it took the precaution of saying that the ensuing discussions on Norwegian debt reduction would take place within the Paris Club framework. It can be seen that the Paris Club fears potential contagion and prefers not to draw attention to those that do not repay or those that cancel debts without going through them. The Paris Club's wiggle room for maneuver is further reduced by the increasingly active role of China, which is not a member, as an international lender.

Instead of any form of compromising with the grouped creditors, it is perfectly possible to adopt a firm and dignified attitude by refusing categorically the dictates of the Paris Club and by ending all dialogue with this illegitimate entity.

QUESTION 23
What is the role of the World Trade Organization (WTO)?

At the end of the Second World War, the IMF and the World Bank were not the only two organizations that were supposed to be set up to build the postwar world economy. The allies, mainly the United States and

Great Britain, had decided to create the International Trade Organization. But although it was envisioned, the ITO never actually came into existence because the United States abandoned the idea. Fifty-three countries signed the ITO charter in Havana in March 1948, but the U.S. Congress did not ratify the document.[110] What did survive from the preparation of the ITO charter was the lowering of tariff barriers, which had been agreed upon and signed at the beginning of 1948. The committee that had been set up to organize the negotiations, and which by definition was supposed to be a temporary structure and had always had a very limited institutional status, remained in existence under the name of the agreement—the GATT, General Agreement on Tariffs and Trade.

Basically over the next fifty years, the GATT organized eight rounds of negotiations, each one liberalizing trade further than the one before. The last of these rounds, the Uruguay Round (1986–94), ended with the creation of the World Trade Organization in April 1994 at the Marrakech Conference. The "Final Act" of this round was, in the words of the WTO, an "umbrella agreement" widening the scope of negotiations to sectors that had not been part of the GATT, such as agriculture, textiles, and services.[111] It was also the first time that the question of intellectual property rights had been addressed within the context of international trade. The WTO was given the mandate to organize these wide-ranging negotiations and to intensify the liberalization of trade. Free trade had become the impassable horizon of the WTO, even though this free trade was the same as "putting the fox in charge of the hen-house."

Free trade is, in fact, the strategy adopted by those who have become powerful economic actors to ensure that they remain powerful. Once they have reached the top, it is in the interest of the powerful to say, "Now we must allow the market forces to work." For the WTO, to liberalize means obliging developing countries to abandon all forms of protection and to open up their economies to the ferocious appetites of the transnational firms.

Any nation which by means of protective duties and restrictions on navigation has raised her manufacturing power and her navigation to such a degree of development that no other nation can sustain free competition with her, can do nothing wiser than to throw away

these ladders of her greatness, to preach to other nations the benefits of free trade, and to declare in penitent tones that she has hith-
erto wandered in the paths of error, and has now for the first time
succeeded in discovering the truth.

—FRIEDRICH LIST, economist,
The National System of Political Economy, 1841

In the nineteenth century, Great Britain was the dominant power, and
it also used this argument, as Ulysses Grant, president of the United
States from 1868 to 1876, well understood: "For centuries England has
relied on protection, has carried it to extremes, and has obtained satisfactory results from it. There is no doubt that it is to this system that it owes
its present strength. After two centuries, England has found it convenient
to adopt free trade because it thinks that protection can no longer offer it
anything. Very well then, gentlemen, my knowledge of our country leads
me to believe that within two hundred years, when America has gotten
out of protection all that it can offer, it too will adopt free trade." This is
precisely the aim of the WTO.

Each country in the WTO has one vote, and decisions are reached by
consensus. Much pressure is put on countries that are not willing to toe
the line, and the great powers thought at first that this would be enough
to forge ahead with liberalization. Fortunately, this was not the case. That
is why the present general director of the WTO, Pascal Lamy, who is the
former European commissioner for trade and as such used to be the
negotiator representing the European Union at the WTO, has often
expressed his desire for an institutional reform so that the neoliberal
reforms he was defending along with the great powers could no longer be
blocked by informal coalitions of other member countries.[112]

The WTO has its own internal tribunal, the Dispute Settlement Body
(DSB), whose arbitrator makes the final decision when a country contests
an agreement. The arbitrator's decisions are binding for all member
states. Although the Havana treaty specifically referred to the United
Nations and announced the creation of an International Trade
Organization subject to UN laws (such as the Universal Declaration of
Human Rights), the main economic powers made sure that the WTO had
no institutional link with the United Nations.

The WTO hit the headlines toward the end of 1999, when its ministers held a conference in Seattle. Large sectors of public opinion had been very quick to realize the threat of this new international actor, which has such enormous and uncontrolled power. The demonstrations at Seattle were big enough to prevent the summit from taking place, and the representatives of the various countries had to leave without achieving their goals.

The September 11, 2001, attacks in the United States finally enabled the great powers, blocked for two years, to put on the pressure so that the WTO conference in Doha succeeded in launching new negotiations to further increase the liberalization of world trade. It was not by chance that this meeting was held in the highly policed state of Qatar, so far from potential mass demonstrations. In Doha, it was decided that the new round of negotiations should be completed before the end of 2004, but after that the divisions between industrial countries, developing countries, and poor countries remained strong. At the next conference, which took place in Cancún, Mexico, in 2003, the developing countries formed an alliance that was dubbed the G20, and stood up to the great powers of the North.[113] The intransigence of the rich countries, especially in the negotiations concerning agriculture, led Mexico to walk out of the summit. After Seattle, this was the second setback for the WTO.

Negotiations were still deadlocked in August 2008. The United States and the European Union have been negotiating mainly with Brazil and India to try to reach an agreement. These two countries both hope to become included in the great powers, even if it means sacrificing their populations. However, even these negotiations have not yet led to an agreement. This is a good thing, as it has become a matter of urgency to stop the privatization of basic common goods such as water, education, health, and access to seeds through the elaboration of agreements such as the agreements on services (GATS) and on intellectual property rights (TRIPS).

Along with the IMF and the World Bank, the WTO completes the powerful war machine set up to prevent the Southern countries from protecting their economies against the ferocious appetite of the multinationals, which are now so vital for them. For example, Article III of the Marrakech agreement establishing the WTO says, "With a view to achieving greater coherence in global economic policymaking, the WTO shall cooperate, as appropriate, with the International Monetary Fund and with the International Bank for Reconstruction and Development and its affiliated agencies."

How does this cooperation work? The IMF and the World Bank impose very strict neoliberal conditionalities that force indebted countries to open up their economies to a world market dominated by the most industrialized countries and the multinational companies that usually have their headquarters in them. The way the economies of developing countries are linked to the world market is always to the detriment of local producers, the internal market, and the possibility of developing South-South relations. Contrary to what the neoliberal dogma would have everyone believe, a more open economy, with more connections to the world market, is a handicap to development, with only a few exceptions like China.[114] Integrating a developing country into the world market generates a structural deficit in the balance of payments, since imports increase more quickly than exports, and this deficit tends to be closed by borrowing from abroad, which increases the debt.[115] Most developing countries have entered the downward spiral of debt and dependence.

The actions of the WTO affect much more than mere trade. The WTO is a key element in the system set up to give free rein to neoliberal interests. The policies promoted by the trio of the World Bank, the IMF, and the WTO are mutually coherent and follow a clear-cut agenda with many facets (political, economic, financial, and geo-strategic), which the social movements must continue to oppose.

Countries seeking free trade agreements with the United States should meet criteria beyond those of an economic and commercial nature. At the very least, those countries should cooperate with the United States in its external policy and its national security objectives.
—ROBERT ZOELLICK, U.S. Trade Representative, 2001 to 2005[116]

CHAPTER SIX

The Structure
of Developing Countries' Debt

Of what does the external debt
of developing countries consist?

In 2007, the total external debt of developing countries was estimated at approximately $3.36 trillion dollars. For the borrowers, this debt stock is made up of approximately equal amounts of public and private debt.

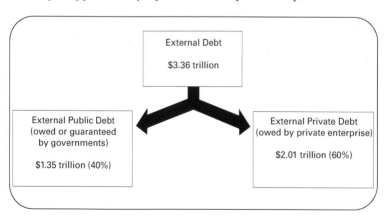

The holders of the external debt can be broken down into: multilateral holders, $380 billion; bilateral holders, $280 billion; and private holders, $2.7 trillion.

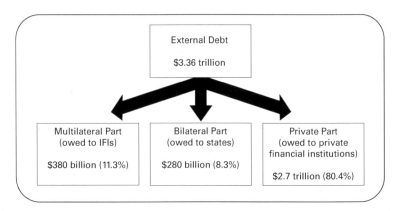

Private banks hold by far the greatest part of the external debt.

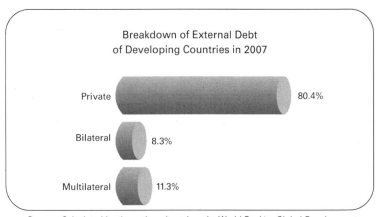

Source: Calculated by the authors based on the World Bank's, *Global Development Finance 2008*

The most industrialized developing countries have the largest debt (see diagram page 148).[118]

The type of creditor varies from one country to another. Countries that have strategic natural resources or that have reached a certain level of industrialization have a higher credit rating. Private financial institutions (banks, pension funds, insurance companies, various speculative funds) are therefore happy to lend them money, and most of the debt of these countries is held by private financial institutions. This is the case for countries such as Brazil, Argentina, Chile, Venezuela, Mexico, South Africa, China, India, Malaysia, and Turkey.

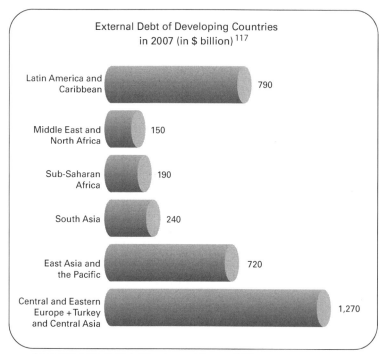

External Debt of Developing Countries
in 2007 (in $ billion) [117]

Latin America and Caribbean — 790

Middle East and North Africa — 150

Sub-Saharan Africa — 190

South Asia — 240

East Asia and the Pacific — 720

Central and Eastern Europe + Turkey and Central Asia — 1,270

Source: World Bank, *Global Development Finance 2008*

However, some very poor countries with mineral resources also get considerable loans from private financial institutions, but the percentage of the total debt in this case is not generally the major part. This is the case for Bolivia, Côte d'Ivoire, Congo-Brazzaville, Mauritius, and Sudan.

By contrast, the poorest countries that do not have large quantities of mineral resources are of little interest to private creditors. The private creditors withdrew from these countries at the beginning of the debt crisis in the early 1980s after collecting repayment of their existing debts without granting new ones, except for short-term loans at exceptionally high interest rates. The public creditors (bilateral and multilateral) took over, lending money to the poorest countries to enable them to repay these private creditors.

The multilateral creditors, in particular the World Bank and the regional development banks, have reached the point where they are by far the main creditors of some of the most heavily indebted countries. Thus

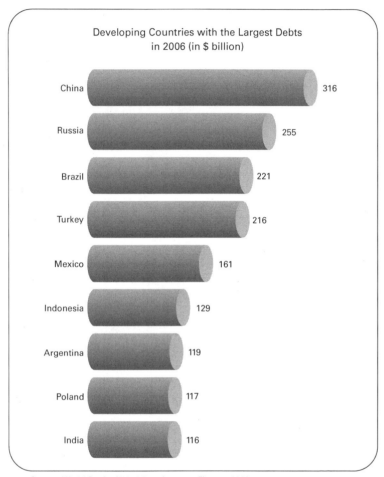

Source: World Bank, *Global Development Finance 2008*

they hold over 75 percent of the debts of Burkina Faso, Chad, Gambia, Madagascar, Niger, Mali, Malawi, Uganda, Haiti, and Nepal.

States of the North are the main creditors in other indebted countries, as for example in Cameroon, the Democratic Republic of the Congo, Egypt, Gabon, and Vietnam. This is due to the fact that, for historical reasons, a considerable proportion of the bilateral debt is money owed to private firms of the former colonial power, private firms whose loans are guaranteed by their governments, essentially through export credit agencies, such as Coface in France or Ducroire in Belgium.

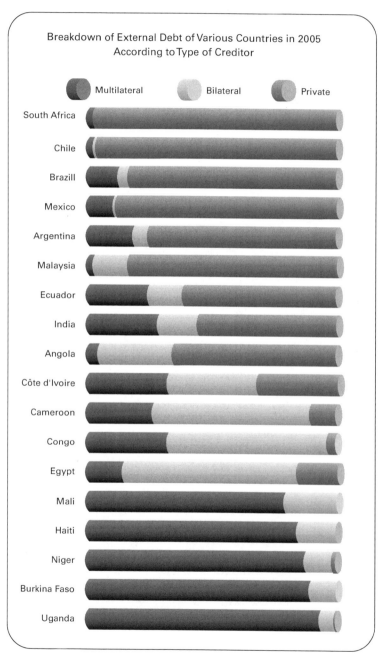

Source: World Bank, *Global Development Finance 2007*

QUESTION 25
How has the debt changed since 1970?

Before the debt crisis began, the external debt of all the countries had increased eight-fold between 1970 and 1980.

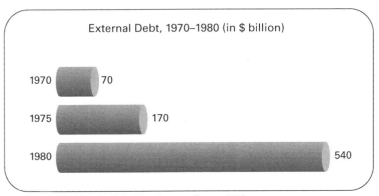

External Debt, 1970–1980 (in $ billion)

1970   70

1975   170

1980   540

Source: World Bank, *Global Development Finance 2008*

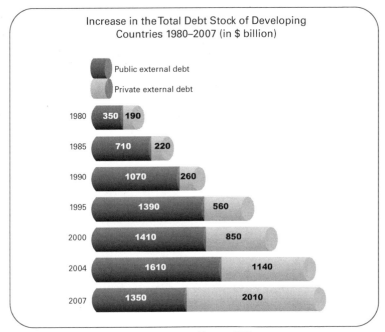

Increase in the Total Debt Stock of Developing Countries 1980–2007 (in $ billion)

Public external debt

Private external debt

1980   350 190

1985   710 220

1990   1070 260

1995   1390 560

2000   1410 850

2004   1610 1140

2007   1350 2010

Source: World Bank, *Global Development Finance 2008*

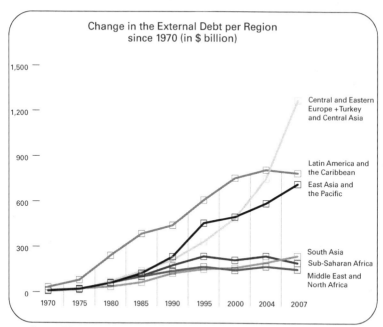

Source: World Bank, *Global Development Finance 2008*

Since 1980, the external debt of developing countries has continued to increase. A preliminary analysis shows that the debt has increased greatly for all the developing countries in all six regions since 1970.

From the diagrams, we can see that Latin America had an enormous external debt early on and thus it was not just a coincidence that the 1982 debt crisis began there. Although it cannot be seen on the above graph (see Q29), the Latin American countries have greatly increased their internal public debt over the last few years while their external public debt has gone down slightly, essentially as a result of early repayments.

On a different scale, Sub-Saharan Africa has followed a similar pattern, namely a large external debt in the early 1980s (close to that of East Asia), a debt crisis that devastated the continent, and rates of repayment that were crippling the countries. Then, in the mid-1990s, the widely publicized debt reductions, though bringing the *increase* in total debt stock to a halt, only managed to reduce the *total* stock to just slightly below $200 billion.

For East Asia, the changes were very different. The external debt was low during the 1980s, but then grew rapidly during the first half of the

1990s. This led to the 1997–98 crisis, followed by very large repayments by the countries concerned.

After the Berlin Wall fell in November 1989, the countries of the former Soviet bloc plunged into the neoliberal ethos—and their debt soared. This is the region with the greatest increase in public external debt in 2007.

QUESTION 26

Do developing countries repay debts?

Although major economic problems sometimes prevent some developing countries from continuing their repayments over limited periods, the immense majority honor their financial commitments. Thus the total amount paid in debt servicing for 2007 came to $520 billion, distributed over the six developing countries regions as follows:

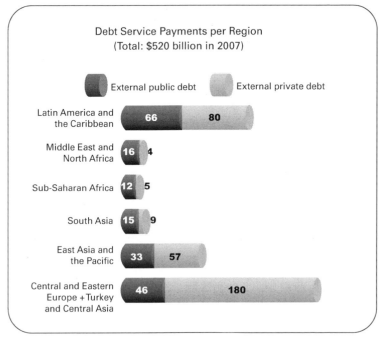

Source: World Bank, *Global Development Finance 2008*

The amount paid in servicing the debt over the period 1970–2007 increased parallel to the debt itself:

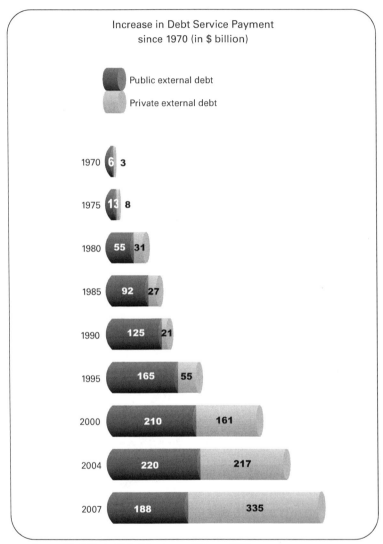

Source: World Bank, *Global Development Finance 2008*

The total amount repaid by the developing countries between 1970 and 2007 was an astronomic $7.15 trillion, distributed over the regions as follows:

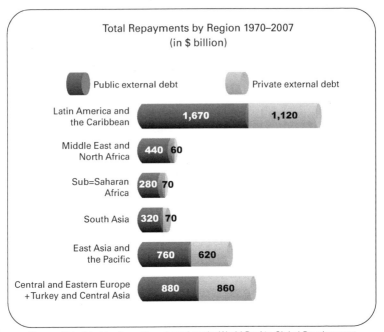

Source: Calculated by the authors based on the World Bank's *Global Development Finance 2008*

Basically, the debt is an incredible levy imposed on the economy of developing countries:

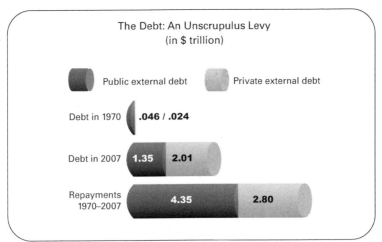

Source: Calculated by the authors based on the World Bank's, *Global Development Finance 2008*

What do the graphs really show?

*Between 1970 and 2007, the total external debt of the developing
countries was multiplied by 48—during which time they
repaid 102 times the amount they owed in 1970*

For decades now, the amount to be repaid has become so large that that it
has led to a snowball effect, with the developing countries taking out new loans
to service the existing loans. This can clearly be seen by looking at the long-
term debt figures for the year 2007.[119] The governments of developing countries repaid $123 billion of outstanding principal and $65 billion interest.
During the same time, they received $169 billion in new loans, which they will
have to repay, both principal and interest, in the coming years. Since 1970, the
figures are even more spectacular: the governments of developing countries
have received $3.89 trillion in loans, but the principal repayments total $2.83
trillion and the interest repaid, $1.52 trillion; that is, developing countries have
repaid a total of $4.35 trillion, which means the creditors have already made a
profit of $460 billion since 1970,[120] and that is without even taking into
account the amount that still remains to be repaid.

In other words, the debt for which repayment is being demanded
from the developing countries today has nothing to do with money that
has been injected into the economy of these countries. It is a Sword of
Damocles hanging there, obliging them to transfer the greater part of their
wealth to their creditors and to make them reform their economies
uniquely in order to service the debt.

Servicing the debt is the visible sign of allegiance.
—JEAN ZIEGLER, *L'empire de la honte* (The Empire of Shame), 2005

QUESTION 27
What about the external public debt
of developing countries?

Let us now look at the external public debt, that is to say, the debt repaid
or guaranteed by the governments of developing countries. Unlike the

debt a private company owes to foreign institutions, the public debt weighs directly on the population of the Southern countries, since their governments have to draw on the state budget to repay it. It is this part of the debt that we are most concerned with, especially when demanding that debts be canceled (see chapter 10).

This question concerns the external *long-term public debt*—evaluated at $1.35 triillion. It is distributed per creditor as follows:

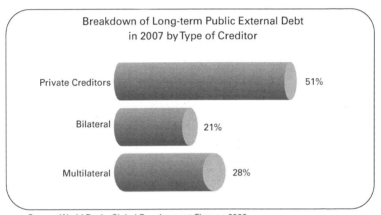

Breakdown of Long-term Public External Debt
in 2007 by Type of Creditor

Private Creditors — 51%

Bilateral — 21%

Multilateral — 28%

Source: World Bank, *Global Development Finance 2008*

And by region:

Long-term Public External Debt by Region in 2007 (in $billion)	
Latin America and Caribbean	400
Middle East and North Africa	110
Sub-Saharan Africa	130
South Asia	160
East Asia and Pacific	260
Central and Eastern Europe +Turkey and Central Asia	290

Source: Calculated by the authors based on the World Bank's *Global Development Finance 2008*

The most heavily indebted governments in absolute figures are:

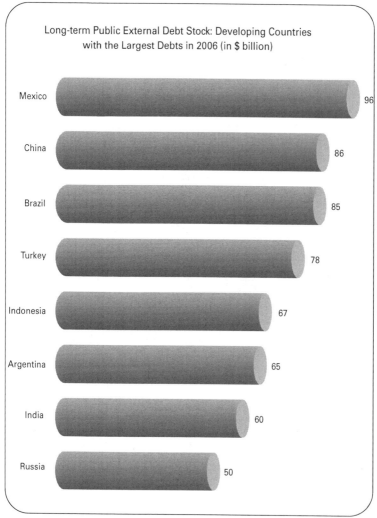

Long-term Public External Debt Stock: Developing Countries
with the Largest Debts in 2006 (in $ billion)

Country	$ billion
Mexico	96
China	86
Brazil	85
Turkey	78
Indonesia	67
Argentina	65
India	60
Russia	50

Source: Calculated by the authors based on the World Bank's *Global Development
Finance 2008*

In relative figures, it is interesting to compare the total debt stock with the number of citizens of each country. The external public debt per inhabitant gives a very different picture:[121]

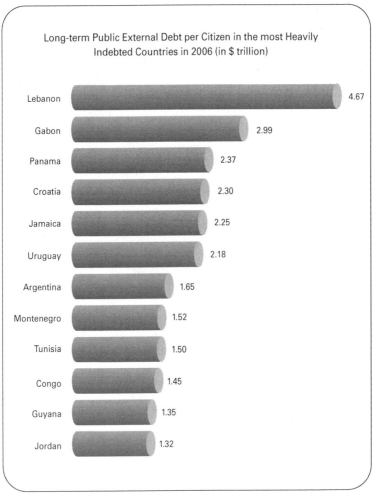

Long-term Public External Debt per Citizen in the most Heavily Indebted Countries in 2006 (in $ trillion)

Lebanon	4.67
Gabon	2.99
Panama	2.37
Croatia	2.30
Jamaica	2.25
Uruguay	2.18
Argentina	1.65
Montenegro	1.52
Tunisia	1.50
Congo	1.45
Guyana	1.35
Jordan	1.32

Source: Calculated by the authors based on the World Bank's, *Global Development Finance 2008* and *World Development Indicators 2008*

Between 1970 and 1995, the total debt stock soared, before rising more gradually and later starting a slight drop in 2005:

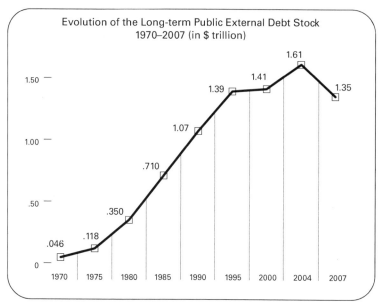

Source: World Bank, *Global Development Finance 2008*

In 2007, servicing the total external public debt amounted to $188 billion distributed as follows for the six regions:

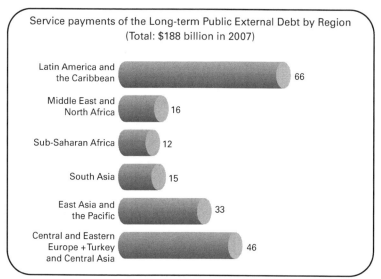

Source: Calculated by the authors based on the World Bank's, *Global Development Finance 2008*

The change in the amount repaid over the period 1970–2006 directly reflects the change in the debt itself:

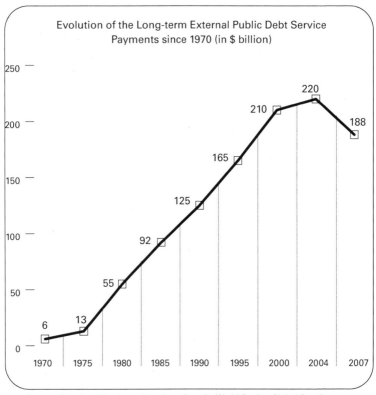

Evolution of the Long-term External Public Debt Service Payments since 1970 (in $ billion)

Source: Calculated by the authors based on the World Bank's *Global Development Finance 2008*

Over the period of reference, 1970 to 2007, which is approximately the duration of a "long cycle" in an economy, the long-term external public debt of the developing countries rose from $46 billion to $1.35 trillion, whereas the developing countries repaid a total of $4.35 trillion. That is to say:

Between 1970 and 2007, the external public debt of the developing countries was multiplied by twenty-nine. During this time, they repaid the equivalent of ninety-four times the amount owed in 1970.

How are debt-related financial flows directed?

Enormous repayments have to be balanced against considerable new loans to find out if, in the end, the governments of developing countries receive more in new loans than they are paying out to service existing debts. In other words, is the debt-related financial flow from North to South or from South to North?

To answer this question, the net transfer on the debt is taken as the difference between the amount provided by new loans and the total amount repaid. If it is positive, the country has received more than it has paid out, even if it implies that large repayments due in the future will make the net transfer negative in the coming years. If it is negative, that means that the debt is directly draining the wealth of the developing countries to enrich the creditors.

Unsurprisingly, in 2007 the net transfer on the public long-term external debt was negative: minus $18.9 billion. But with clear differences: it was positive for South Asia and Sub-Saharan Africa, practically null for countries from Central and Eastern Europe, Turkey and Central Asia, and negative for the other regions.

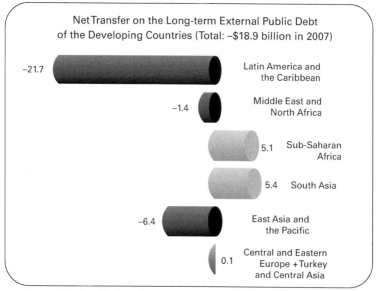

Net Transfer on the Long-term External Public Debt of the Developing Countries (Total: –$18.9 billion in 2007)

–21.7	Latin America and the Caribbean
–1.4	Middle East and North Africa
5.1	Sub-Saharan Africa
5.4	South Asia
–6.4	East Asia and the Pacific
0.1	Central and Eastern Europe +Turkey and Central Asia

Source: Calculated by the authors based on the World Bank's, *Global Development Finance 2008*

It is as if the population of the developing countries had directly sent $18.9 billion to their creditors in 2007! Although not shown in the chart, the large negative transfer to the IMF particularly stands out; the IMF alone received $5 billion.

This is a perfect example of the "debt spiral." After the debt crisis, the governments of developing countries had to take out new loans to make the enormous repayments of existing debts. The net transfer on the external debt remained positive, as long as new loans were coming in and the rate of repayment remained reasonable, whereas the net flow became negative from 1985 on, when the level of repayments soared, apart from two periods that stand out: 1993, when money started to flow into Latin America, just before the crisis broke out in Mexico in 1994; and then in 1998, when the IMF and the G8 poured money into Asia to counter the Asian crisis (see diagram on facing page).

But even these figures do not tell the whole story, since a true estimation of the real flows would not only take into account repayments of the external debt but would have to include all of the following: capital flight when rich people in the developing countries invest abroad; the repatriation of profits by multinationals, including invisible transfers, especially using methods of "over-" or "under-charging." According to what is more favorable and depending on a variety of factors, a transnational corporation may choose to declare its profits in any of the countries where it is located. Internal over- and undercharging is one of the techniques commonly used: the prices for intra-company imports and exports can be set well above and below market prices, thus helping to shift profits from one place to another; the acquisition of businesses in developing countries at rock-bottom prices by the dominant classes of the industrialized countries under privatization policies; the low-cost purchase of basic goods produced by the populations of developing countries (with deteriorating exchange rates); the "brain drain"; and the theft of genetic resources.

Between 1985 and 2007, developing countries sent to their creditors the equivalent of 7.5 Marshall Plans.

At the end of the Second World War, the Marshall Plan for the reconstruction of Europe, financed by the United States, cost about $100 bil-

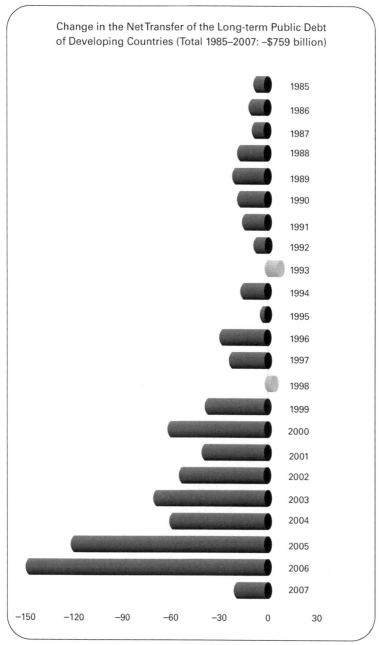

Change in the Net Transfer of the Long-term Public Debt of Developing Countries (Total 1985–2007: –$759 billion)

Source: World Bank, *Global Development Finance 2008*

lion at today's value. Between 1985 and 2007, the governments of developing countries paid back $759 billion more than they received in new loans—that is, $759 billion, the total net transfer over this period. Thus it is as if the citizens of the developing countries had sent the equivalent of 7.5 Marshall Plans to their creditors, with the local capitalist elite taking their commission on the way. It is a well-oiled mechanism, with part of the money coming back to the South in the form of new loans to ensure that the transfers continue. Inevitably, the debt becomes self-perpetuating. Thanks to the debt, the wealth of the citizens of the South is being transferred under our very eyes to the elite of the North, with the complicity of the elite of the South.

QUESTION 29
What about the domestic debt of developing countries?

World Bank statistics give details concerning foreign debt, but there is less information available concerning internal public debt. However, the part played by internal debt has increased in importance over the last few years.

The internal public debt of developing countries increased sharply from 1995 onward. Major increases in a large number of middle-income countries are especially worrying. Even though certain very poor countries are not yet affected by the phenomenon, there is clearly an upward trend in the internal public debt of developing countries.

According to the World Bank, the total domestic public debt of the developing countries rose from $300 billion in 1997 to reach $3.5 trillion in September 2005 (two and a half times the external public debt, which in 2005 reached the figure of $1.415 trillion).[122] What is more, in 2007 repayments of the domestic public debt amounted to approximately three times those of the external public debt, that is, $600 billion. This means that repayments of all public debt (both internal and external) paid out each year by the public authorities of developing countries exceed $800 billion.

Take the example of Colombia. Like other Latin American countries, it was hit by the debt crisis of the 1980s but "benefited" from the huge but

Domestic and External Public Debt in Colombia

YEAR	DOMESTIC (% of GDP)	EXTERNAL (% of GDP)	TOTAL (% of GDP)	DOMESTIC PUBLIC DEBT AS PERCENT OF TOTAL PUBLIC DEBT
1990	1.90	12.87	14.76	12.9
1991	1.55	12.48	14.03	11.0
1992	2.93	12.06	14.99	19.5
1993	4.47	10.08	14.55	30.7
1994	4.58	8.08	12.66	36.2
1995	5.75	8.14	13.89	41.4
1996	6.62	7.81	14.43	45.9
1997	8.83	8.93	17.76	49.7
1998	10.60	11.51	22.11	47.9
1999	14.45	15.07	29.52	48.9
2000	18.65	18.25	36.90	50.5
2001	22.02	22.14	44.16	49.9
2002	24.97	25.35	50.32	49.6
2003	25.63	25.09	50.72	50.5
2004	25.73	20.70	46.43	55.4
2005	29.90	16.68	46.57	64.2
2006	28.48	16.38	44.85	63.5

Source: Banco de la República de Colombia and Ministerio de hacienda y crédito público

ephemeral capital investment that took place at the beginning of the 1990s. It seemed as if the neoliberal model had triumphed, but in fact it was leading Colombia to an impasse of financialization and excessive public debt. The country's domestic public debt increased enormously.

Colombia's domestic public debt expressed as a percentage of its GDP rose fifteen-fold between 1990 and 2006; its external debt increased over the same period but only by one and a half times.

The same kinds of policies were applied in Brazil, Argentina, Venezuela, and Mexico. In developing countries everywhere, there was a huge increase of public debt, mainly internal debt. The figures published in April 2005 by the World Bank speak for themselves.[123] Taking developing countries as a whole, both external and domestic public debt, which accounted for 46 percent of GDP in 1990, increased to 60 percent of overall GDP in 2003. However, external public debt as a percentage of GDP decreased slightly between 1990 and 2003, from 31 percent to 26 percent. On the other hand, domestic public debt doubled its share of the total, increasing from 15 percent to 34 percent of GDP.

The financial crises that affected the developing countries between 1994 and 2002, resulting from the deregulation of the market and the private financial sector as recommended by the World Bank and the IMF, led to an enormous increase in internal public debt. In short, by following the Washington Consensus, governments of developing countries had to give up their currency and capital controls. This was combined with the deregulation of the banking sector in different countries. Private banks had to take more and more risks, which led to numerous crises, beginning with Mexico in December 1994. Capital was massively withdrawn from Mexico, sparking off a chain reaction of bank failures. The Mexican government, supported by the World Bank and the IMF, transformed the banks' private debt into internal public debt. This took place in exactly the same way in countries as different as Indonesia (in 1998) and Ecuador (in 1999/2000).

In addition, even in those developing countries whose banking sectors had not collapsed, the World Bank advised the governments to increase their internal debt. Although difficult to believe, the World Bank actually considered that this was a positive development, and advised foreign investors to invest in the rapidly growing internal debt market. It advised governments of indebted countries to encourage large foreign banks to take over local banks—something already very prevalent in Latin America. Large Spanish banks have massively invaded the banking sector in South America, and U.S. banks dominate banking in Mexico.[124] The World Bank also supports the privatizing of pension schemes and encourages the use of workers' savings (which constitute their future pensions) to buy securities in domestic public debt. The governments of Brazil, Chile, and Argentina applied this policy of partial privatization of pension schemes, and pension funds have become significant buyers of domestic debt securities.

This development does not concern only Latin America. Domestic public debt has risen the most in Asia in the last few years, mainly as a result of the Asian crisis of 1997–98 and of the policies imposed by the IMF and the World Bank.

Instead of being invested productively, under the supervision of either the public authorities or the private sector, the savings placed in banks have systematically been diverted to serve the parasitic investment model. Banks lend money to the public authorities that must be repaid at excessively high rates. It is less risky for them to lend to the state than to give loans to small or medium producers. A state rarely defaults on its domestic debt. Encouraged by the World Bank, central banks of developing countries often impose very high interest rates. This leads to the situation that local banks borrow short term, at fairly low rates, on foreign financial markets (the United States, Japan, and Europe) and then lend this money long term in their country at a high interest rate. The banks make a good profit until interest rates begin to escalate in the North, which can lead to bankruptcy. And there is always the risk that the state will take over their private debts again, thus increasing the domestic public debt. And so we have the vicious circle of internal/domestic public debt, which accompanies that of external/foreign public debt.

Brazil is a typical example. Its internal public debt is eight times higher than its external public debt. In 2008, its internal public debt reached $869 billion ($1.4 trillion *reals*), an increase of 40 percent in barely two years.[125] Repayments on Brazil's domestic debt are twelve times higher than those of its external debt. The percentage of Brazil's budget spent on debt repayment (internal and external together) is four times greater than the percentage spent on education and health.[126] Guatemala's internal public debt is four times higher than its foreign debt.

In Argentina, even though the government managed to achieve a reduction of its external public debt in 2005 (by suspending repayments to private creditors for three years) its domestic public debt increased, and as a result there was once again a dramatic increase of Argentina's total public debt.[127]

Another phenomenon that triggers an increase of domestic public debt is the accumulation of huge foreign exchange reserves by those developing countries that export oil, gas, minerals, and certain agricultural products whose price has increased since 2004. This phenomenon also affects China, which is accumulating an enormous amount of foreign

Argentina's Public Debt (in $ billion)

PERIOD	TOTAL DEBT	EXTERNAL DEBT	DOMESTIC DEBT
Dec. '94	80.7	60.9	19.8
Dec. '95	87.1	66.4	20.7
Dec. '96	97.1	72.9	24.2
Dec. '97	101.1	72.9	28.2
Dec. '98	112.4	81.2	31.2
Dec. '99	121.9	82.5	39.4
Dec. '00	128.0	81.4	46.6
Dec. '01	144.5	84.6	59.9
Dec. '02	137.3	87.6	49.7
Dec. '03	178.8	102.0	76.8
Dec. '04	191.3	111.6	79.7
Dec. '05	128.6	60.9	67.7
Dec. '06	136.7	56.2	80.5
Dec. '07	144.7	62.1	82.6

Source: Ministerio de economia y producción, subsecretaria de financiamiento

exchange reserves because it is swamping the world market with manufactured products, thus acquiring a permanent trade surplus. The central banks of these countries invest a large proportion of their reserves in U.S. Treasury bonds (or in treasury bonds of other countries, especially those in Europe). In other words, they are lending money to the U.S. government so that the huge deficit of the United States can be absorbed.

Paradoxically, though some developing countries have an abundance of reserves, this policy of transforming them into international reserves generally leads to taking out new loans. However surprising and ridiculous it may seem, though national currency reserves are partly invested in industrialized countries' treasury bonds (as recommended by the World Bank and the IMF), governments have to borrow in order to pay back the public debt. And the return on reserves invested in treasury bonds is always lower than the interest paid when borrowing, thereby leading to a loss for the treasury of the country concerned.

Furthermore, the existence of an abnormally high amount of foreign currency in a country often causes the central bank of that country to become indebted. The surge in capital inflow in the form of foreign currency is in the hands of resident brokers who exchange it for domestic currency in their banks. This can swell the volume of domestic currency and become a potential source of inflation. To prevent this from happening, the monetary authorities intervene to "sterilize" these reserves, either by increasing statutory reserve requirements—that is, the proportion of assets that commercial banks must hold on deposit with the central bank; in which case, increased interest rates on bank loans makes credit more expensive and slow down the creation of money in the form of bank loans—or by issuing public debt shares. (The sale of these treasury bonds should allow the central bank to recover some of this excess domestic currency and thus remove it from circulation.)[128]

An overwhelming majority of governments prefer this neoliberal policy, and therefore domestic public debt is increasing to counterbalance their high foreign exchange reserves.[129] This is true for China and for Latin American, Asian, and African countries.

Instead of amassing mountains of foreign exchange reserves and simultaneously increasing their domestic public debt, it would be better for governments of developing countries to 1) introduce controls for capital and foreign exchange (which would be a much more efficient means of protecting themselves against speculation and would also fight against the flight of capital); 2) use a large part of their reserves to invest productively in industry, in agriculture (agrarian reform, development of food independence), in the infrastructure, in environmental protection, in urban renewal (urban reform, renovation, and construction of housing), in the health services, education, culture, research; 3) pool part of their reserves to create one or more joint financial organizations (a Bank of the South or a Southern Monetary Fund); 4) set up a coordination of indebted countries to stop paying the debt; 5) reinforce and establish a cartel of countries that produce basic products so that their prices can be stabilized at a higher level than at present; 6) develop barter agreements similar to those between Venezuela and Cuba and recently extended to Bolivia and Nicaragua.[130] These alternatives will be analyzed further on.

CHAPTER SEVEN

Deciphering the Official Discourse
on Debt Relief

How did the debt relief initiative come about?

Creditors are not in the habit of canceling debts, much less giving something away for free. Yet in the press we regularly read about debt relief and debt cancellation. So what's the real situation?

The 1988 G7 Summit in Toronto marked a turning point: the debt was finally recognized as a structural rather than an economic problem. It was no longer a question of helping out a few countries that had managed their finances badly but of finding a solution to a problem that concerns the economic model as a whole. There was a real risk—which still exists— that the debt would cause the entire system to collapse. This was not in the creditors' interest because for them, debt equals power. They therefore agreed to waive a number of debts—the least possible—if by so doing they could maintain and even increase their domination.

Starting in 1988, therefore, the major moneylenders set themselves a dual objective: maintain stricter control of the behavior of indebted countries and allow those that accepted neoliberal measures to benefit from a systematic restructuring of their debt. But the conditions underlying this restructuring were so untimely and restrictive that the situation continued to deteriorate. Hence the present paradox: debt cancellation continues to make headlines while the debt problem remains unchanged.

Must we really let our children die of hunger to repay our debts?
—JULIUS NYERERE, president of Tanzania, 1964 to 1985

Up until 1996, the IMF and the World Bank, in their role as priority creditors, hid behind their statutes in order to refuse all debt relief: according to these two institutions, their statutes forbade them to envisage such an eventuality.

As for the Paris Club, it was given the job of orchestrating the different decisions of the G7 summits after 1988. At the Toronto summit, it was decided that 33 percent of non-ODA debt contracted before the cutoff date[131] would be canceled for the poorest countries. With the passing years, the percentage of debt to be canceled was revised upward, since the original figure did not allow countries to get out of the spiral of overindebtedness. It was therefore raised to 50 percent in London in 1991 and to 67 percent in Naples in 1994. But let's not be dazzled by these glittering percentages—they concern not the total debt but only the non-ODA debt contracted before the cut-off date. The reality is a world away from appearances, and the debt has reached new summits.

At the 1996 G7 summit in Lyon, in view of the scale of the debt crisis and under pressure from many organizations within the Jubilee movement (see Q59), the world's major moneylenders were forced to come up with another debt relief initiative, which received a lot of press and was not without its own hidden agenda: the HIPC (Heavily Indebted Poor Countries) initiative. As too few countries managed to fulfil the conditions imposed, the initial initiative was beefed up in 1999 at the G7 summit in Cologne.

Officially, this initiative was a revolution. It would allow the countries concerned to meet their "current and future external debt service obligations in full, without recourse to debt rescheduling or the accumulation of arrears, and without compromising growth." The big innovation was the involvement for the first time of the IMF and the World Bank: "The initiative marked a major departure from past practice, which had resisted any reduction of debt owed to multilateral financial institutions on the grounds that this would undermine their 'preferred creditor status.'"[132]

Far from providing a solution to the debt problem of developing countries, the initiative was essentially a restrictive one: it applied only to the poorest countries (annual per capita income less than $865), and these had to have access to the concessional financing of IDA (a branch of the World Bank) and to the IMF Poverty Reduction and Growth Facility (PRGF). Only eighty-one developing countries met these criteria.

But as if that wasn't enough, two other conditions were added: the country's debt burden had to be deemed intolerable, even after the traditional relief mechanisms, and the countries had to successfully apply, according to the World Bank, "strategies aimed at reducing poverty and laying the foundations for sustainable economic growth." This last criterion was debatable, since the policies imposed by the international institutions to promote growth went counter to the poverty reduction objective. As a result, only forty-two countries were selected to participate in the initiative: Angola, Benin, Bolivia, Burkina Faso, Burma, Burundi, Cameroon, Central African Republic, Chad, Comoros, Congo, Côte d'Ivoire, Democratic Republic of the Congo, Ethiopia, Gambia, Ghana, Guinea, Guinea-Bissau, Guyana, Honduras, Kenya, Laos, Liberia, Madagascar, Malawi, Mali, Mauritania, Mozambique, Nicaragua, Niger, Rwanda, São Tomé and Príncipe, Senegal, Sierra Leone, Somalia, Sudan, Tanzania, Togo, Uganda, Vietnam, Yemen, and Zambia.[133]

The HIPC initiative did not relieve the debt burden, because behind the declared objective lurked another: the HIPC initiative simply made the external debt of these countries sustainable. In other words, the official creditors agreed to reduce the debt slightly to put an end to late payments and applications for debt restructuring. But above all they took advantage of this initiative to once again impose the logic of structural adjustment—a much discredited policy since the 1980s. With the HIPC initiative, the Bretton Woods institutions and the G7 sought to give new legitimacy to the neoliberal logic and their position of dominance by oiling the cogs of globalization.

QUESTION 31
What is the Heavily Indebted Poor Countries (HIPC) initiative?

To benefit from debt relief in the framework of the HIPC initiative, a country must go through a number of grueling and excessively time-consuming stages. It is a long, uphill battle driven by the neoliberal drill sergeants.

First of all, countries deemed to be eligible must, according to the IMF, "face an unsustainable debt burden" and "have established a track record of reform and sound policies through IMF- and World Bank-supported programs." A country concerned by this initiative must first sign an agreement with the IMF to pursue, over a period of three years, an economic policy approved by Washington. This policy is based on the terms of a Poverty Reduction Strategy Paper (PRSP). This document, which needs months at least to prepare, is a first, temporary step. It must present the economic situation of the country and list in detail all privatizations and economic deregulation measures that would enable the country to generate resources for debt repayment, and it must also describe how the funds derived from debt reduction will be used, in particular in the fight against poverty. Thus, in drawing up this paper, the country is forced to assume a contradiction, since the measures imposed are bound to ensure rampant poverty for the majority of the population.

Officially, the PRSP is to be drawn up "through a broad-based participatory process," in collaboration with local civil society. However, numerous cases show that collaboration with civil society has been very partial and selective, since many organizations do not have the technical or financial means to influence discussions, especially those located outside the capital, and others have been set up and lavishly financed by the establishment to convey the official discourse. There was often strong pressure to sign agreements quickly, without making waves, and in general the consultation process was cut short so that the international institutions and African leaders could have their way, as the UNDP confirms: "Take Burkina Faso, where participation in the HIPC/Poverty Reduction Strategy process took the form of a one-and-a-half-hour meeting of donors and civil society."[134]

In this way the structural adjustment process gets the apparent approval of civil society, thereby weakening any criticism of the economic measures implemented. This phony consultation process means that social movements are only invited to state their positions on how a few modest sums will be used while the HIPC initiative promoters make sure they get no say in the overall running of the economy. Decision making remains in the hands of the international institutions, which won't give an inch.

A close examination of the macroeconomic and structural adjustment policy contents of PRSPs shows that there is no fundamental
departure from the kind of policy advice espoused under what has
come to be known as the Washington Consensus.
                —UNCTAD, "Adjustment to Poverty Reduction: What's New?"
                                                        September 26, 2002

After these three years of structural-adjustment-inspired reforms
comes the "decision point" to determine whether a country's debt is
still unsustainable. How is this done? The international institutions
have decided—arbitrarily—on a criterion of unsustainability.
Arbitrarily, because the main criterion for progressing to the next stage
is mathematically nonsensical! This criterion, that the ratio of net present value of debt[135] to annual exports must exceed 150 percent, is
absurd because it means comparing a debt stock (accumulated over several years) with an annual flow of capital based on exports that do not
all benefit the state in question.[136]

At the "decision point" stage, the IMF and the World Bank use this
criterion to decide if the country's debt is sustainable or not. Four countries (Angola, Kenya, Vietnam, and Yemen) in this way learned that they
did not come under the HIPC initiative: their debt was deemed sustainable, and they were therefore not eligible for HIPC debt relief. If one also
removes from the list Laos and Burma, which refused to join the initiative,
only thirty-six countries remain eligible.

These "survivors" must therefore continue to carry out the economic reforms required by the IMF and the World Bank for a period of
one to three years. The PRSP must be finalized and meet the requirements of the international institutions. Naturally these same institutions
announce when the "completion point" has been reached, by which
time the debt relief assistance will actually be delivered. This assistance
is calculated so that the debt will finally become sustainable again. In
principle, the NPV of debt to exports ratio should fall below the 150
percent threshold.

The debt was invented by the devil. Go for a walk in Africa and ask where the debt is! No one knows where the debt we are being made to pay comes from. The debt is worse than AIDS. At least with AIDS there is hope for the future, whereas with the debt . . . Future generations are condemned to pay for it, not just the debt stock, but interests, too. I don't talk about the debt because I know we can't get rid of it. They mess about, they reschedule, they throw a few crumbs — it's like giving aspirin to a cancer patient.

—ABDOULAYE WADE, president of Senegal,

in *Libération*, June 24, 2002

The portion of debt due to countries of the Paris Club is then reduced in the following manner:[137] ODA loans (contracted at lower than market rate) are rescheduled over 40 years including 16 grace years;[138] "commercial" or "non-ODA" debts are canceled up to 90 percent, the remainder being rescheduled at the market rate over twenty-three years, including a six-year grace period. The other bilateral creditors (countries outside the Paris Club such as Gulf States or emerging countries) and multilateral creditors (IMF, World Bank, and regional development banks) must complete this procedure in order to make the debt sustainable. Certain rich countries, including France, have granted additional relief, going as far as 100 percent cancellation in the case of commercial loans. Following this methodology, goes the official line, the debt problem has finally been settled.

Actually nothing could be further from the truth. The HIPC initiative has proved to be a fiasco. A full audit should be made, because a great many citizens, especially in the South, think that the HIPC initiative is more of a problem than a solution for the world's indebted countries.

QUESTION 32
Has the HIPC initiative achieved its goal?

If the goal was to provide a broad, fair, and lasting solution to the huge debt problem, then the HIPC has failed, and failed miserably.

A FAILURE IN TERMS OF TIME SCALE

In principle, the HIPC initiative should have been completed within six years: three years to reach decision point, three more years to reach completion point. According to this reasoning, in July 2008, twelve years after it was launched, everything should have been tied up long ago. This was far from being the case, since the initiative had accumulated a number of delays. Some countries had not yet reached the decision point, and others had reached it seven years before without being able to get to the completion point! The initiative is so far behind that its planned closing date (sunset clause) has had to be extended several times.

However, it sometimes happens that certain stages are completed very rapidly. For example, in April 2006, knowing that other countries "deserved" to be part of the HIPC initiative, the IMF and the World Bank proposed adding seven countries to the list, namely, Afghanistan, Bhutan, Eritrea, Haiti, Kyrgyzstan, Nepal, and Sri Lanka. Haiti reached decision point as early as the end of 2006, followed by Afghanistan in July 2007. These happen to be two countries in which the United States has a vested interest: it had troops in Haiti in February 2004 to hasten the departure of President Jean-Bertrand Aristide; it has a military presence in Afghanistan, a country it invaded on the pretext of the 9/11 attacks and in which it has set up a puppet government. Where there is a will, there is a way.

Bhutan and Sri Lanka quickly conveyed their refusal to join the HIPC initiative. After Laos and Burma, that makes four out of forty-nine that have turned down the invitation—a remarkable proportion for an initiative presented as a generous one. If one also takes into account the four countries removed from the group, that leaves only forty-one eligible for inclusion out of a total of 145 developing countries. This can hardly be called making headway.

At the end of July 2008, thirty-three countries had reached decision point, of which only twenty-three had gone on to reach completion point:

Status of Implementation for the HIPC Initiative in July 2008

COMPLETION POINT REACHED		DECISION POINT REACHED		PENDING
Uganda	May 2000	Guinea-Bissau	Dec 2000	Côte d'Ivoire
Bolivia	June 2001	Guinea	Dec 2000	Comores
Mozambique	Sept 2001	Chad	May 2001	*Eritrea*
Tanzania	Nov 2001	D.R. Congo	July 2003	*Kyrgyzstan*
Burkina Faso	Apr 2002	Burundi	Aug 2005	*Nepal*
Mauritania	June 2002	Congo	Mar 2006	Somalia
Mali	Mar 2003	*Haiti*	Nov 2006	Sudan
Benin	Mar 2003	*Afghanistan*	July 2007	Togo
Guyana	Dec 2003	C. African Rep.	Jan 2008	**COUNTRIES THAT**
Nicaragua	Jan 2004	Liberia	Mar 2008	**REFUSED**
Niger	Apr 2004			Laos
Senegal	Apr 2004			Myanmar
Ethiopia	Apr 2004			*Sri Lanka*
Ghana	July 2004			*Bhutan*
Madagascar	Oct 2004			
Honduras	Apr 2005			**COUNTRIES REMOVED**
Zambia	Apr 2005			Angola
Rwanda	Apr 2005			Kenya
Cameroon	Apr 2006			Vietnam
Malawi	Sept 2006			Yemen
Sierra Leone	Dec 2006			
Sao Tomé/Principe	Mar 2007			
Gambia	Dec 2007			

Note: Names in italics are countries added to the list in 2006

A FAILURE IN TERMS OF SCOPE

The criteria used for country selection excluded the most highly populated developing countries (for example, Nigeria—120 million inhabitants—which was on the very first list in 1996) and kept only small countries that are both very poor and heavily indebted. Even after the addition

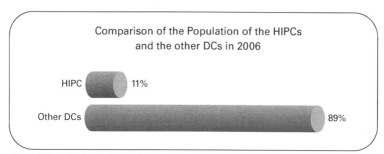

Source: World Bank, *World Development Indicators 2007*

of certain states to the HIPC list in April 2006, the countries where the majority of the world's poor people live are not included: China, India, Indonesia, Brazil, Argentina, Mexico, the Philippines, Pakistan, Nigeria, and the like. In fact, the initiative concerns only about 11 percent of the total population of developing countries. What chance do all the developing countries have of getting out of the present financial impasse with such an initiative?

A FAILURE IN TERMS OF RELIEF

The IMF and the World Bank regularly publish status reports on the HIPC initiative. According to the September 2007 report, only thirty-one countries had reached decision point. Statistics on the debt servicing of these countries show a slight decline in the first years, but since 2002 it has risen again (the year 2006 will be discussed below).

For the analysis to be complete, it must be noted that to benefit from the HIPC initiative, the countries concerned had to be free of arrears to the IMF and the World Bank. To qualify, therefore, they had to pay any arrears at the start of the initiative, which caused the amount of debt service to rise. This was the case for the DRC after Joseph Kabila was elected president in 2001. The country suddenly had to borrow to pay back its arrears to the two Bretton Woods institutions before reaching decision point. The drop associated with the HIPC initiative had nothing to do with the extravagant percentages announced in the media.

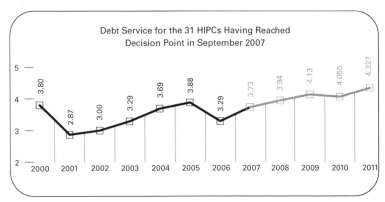

Source: IMF and IDA, HIPC Initiative and MDRI—Status of Implementation, September 27, 2007. In $ millions; in gray, estimates that reflect only the HIPC initiative

Is the initiative enough to make the debt sustainable for the countries concerned? By 2004, UNCTAD was convinced of the contrary:

> There now seems to be an emerging consensus, however, that many African countries continue to suffer from a debt overhang despite the HIPC Initiative and various actions in the context of the Paris Club. The fact that even those countries that have reached (or are about to reach) the so-called completion point will soon find themselves in an unsustainable debt situation gives credence to the arguments advanced by critics with respect to the inappropriateness of the criteria applied in the debt sustainability analysis. And the fact that several more debt-distressed African countries are not eligible for HIPC debt relief reflects the lack of objectivity in the eligibility criteria. . . . According to the IMF and the World Bank's own analysis, some completion point countries (notably Uganda) currently have debt ratios exceeding sustainable levels as defined by the Initiative. There are various reasons for this, including the drastic fall in commodity prices from the late 1990s to the end of 2002, overoptimistic assumptions for economic and export growth, and in some cases new borrowings.
>
> —UNCTAD, *Economic Development in Africa.*
> *Debt Sustainability: Oasis or Mirage?* September 2004

Debt–Exports Ratio for Countries at Decision Point versus Completion Point

COUNTRY	COMPLETION POINT YEAR	TARGET RATIO AT DECISION POINT	RATIO OBSERVED AT COMPLETION POINT
Burkina Faso	2002	185.5%	207.5%
Ethiopia	2004	173.5%	218.4%
Niger	2004	184.8%	208.7%
Rwanda	2005	193.2%	326.5%
Malawi	2006	169.0%	229.1%
Sao Tomé / Principe	2007	139.7%	298.7%

Source: IMF, HIPC Initiative and MDRI—Status of Implementation, 27 September 2007

For example, according to figures published in 2007, six countries that had reached completion point still had a largely unsustainable debt, to such a degree that additional relief had to be provided. Let us look at the NPV of debt/exports ratio of these countries, bearing in mind that the objective of the initiative was to bring it below the threshold of 150 percent.

Why this huge discrepancy? As stated below by UNCTAD, the IMF used growth and exports statistics that were far too optimistic. Willfully ignoring the disastrous consequences of Structural Adjustment Programs since 1980, the IMF persists in thinking that by applying the measures it imposes, growth can be generated at the touch of a wand. Experience once again proves it wrong.

> It is now widely recognized that, in a certain number of cases, the initial analyses of intolerable indebtedness greatly overestimated the potential of the HIPC in terms of export revenues and economic growth.
>
> —KOFI ANNAN, *UN Secretary General's Report on the External Debt Crisis*, August 2, 2001

This means that even countries that conscientiously fulfill IMF and World Bank requirements still fail to have a sustainable debt at the end of the process. The HIPC initiative has not been able to make an unsustainable debt sustainable, though this was its declared goal.

A FAILURE IN TERMS OF OBJECTIVE

The sustainability objective is in itself highly questionable. The HIPC initiative's goal was not to guarantee fundamental human rights, eradicate poverty, or enable the people in the South to affirm their full sovereignty. Its purpose was simply to enable developing countries to repay their debt regularly, without default, but to the maximum of their financial capacity. The creditors wanted to be sure of receiving repayments without the risk of a sudden stoppage on the part of one country or another.

> For a creditors' club, debt sustainability is an essential goal, because it maximizes the long-term probability that the debt will be fully repaid and that normal and mutually profitable relations can be established and developed on a lasting basis. It is therefore a matter not of generosity, but of common interests supported by solidarity.
> —MICHEL CAMDESSUS, declaration on the occasion of the 50th anniversary of the Paris Club, June 14, 2006

The threshold determined by the HIPC initiative corresponds to an estimated threshold below which a HIPC would not be able to make regular repayments. Thus it corresponds to the maximum debt a country can bear without requiring a restructuring process. The HIPC initiative merely brings the debt below this maximum amount—and as we have seen, it usually fails to do even that! The HIPC initiative therefore aims to cancel debts that cannot be repaid and thus to avoid having these countries suspend their repayments.

> The majority of countries concerned were not paying more than 50 percent of debt service before the initiative was implemented. A proportion of the debts contracted by the HIPCs were not actually repaid. Therefore the debt relief only regularizes—on an average basis—a situation that already exists. In this context, the reductions in debt

service that have been presented . . . appear to overestimate the impact of the initiative. In fact, the agreed relief measures concern in part these non-recoverable debts. That is why the reduction in the levels of effective repayments by HIPCs is slight in relation to the announced reduction in debt stock. . . . Moreover, the reduction of debt service over exports remains closely linked to the IMF's hypotheses concerning export gowth, that is, an average annual growth of 10 percent between 2005 and 2007.

—STÉPHANE ALBY and GAËLLE LETILLY, BNP Paribas,
"Les annulations de dette des pays pauvres:
pour quels résultats?" in *Conjuncture*, March 2006

A FAILURE IN TERMS OF TRANSPARENCY AND HONESTY

In this context, it is reasonable to ask how the debt of the HIPCs has evolved. We have just observed some alarming facts: for many countries, the debt remains unsustainable; this initiative simply confirms that the HIPCs were not repaying all they owed, which no doubt obliged them to borrow again in order to honor the debt. Strangely, the report published by the IMF and IDA presents the evolution of debt service, but it is not at all forthcoming on the evolution of the debt stock. It simply states that the

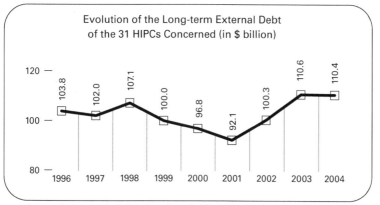

Source: Authors' calculations based on the World Bank's *Global Development Finance 2008*

HIPC initiative should lead to a reduction in debt of $63 billion for the thirty-one countries that had reached decision point in September 2007. We thought this required further examination, and thanks to the country by country figures published by the World Bank, we have been able to reconstitute the long-term external public debt stock of this group of thirty-one countries.

Clearly, it cannot be said that the reduction was significant and lasting.

A NEOLIBERAL SUCCESS

For the experts who devised the HIPC initiative, relieving the burden of a heavily indebted country is not an end, but simply a means. The real goal is to guarantee continuity in the matter of repayments and cast a veil of generosity over the heightened structural adjustment measures.

> Countries applying for the HIPC initiative must adopt a Poverty Reduction Strategy Paper (PRSP), under the auspices of the IMF and the World Bank. This document must indicate the use that will be made of the resources made available by this initiative, and contain a certain number of commitments relating to the implementation of classic structural adjustment measures: privatization of public companies, reduction of the salaried workforce, reduction of grants, elimination of government subsidies, deregulation of the labor market. In other words, the whole arsenal of ultra-liberal measures which have contributed to the impoverishment of African populations, to the degradation of social services, to a fall in life expectancy of over seven years, to the return of diseases we had thought eradicated, to increased unemployment for young graduates, to setting back industrialization, and to the creation of chronic food shortages.
> —MOUSSA TCHANGARI, "Un projet néo-libéral pour l'Afrique"
> (A Neoliberal Project for Africa), in *Alternative* (Niger),
> July 24, 2002

The message is, more or less, "If you adopt the policies we tell you to, you will no longer have an unsustainable debt burden. Better still, we will lend you money so that you can carry out the policies we recommend. This will also allow you to buy consumer and capital goods as well as the services you need from the creditor countries." The HIPC initiative is thus part of the whole arsenal of debt used by the creditors, with the complicity of the leaders of the countries concerned, with the agenda of maintaining and increasing domination. In addition, it places all the responsibility for overindebtedness on the countries of the South: the moneylenders take not the slightest responsibility, since in the framework of the HIPC initiative it is up to the country—advised, one might add, by two of its main creditors (the IMF and the World Bank)—to reform its economy in order to be allowed to reach completion point. This implies that the only solutions envisaged must come from within the countries, together with all the obligations. Yet it is the logic of structural adjustment, deriving from the logic of plunder, slavery and colonialism, that keeps these countries under the yoke.

After almost two decades of applying Structural Adjustment Programs, poverty levels in Africa have risen, slow and erratic growth are the norm, rural crises have intensified and deindustrialization has damaged future growth prospects. [For the last two years poverty reduction has become the fundamental aim of the programs and activities of the international financial institutions in Africa and other countries with low revenue].

—UNCTAD, Press release, September 26, 2002

The IMF and the World Bank have changed the words, changed the acronyms, changed their methods of consultation, but they have not changed an iota of their creed.

—DETLEF KOTTE, UNCTAD, in *Libération*, "FMI et Banque mondiale: le fiasco africain," September 27, 2002

To get these countries to accept their dubious remedies, the IMF and the World Bank have made a show of prescribing poverty reduction strategies. They have given themselves an alibi (paltry sums sprinkled over a very few social projects) while taking care to hide the serious secondary effects involved: for example, in countries where more than 40 percent of the budget goes to repaying the debt, governments are not allowed to recruit and train a sufficient number of teachers, nursing aids, doctors, and other essential workers in the name of the sacrosanct principles of a leaner civil service and a balanced budget. The various small amounts freed up by the HIPC initiative are no more than window dressing: a few schools or dispensaries are built, but as the state is not allowed to recruit the necessary staff, apart from underqualified and underpaid substitutes, it is obliged to apply a cost recovery policy: each family must pay a contribution for the schoolmaster's wages, for medication, compresses, food for sick people in hospital, and such. The right to an education and health care is always the first to be forgotten.

The HIPC initiative has achieved its hidden goal: countries have continued to open up their economies, privatize their public companies, reduce their social spending, repay their debt, and show an appropriate docility. Their leaders have been able to boast the support of the international financial institutions and declare in the press that debt cancellation will reduce poverty. They can also take cold comfort from the fact that their countries were poor enough and indebted enough to be eligible for this initiative.

Certainly, seen from this viewpoint, the HIPC initiative has fulfilled its mission.

QUESTION 33
What was contained in the latest debt relief announced by the G8 in 2005?

In 2005 only eighteen countries concerned by the HIPC initiative had completed the course (in other words, less than half the countries eligible), and many of these still had an unsustainable debt. More than twenty others were still bogged down in the complicated process. However, as long as repayments by the HIPCs continued, the creditors were reluctant to go further.

A flagship international debt relief scheme for the world's poorest countries is failing to free many countries from debt as it becomes clear that its forecasts were too optimistic, the IMF and World Bank have admitted. . . . The bank's governing board, which met earlier this week, showed no enthusiasm for making the scheme more generous despite pressure from non-governmental organizations, bank officials said.

—*FINANCIAL TIMES*, "Debt Relief Scheme Missing Targets, says IMF," September 5, 2002

But in 2005 changes in the international situation altered the picture: oil prices started to surge, due to the boom in Chinese demand, to the difficulties experienced by Mikhaïl Khodorkovski's oil company, Yukos, under pressure from Vladimir Putin, and to high tension in oil-producing countries such as Iraq and Nigeria. The barrel of Brent crude oil rose from an average $29.40 in August 2003 to $49.80 in October 2004 and topped the $55 mark in March 2005.[139]

The majority of countries eligible for the HIPC initiative are poor, non-oil-producing countries, so this vast increase in oil prices hit them hard. The slight relief afforded them by the HIPC initiative often turned out to be lower than the extra costs incurred by higher import prices.

The major powers were then forced to make an additional effort. In 2005, the G8 was hosted by Great Britain where prime minister Tony Blair was facing difficulties on the domestic front due to several embarrassing affairs involving some close colleagues and Labor executives. The international situation would be an opportunity for him to regain some prestige, and his close relationship with U.S. President George W. Bush would help him in this regard.

On June 7, 2005, following a meeting with Blair, Bush declared: "Our countries are working on a proposal that will eliminate 100 percent of the debt of the poorest countries." A deceptive declaration—since only four days later, the finance ministers of the G8 announced in London the "historic" cancellation of the debt of eighteen poor countries owed to three creditors: the IMF, the World Bank, and the African Development Bank (ADB), for an amount estimated at $40 billion. Eventually, twenty other countries could benefit from the measure, bringing the total to $55 billion. The G8 summit, held in Gleneagles, Scotland, the following month, ratified this decision which was to be known as the Multinational Debt Relief Initiative (MDRI).

So which were these eighteen countries? No prize for the right answer: of course it was precisely those eighteen HIPCs that had reached completion point at that time. The next twenty countries were the HIPCs that were still working toward completion point. From the very outset, the MDRI slipped neatly into the wake of the HIPC initiative: the countries concerned had to bow to all the conditionalities—criticized and questioned as they were—of the HIPC initiative.

It is interesting that this caused some ruffled feathers in the plush ambience of official meeting rooms. The leaders of "small" rich countries did not appreciate being presented with a fait accompli by the G8. The announcement made on June 11, 2005, was indeed a presumptuous one: eight countries had decided put the debts held by the IMF and the World Bank behind them and move on without consulting these small countries, whereas, officially at least, decisions have to be taken by all member states.

On June 22, 2005, Willy Kiekens, IMF executive director, Belgium, floated the idea of an instrument by which the full, irrevocable and unconditional debt relief decided by the G8 could be bypassed. Kiekens would continue to demand repayments: the IMF would only refund these amounts to the indebted country if that country applied "adequate" economic policies. A week later, the IMF representatives of Belgium, Switzerland, Norway, and the Netherlands delivered a memorandum demanding the continuation of strict conditionalities in exchange for debt cancellation, since, in their words "conditionality is a key feature for effective use of resources that are freed up by debt relief." Such a proposal was in stark opposition to the announcements of the G8 and would have caused it to lose face.

The contest movement led by Belgium, Switzerland, Norway, and the Netherlands was far from being a lost cause, since the four of them, each at the head of some ten countries, held 16.32 percent of voting rights, which is enough to block the IMF where major decisions require 85 percent. Normally, this allows the United States to block any development it does not approve. In September 2005, during the IMF and World Bank Assembly, the G8 countries had to agree to pay the cost of the MDRI to quell the uprising. Note that the IMF included in the list two non-HIPC countries, Cambodia and Tajikistan—countries that, of course, had already accepted the IMF's conditionalities.

It is important at this point to examine the concrete results of the MDRI for the countries concerned. The figures published by the IMF and the World Bank are as follows:

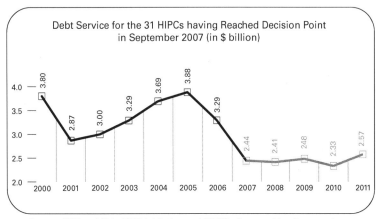

Source: IMF and IDA, HIPC Initiative and MDRI—Status of Implementation, September 27, 2007. In gray, estimates taking into account the HIPC initiative and the MDRI.

Assuming that these forecasts are confirmed in the coming years (we have seen with the HIPC initiative that IMF estimates are often unreliable and are mainly designed to serve the ideology upheld by its experts), this chart calls for two comments. First, one observes a variation comparable to that seen at the start of the HIPC initiative: a drop when the initiative was launched, and then a return to an upward trend. It would thus be tempting to expect a similar "success." Second, the economy linked to the MDRI for the 31 HIPCs appears to be between $1.2 billion and $1.8 billion per year, that is, less than $60 million per country. Such amounts are derisory, especially as these sums can be deducted from the aid they will receive if they do not fulfill the criteria imposed by the rich countries that will pay in their place. In comparison, in 2007 the G7 countries devoted $790 billion to military spending (including $550 billion by the United States alone) and $350 billion to agricultural subsidies that seriously penalize small Third World producers.[140] The war waged in Iraq by the United States and its allies since 2003 cost them some $20 billion per month in 2008.[141] The annual cost of the MDRI for the rich countries is therefore less than U.S. spending in three days on the Iraq conflict.

For the countries concerned, the MDRI is no gift from heaven. It was introduced after long years of neoliberal reforms imposed by the IMF and the World Bank. These countries have therefore paid dearly, and in advance, for eligibility. The HIPC initiative's logic has been extended to the MDRI: because of the former's shortcomings, the creditors have simply stepped up the process to close the most serious gaps.

The straitjacket of structural adjustment is as present and non-negotiable as ever for those who bear the debt burden. The failure of its logic is clear: since 1988 each debt relief scheme for the poorest countries results in another, always too late and always ill-adapted. It must not be forgotten that debt is much more than a financial mechanism: it is a powerful instrument of domination that for decades has allowed the leaders and big businesses of rich countries, with the complicity of the South's ruling class, to impose an economic model that serves their interests.

By sending their deliberately confusing messages, the world's big moneylenders tried to quell protest concerning the debt and give the impression that the debt of developing countries was a thing of the past. The Gleneagles decision is above all proof of the failure of the HIPC initiative: if it were not so, the debt of these eighteen countries would not have needed further relief.

However, a new element has emerged to upset the debt machine. Until recently, it was mainly the G7 countries and the multilateral institutions that supported the HIPC initiative and the MDRI. But now China has stepped in. According to the interpretation given to the situation by the Bretton Woods institutions and the G7, China has taken advantage of the improved solvency of the HIPCs to lend them money that they use to buy cheap Chinese goods and services (rather than buy them from the companies of the G7 countries). At the same time, China is thus assured of acquiring supplies of the raw materials vital to its economic growth. Since China is not a member of the Paris Club, it is not bound by the debt relief promises that are negotiated there. China grants new loans to developing countries without any political conditionalities whatsoever, as opposed to the Bretton Woods institutions and the members of the Paris Club. Given all these reasons, the countries of the South that thus benefit from a new source of financing are less and less willing to do the bidding of the IMF and the World Bank. The grace period granted for rescheduled repayments in the context of the HIPC initiative (see Q31) allows HIPCs to enter into trade agreements with China as soon as they reach completion point and their debt starts to increase. When the period of grace comes to an end and the loans contracted with China begin to be repaid, it is likely that the HIPCs will again be unable to sustain repayments and that a new debt relief phase will be necessary. Worried at being deprived of the benefits of an initiative they paid for, the G7 countries have attempted to involve China in the process but China has firmly declined thus far. The rich countries have little influence over China—a fact they find irksome to say the least.

CHAPTER EIGHT

The Sham of the Dominant Model

QUESTION 34
Does Official Development Assistance (ODA) help
to mitigate the effects of the debt?

Since 1970, most governments of rich countries have never honored their commitment to allocate 0.7 percent of their Gross National Income (GNI) to Official Development Assistance (ODA) for countries of the South. This does not stop them bringing this empty promise to the fore at every occasion, such as during the G8 summit of 2005, where it was renewed through to 2015. But the very notion of ODA is highly questionable. Isn't it more an alibi used by supposedly generous states whose political and economic agenda in the Third World, in fact, blocks any attempt at independent development?

It would actually seem that the steep downward trend of ODA during the 1990s is back again. The figures published by the Development Assistance Committee (DAC), which centralizes ODA information for the OECD, show that after decreasing by a third relative to the GNI of DAC member countries (from 0.33 percent in 1990 to 0.22 percent in 2001), the ODA did increase to 0.33 percent in 2005 but then fell again to 0.28 percent in 2007, when it stood at $103.7 billion. The 0.7 percent objective has been reached only by a few countries of Northern Europe: Norway, Sweden, Luxembourg, Denmark, and the Netherlands. On the other hand, five countries commit less than 0.2 percent of their GNI to ODA: Italy, Portugal, Japan, Greece and the United States. All this shows what a fiasco such international commitments are. Will the 0.7 percent promise have a better chance of being upheld in 2015 than in 1970?

The commitments taken during the G8 summit in 2005 were clear: a significant increase in ODA, and specifically a doubling of ODA to Africa by 2010. According to the OECD, this "implied lifting aid from US$80 billion in 2004 to $130 billion in 2010 (at constant 2004 prices)." The verdict is bleak: "Overall, most donors are not on track to meet their stated commitments to scale up aid; they will need to make unprecedented increases to meet their 2010 targets."[142] In other words, the targets will not be met and this has been the case for nearly forty years. It would seem that you cannot take a G8 leader at their word.

However, the very nature of ODA is questionable. The definition provided by the DAC   clearly illustrates the limits of ODA, and the roots of future transgressions are already contained in this definition. ODA consists of "grants or loans to countries and territories on Part 1 of the DAC list . . . undertaken by the official sector, with promotion of economic development and welfare as the main objective." The DAC thus holds an updated list, called "Part 1," composed of 150 countries and territories of low or medium revenues, which are beneficiaries of ODA. The other countries are the "in transition" countries that make up "Part 2," including the ex-Soviet bloc and other more advanced countries: the grants and loans to these countries do not count as ODA, but as Official Aid (OA).

Loans are included as ODA, as long as they are given to eligible countries at a "preferential" rate, namely at less than 25 percent the market rate. The size of loans in ODA is far from negligible: at the end of 2007, countries of the South had contracted debts at preferential rates to other states, to the tune of $230 billion.[143] That is to say that ODA, by its own definition, creates debt.

Consequently, the subsequent repayments cause a hemorrhage of capital from countries of the South. In terms of bilateral debts at preferential rates, between the end of 1994 and the end of 2007, the governments of developing countries had paid back $82.4 billion more than they had received in new loans.[144] This net negative transfer reveals the hidden aspects of aid: in the final analysis, ODA also helps donor countries to enrich themselves at the expense of countries that they claim they help.

Furthermore, the definition of the purpose of these grants and loans is sufficiently vague to leave it open to various statistical manipulations. With the result that the main projects financed are far removed from the top-priority requirements of the populations.

An assessment of the figures published by the OECD in 2008 shows that in 2007, ODA fell by 8.4 percent in real terms. Out of the $103.7 billion ODA in 2007, $8.7 billion went toward debt remission, which does not create any positive financial flux for the indebted countries. The increase in ODA between 2001 and 2005 owed much to remission of bilateral debt that was subsequently reduced. For Iraq and Nigeria, debt remission has diminished, and the HIPC initiative is running out of steam. To count debt remission in ODA is scandalous. Often, the canceled debts are old, costly, and dubious debts that were cluttering up the accounts of the creditors. Their cancellation is merely a cleaning up of the accounts, and the creditor countries actually create a double PR bonus from it, since they can loudly announce a reduction of the debt one year, before proclaiming a rise in their ODA the following year, even though it concerns one and the same financial operation. ODA figures are thus easily manipulated. In this way, the fact that over 40 percent of France's ODA in 2003 was taken up by debt remission meant that the government could announce a rise in ODA, whereas outside debt remission, their ODA, had actually decreased.[145] Similarly, the remission of a Democratic Republic of the Congo debt enabled Belgium to announce a net increase in ODA in 2003, when it claimed to have reached 0.6 percent of GNI, compared with 0.43 percent in 2002, but then in 2004 the figure immediately fell back to 0.41 percent, revealing the masquerade. The record for 2004 is held by Portugal, whose ODA jumped by 187.5 percent due to an exceptional debt remission to Angola.[146]

Moreover, the accounting on these remissions is questionable. According to the OECD, in the case of a cancellation, only the interests of ODA creditors should be included in ODA (since the principal had already been counted as ODA during the loan's year), contrary to the non-ODA debts for which the total (principal and interest) are included as ODA at the time of their cancellation. Basically, this means that a commercial loan contracted in 1990 and canceled in 2006 can be given as an increase in ODA to the tune of the principal and the potential interest on this remaining principal. On paper, it looks as if these funds were distributed again, whereas in reality nothing takes place.

Moreover, it is the nominal value of the canceled debts that is factored in. Yet in view of difficulties faced by these countries, the real value of these debts is much lower because if a creditor tried to sell such a debt today, it would have to reduce the price to find a willing buyer. In fact, "the United States Government—which is congressionally mandated to estimate the present value of its loan portfolio—applies a 92 percent discount to the debt of HIPCs."[147] Since this is clear, actually including the nominal value of canceled debts in ODA, as the governments of industrialized countries (including the United States) do, is deliberate embezzlement. The *Financial Times* is spot on: "The aid that isn't. Writing off official commercial debt should not count as aid."[148] ODA is a game of creative accounting.

Furthermore, technical cooperation, which constitutes over a quarter of ODA, includes "grants to nationals from aid-receiving countries who benefit from an education in their country or elsewhere" and "payments toward fees for consultants, advisors and analogous personalities, as well as teachers and administrators on special assignment in the aid-receiving countries." Yet, it is well known that expatriate teachers from countries of the North work in schools that are mostly attended by the children of other expats.

Moreover, some countries include tuition fees in their ODA accounts, that is, the cost of financing the secondary and tertiary education of students from ODA-receiving countries. Initially, the DAC tolerated the inclusion of tuition fees as long as the studies were oriented toward issues of development and the students returned to their countries to work. However, in reality this does not happen, since on the one hand, the costs are integrated before they can verify if an effective return took place, and, on the other, it also concerns foreign students born in countries of the North who mostly stay put. The costs are significant: around 900 million euros for France in 2006, twice that of 2001.[149]

"Aid to refugees" costs are also included in ODA. Yet, according to the French parliamentarian Henri Emmanuelli, "France declares virtually all costs incurred in hosting foreigners. Considering which organizations receive financing, especially l'Office français de protection des réfugiés et apatrides (OFPRA) [Office for the protection of refugees and stateless], these expenses are primarily used for regulating migration and dealing with asylum seekers on French soil, rather than for aiding refugees. The argument that hosting refugees provides relief to countries to which victims of neighboring crisis or conflict zones does not convince your Special Rapporteur that the costs involved can be considered development aid."[150] This is how people seeking asylum in countries of the North, to escape repression or to ensure the survival of their families who remain in their countries of origin, enable French ODA to announce an increase of 450 million euros in 2006.

According to the OECD, nearly three-quarters of bilateral ODA is made of "special-purpose grants," such as technical cooperation, debt remission, emergency aid and administrative costs. The World Bank adds: "Although special-purpose grants are an essential element of the development process and have budgetary consequences for donor countries, they do not provide additional financial resources to recipient countries to support programs that are needed to achieve the Millennium Development Goals (MDGs)."[151] Indeed, a significant part of the official sums are fictive or move back to "donor" countries (purchase of food, medicine, equipment, expert missions), as Robert McNamara, World Bank president from 1968 to 1981, recognized: "The portion of aid (ODA) that remains in developing countries is very small. Practically, all the money donated returns rapidly to the rich countries in the form of imported products."[152] According to James Wolfensohn, World Bank president from 1995 to 2005, there were more than 63,000 projects in progress in all developing countries, but the costs of feasibility studies, travel and lodgings of experts from industrialized countries alone absorbed between 20 and 25 percent of the total aid.[153]

It is to be said, too, that France includes in its ODA some of the costs incurred in Mayotte and Wallis-et-Futuna, two overseas territories under French control, for a total of €200 million in 2006. Once debt remissions (€2.5 billion in 2006), schooling, hosting of refugees and costs toward overseas territories are removed, the French ODA is reduced by half to €4.2 billion (0.24 percent of GNI) instead of the €8.3 billion (0.47 percent of GNI) announced in 2006.

The amount announced has once again been inflated by including
debt cancellations which are not even sure to become effective in
the near future, as well as including costs that do not contribute to
development, such as tuition fees for foreign students, grants to
research institutes or the costs of hosting refugees. Moreover the
part allocated to such costs is even greater this year than last year.
—HENRI EMMANUELLI, French Member of Parliament[154]

Therefore, the portion of aid that actually reaches the populations of
developing countries is very small. Even in the case of emergency humanitarian aid, where the need is blatant, ODA still inflates the aid received.
When a country of the North decides to send a planeload of food and
medicines to a country in distress, the cost of chartering the plane, of buying the food and drugs, the salaries of those who prepare or go with the
cargo, are all included in the amount of aid that has been given, but the
corresponding sums stay in the North. The only thing that may, with
hope, get to the destination, is the product itself, but the ODA is calculated on all the costs incurred in sending it, which is far more than what
is received at the other end. On the contrary, when a debt is serviced, the
entire amount does leave the economy.

Hence, a series of statistical manipulations is deployed to mask the
weakness of the aid given by rich countries. Moreover, this aid does not
necessarily prioritize the countries that are most in need of it, but it is
mainly directed toward those that serve the geostrategic interests of the
donors, independent of the real needs of the countries of the South. As
such, apart from Iraq and Afghanistan, the main recipients of aid from the
United States are Sudan, Colombia, and Israel. In 2002–3, only 41 percent of global ODA went to the fifty Least Developed Countries
(LDCs),[155] meaning that *"strategic interests continue to play a major role
in the allocation of ODA to receiving countries."*[156] The main objective of
the donors is to strengthen their zones of influence by giving political
support to allied governments in the South, so that they can impose economic decisions on them and control their political positions at international summit meetings.[157]

Severe Criticisms of ODA by the UNDP

The 1994 report of the UNDP is particularly severe in its criticisms of ODA and its content should be more widely available. Not only is aid granted without any conditions concerning the respect of human rights, but according to the UNDP (1994), it seems to be systematically directed toward countries with unsatisfactory records in this area. "Indeed, for the United States in the 1980s, the relationship between aid and human rights violations has been perverse. Multilateral donors also seem not to have been bothered by such considerations. They seem to prefer martial law regimes, quietly assuming that such regimes will promote political stability and improve economic management. After Bangladesh and the Philippines lifted martial law, their shares in the total loans given by the World Bank declined."

The same applies to military spending. "Until 1986, bilateral donors on average gave five times as much assistance per capita to high military spenders as they gave to low military spenders. And even in 1992, the high military spenders were still getting two and a half times as much per capita as the low military spenders."

Thus these geopolitical criteria play a decisive role and can even distort the very notion of aid. "If aid were directly linked to achieving certain human development priority objectives and emerging global human security threats, this would have a profound impact on its distribution. ODA allocations would be determined by how much each country could contribute toward meeting these objectives. Rather than being doled out to favorite clients, ODA would go where the need was greatest." In fact, writes the UNDP, "on average, [the donor countries] allocate only 7 percent of their aid to human priority concerns."

As far as technical aid, supposed to strengthen the self-sufficiency of developing countries, is concerned, the situation is no more encouraging. "Perhaps most disturbing is that, after 40 years, 90 percent of the $12 billion a year in technical assistance is still spent on foreign expertise—despite the fact that national experts are now available in many fields." The UNDP deplores that "unless attitudes and institutions are changed, the assistance 'does not take.'" For example, about a quarter of total annual aid destined for Sub-Saharan Africa is swallowed up financing "failed economists' visits." What could be clearer!

—UNDP, *Human Development Report, 1994*

QUESTION 35

Is micro-credit a solution to the excessive debt of developing countries?

When the 2006 Nobel Peace Prize was given to Muhamma Yunus, founder of the Grameen Bank in Bangladesh, micro-credit became a hot news item. What if micro-credit could save the world? Loans of tiny sums of money, targeting mainly poor women or small craftsmen who were excluded from the classical banking system, would provide the missing resources to start or develop a business. The necessary sums were often very small, just tens or hundreds of dollars, and established banks refused to deal with such loans, on the one hand because the amount was too small, and on the other because the potential debtors were considered to be insolvent.

The money injected in this way has proved to have local repercussions, since the borrowers use it to improve access to basic social services (namely through local systems of social protection such as village mutual aid) or to develop handicraft or agricultural activities that are essential for the local economy. On top of which, experience has shown that such loans have a very high rate of reimbursement: the borrowers are able to gather sufficient capital to be in a position to pay back their debts. Moreover, the position of women is often enhanced by micro-credit since they are the main beneficiaries of these loans in the family. But at what price?

And here is the snag: micro-credit organizations impose high interest rates on the population, often annual rates of over 20 percent. Thus these organizations make significant profits and amass a major part of the wealth they have helped to create. Generally, the economic activity created or preserved does not really improve living conditions: it makes survival more organized, while the lenders are making profits. This is the reason why many organizations of the North, including established banks, have tried to capture a share of the market, which they consider profitable. It's the case, for example, of Jacques Attali, ex-advisor of the French president François Mitterrand and former president of the European Bank for Reconstruction and Development (EBRD), who had to resign in the wake of the scandal caused by extravagant expenses at the bank's headquarters. In 1998, he created PlaNet Finance, with a foothold in sixty countries, which finances and advises microfinance institutions in countries of the South. Not exactly philanthropy, but rather a quest for notoriety without excluding profit making and the added bonus of seeming generosity. The World Bank is also interested, which says it all.

[SIDEBAR]

Banks and Hedge Funds Focus Microfinance in India

Early in 2007, the first international investment fair for microfinance was held in the Indian capital. It gathered forty Indian institutions of microfinance (including SKS Microfinance, Share, Spandana, Basix) and the major private international finance institutions.[158] The microfinance sector is booming and increasingly attracting foreign investors, major banks and hedge funds. There are in India 36.8 million people who use microfinance for loans not exceeding $100 on average. The total volume of loans has increased by 76 percent in 2006–7, reaching $766 million. The rate of debt defaulting is only 2 percent. Some firms such as Sequoia (a U.S. company that invests in Google) or Unitus Equity Fund (another U.S. company that invests in eBay) have bought shares in SKS Microfinance. Western banks such as Citibank and Fortis-ABN-Amro have announced that they will also invest in SKS and other microfinance companies. According to the director of SKS, some hedge funds have also indicated their interest in investing in the sector. All those who have promoted microfinance as a real alternative, from the Brazilian president, Lula, to ex-presidents Jacques Chirac, Bill Clinton, and George W. Bush to the Spanish prime minister, José Luis Zapatero, and Kofi Annan, were surely thinking of a profitable investment for the bankers and

the private investment vehicles. The directors of the Mexican microfinance
company Compartamos became millionaires in 2007.

In the context of a system as violent and iniquitous as neoliberal globalization, micro-credit certainly plays an attenuating role, but it is not an
alternative. It applies bandages haphazardly on some cuts while an actual
economic war rages on. Though its real impact is difficult to evaluate, the
notion of micro-credit is recuperated by the finance establishment. By
definition, micro-credit uses the same mechanisms as the logic of indebtedness and organizes and transfers wealth from the populations of the
South to the creditors. Far from modifying social relations, it articulates
with the capitalist system, in which it integrates perfectly.[159]

QUESTION 36
Have the policies promoted by the World Bank and the IMF contributed to the fight against climate change?

To tackle the problem of global warming, world leaders tried to set up an
organized reduction in the production of greenhouse gases in 1997, with
the Kyoto Protocol. But the fact that the United States went back on their
signature after George W. Bush was elected in 2000 meant the strategy
was doomed to fail. The Bali summit in December 2007 sought to build
new post-Kyoto foundations, but again it led to a dead-end since the
United States refused to commit itself to a binding, quantified agreement.
The leaders of rich countries are thus far from having realized the scale of
the problem. Emission trading was created, meaning that greenhouse
gases can be sold like any other commodity, but so far, the goal has been
to find a mechanism that will not force industrialized countries to reduce
their own emissions, while giving the impression that the problem is
under control.

At the end of October 2006 Nicholas Stern, advisor to the government on the economics of climate change and development, handed
prime minister Tony Blair a 500-page report on the consequences of the
current climate change and measures to counteract this trend. In his

report Nicholas Stern writes: "Climate change will affect the basic elements of life for people around the world—access to water, food production, health, and the environment. Hundreds of millions of people could suffer hunger, water shortages and coastal flooding as the world warms."[160] Implicitly, the diagnosis suggested in the report is a condemnation of policies implemented by the IMF and the WB, where Nicholas Stern was chief economist.

Until the early 2000s, even though several voices had been warning about the dangers of the search for limitless growth resulting in exhausted natural resources, the World Bank and IMF leaders kept claiming that such alarm was totally unfounded. Lawrence Summers, economist and vice president of the World Bank from 1991 to 1996, later secretary of the Treasury under William Clinton, claimed in 1991: "There are no limits on the planet's capacity for absorption likely to hold us back in the foreseeable future. The danger of an apocalypse due to global warming or anything else is nonexistent. The idea that the world is heading into the abyss is profoundly wrong. The idea that we should place limits on growth because of natural limitations is a serious error; indeed, the social cost of such an error would be enormous if ever it were to be acted upon."[161]

> The argument that a moral obligation to future generations demands special treatment of environmental investments is fatuous.
> —LAWRENCE SUMMERS, 1991[162]

Anne Krueger, chief economist at the World Bank during the Reagan administration, before taking up the position of number two at the IMF from 2000 to 2006, concurs with this view. In June 2003, during the Seventh International Economic Forum in St. Petersburg, she said: "Nor have we done irreparable harm to the environment. The evidence shows quite convincingly that economic growth brings an initial phase of deterioration in some aspects, but this is followed by a subsequent phase of improvement. The turning point at which people begin choosing to invest in cleaning up and preventing pollution occurs at a per capita GDP of about US$5,000." The more industrialized countries prove the contrary; they have overreached the per capita GDP $5,000 mark, and yet most of them still implement policies that entail an increase in pollution.

Lawrence Summers predicted that global warming would reduce growth by only 0.1 percent during the next two centuries. Nicholas Stern, on the other hand, concludes: "If we don't act, the overall costs and risks of climate change will be equivalent to losing at least 5 percent of global GDP each year, now and forever. If a wider range of risks and impacts is taken into account, the estimates of damage could rise to 20 percent of GDP or more."

The structural adjustment policies have weakened the capacity of developing countries to respond to natural calamities.[163] The World Bank and the IMF have imposed policies that have led to deforestation and the development of environmentally destructive energy mega-projects. The World Bank has supported projects that destroy natural protectors of coastlines, such as mangroves, which reduce the effects of tidal waves. It has refused to stop its loans to the sector of extractive industries, as recommended by a 2003 impact assessment report, commissioned by the Bank itself. It is responsible for a global fund for the protection of the environment, which is the same thing as leaving the fox to guard the chicken coop.

Since George W. Bush reneged on the Kyoto Protocol concerning the reduction of greenhouse gas emissions by the United States, world leaders have been talking at cross purposes insofar as climate change is concerned. For the developing countries, the countries of the North are the main emitters of carbon dioxide, and in the name of the right to development, the developing countries refuse any ecological constraint as long as the North does not reduce its emissions. On the other side, the leaders of rich countries invoke the rising carbon emissions of the developing countries, especially China and India, as an excuse to refuse to commit to quantified targets, which do not include the developing countries. But what they pretend to ignore is that the problem of global warming is due to the accumulation of carbon dioxide in the atmosphere since the Industrial Revolution of the nineteenth century, whereas the carbon currently emitted does not have an immediate effect. And the existing accumulation was put there exclusively by the industrialized countries.

The populations of poor countries, who have until now contributed very little to the accumulation of atmospheric pollution (less than 20 percent), do not have the means to combat the effects of climate change and are the first to be affected. The responsibility of developed countries in climate change will remain higher for a long time to come even if the developing countries do end up emitting more carbon than the rich countries as will soon be the case.

—JEAN-PASCAL VAN YPERSELE, Belgian climatologist[164]

Climate change thus contributes to even greater inequality, revealing the close link between environmental and social problems.[165] For this, let us consider an analogy developed by Wally Broecker, a professor at Columbia University, the concept of the carbon pie.[166] According to this theory, in order to limit rising temperatures to an average of 2°C, the concentration of carbon in the atmosphere must be limited to twice the level it was before the Industrial Revolution. This means that not only do carbon emissions need to be reduced, but also that there is a "carbon capital" that should not be exceeded, the famous pie that represents a total of 1,025 gigatons (Gt C). Quite a difference!

Yet, since the beginning of the Industrial Revolution, human beings have already taken a large bite: we have emitted about 305 Gt C (of which the countries of the North account for 80 percent, or 245 Gt C) leaving only 720 Gt C.[167] The question is how to share the remaining part of the pie. In an ideal world, the share should be proportional to the population. The countries of the North should have the right to roughly 20 percent of the total pie, that is, 205 Gt C, but this figure has already been exceeded by 40 Gt C. The only solution is for the North to buy back the part of the pie that it has so greedily consumed. In 2006, at the average rate of carbon quotas, on the European market, these 40 Gt C come to around $2.86 trillion, that is, more than twice the external public debt of all developing countries. And this is without factoring in that the North has to buy the part of the pie that it will consume in the future, which is no small portion, in view of current levels of emissions.

For Nicholas Stern, the least industrialized countries, although less responsible than others for global warming, will be worst affected: "All countries will be affected. The most vulnerable—the poorest countries and populations—will suffer earliest and most, even though they have contributed least to the causes of climate change." He adds, contrary to the philosophy of neoliberal globalization, "climate change is the greatest market failure the world has ever seen, and it interacts with other market imperfections." That said, we are under no illusion: Nicholas Stern does not propose any alternative to the productivist model nor to market capitalism. He is simply raising the alarm to preserve the current system. He asserts that humanity can be both "green" and "pro-growth." He explains that the market for the protection of the environment will offer a new avenue for private profits. Finally, he argues that since the developing countries pollute less than industrialized countries yet suffer the most from global warming, they will be able to sell their right to pollute to rich countries. With the revenue obtained from the selling of these rights, they will be able to repair the damage caused to their populations.

Once more, the proponents of the dominant productivist model began by denying the existence of the crucial problem of environmental damage and global warming—and went on aggressively promoting policies making the situation worse. Then, when the situation became untenable, after a public display of regret, they let it be understood that the necessary measures had been identified. In other words, nothing has really changed.

In fact, the Structural Adjustment Programs imposed by the creditors have consistently implicated policies that *inherently* lead to environmental damage by depriving states of the responsibility of managing their own territories, their natural resources, and ecological balance in the common interest. Structural adjustment transfers this responsibility to private parties, often to multinationals that have no stake in the common interest. Their objective is to maximize profits in the shortest time possible.

Obviously, the analysis must not be limited to a North/South contradiction. Capitalism, which dominates the planet, is driven by the search for immediate profit without any consideration for the cost to nature, of which humanity is one element. This logic holds true for all multinationals, both of the North and South. The same logic prevails in the policies embraced by most governments, South and North. The multinationals of the South (the Brazilian Petrobras or the Malaysian Petronas in the oil sector, the South African AngloGold Ashanti in the mining sector, the Chinese multinationals) are destroying the biotope of Southern populations just as gleefully as those of the North are theirs. The explanation lies in the productivist capitalist logic that undergirds their actions. A break with capitalism is at the heart of any serious response to ecological problems. The only just and long-lasting solution is to question the productivist capitalist system, which structurally generates environmental damage and rocketing inequality. We cannot afford not to take this into account.

QUESTION 37
What is NEPAD?

The decolonization of African countries gave rise to great hope. At last the continent was to be able to develop. However, the conditions for such development have not been met, and the social and economic situation has not improved, far from it. The titles of books by the well-known French anti-colonialist ecologist, René Dumont, are telling: from *L'Afrique noire est mal partie* (Black Africa makes a bad start) in the 1960s to *L'Afrique étranglée* (Strangled Africa) in 1980, the continent had sunk ever deeper into poverty.

In 1980, the Lagos Plan was drawn up on the initiative of African leaders within the Organization for African Unity (OAU). It aimed to promote endogenous development and industrialization in Africa. Unfortunately it has remained a dead letter, undermined by the Bretton Woods institutions that launched structural adjustment policies whose objectives were in contradiction with those of the Lagos Plan (see Q15 and Q16).

At the end of the 1990s, two African development plans were constructed by African governments, which received approving nods from governments in the North. On the one hand, the Millennium African Plan was initiated by presidents Thabo Mbeki of South Africa, Olusegun Obasanjo of Nigeria, and Abdelaziz Bouteflika of Algeria, on the theme of African renaissance. On the other hand, the Senegalese president, Abdoulaye Wade, launched the Omega Plan, based on the creation of a blatantly liberal African common market. At the beginning, these plans were sympathetic to several Pan-Africanist circles.

The two plans were merged in 2001 to become the New Partnership for African Development (NEPAD). This aims to provide the dynamics needed to fill the gulf that separated Africa from the industrialized countries; in other words, to bring modern practices and economic growth to Africa. Its stock in trade is to promote private investment to integrate the continent into world markets. Thus Africa, which represents only 2.3 percent of world importations, against 4.5 percent in 1980,[168] is seen as an open playing field for private initiative. At the Dakar Summit in April 2002 on the financing of NEPAD, multinationals of the North, like Microsoft, Hewlett Packard, Unilever, or TotalFinaElf, were very much present.

NEPAD sets out ten priorities, from good governance to access to international markets, from human development to infrastructure. African leaders have also promised to avoid backsliding and to be very vigilant (even though instability and conflict are often partly due to the behavior of multinationals in the country), thus hoping to win the good grace of the moneylenders.

NEPAD's founders were received and encouraged several times by the G8 leaders in 2001 and 2002. This African initiative to attract capital and multinationals, which has won the approval of the big powers, has had the effect of enforcing IMF and World Bank policies across the continent. It is no coincidence that the French representative for dealing with NEPAD is Michel Camdessus, former Director-General of the IMF.

The external conditionalities imposed by the IMF through the Structural Adjustment Programs, described in detail by the press, encounter great reluctance among local populations. The idea of NEPAD was therefore to transform these into internal conditionalities, proposed by the African heads of state themselves. Once again, this partnership is a façade that barely conceals the economic submissiveness of Africa.

The projects under consideration within this new framework still bow to the same logic (see Q10): a gas pipeline from West Africa or between Algeria and Nigeria; a so-called transahelian motorway from Dakar to N'Djamena; railway links between Benin, Niger, Burkina Faso, and Togo (the Geftarail project); the rehabilitation of the oil refinery in Mombasa (Kenya) and the pipeline at Eldoret; the Grand Inga project in DRC to export energy all over the continent, and many others.

Behind this African initiative lies an attempt by four ambitious African heads of state to find a place for themselves in the ongoing economic scheme of things. Far from demanding the cancellation of the debt of

African states or claiming reparation for centuries of pillage and slavery, NEPAD's main actors, especially Abdoulaye Wade, are a little overeager to sweep aside such aspirations, preferring to discuss future investments in Africa.

> We have not come here to be offered money. The idea never crossed my mind. The important thing is the commitment made by the G8, which has accepted the new partnership we are proposing. You know, they did not have to receive us.
>
> —ABDOULAYE WADE, president of Senegal,
> G8 summit, June 2002

But though NEPAD's calculations are based on $64 billion of investment a year and a projected growth rate of 7 percent from now until 2015, these figures are for the time being far from feasible. Indeed, foreign private capital in general prefers to go where the growth is driven by public policies. However, African governments suffer from a lack of funds, precisely because of the debt.

When capital flows in, the attraction is in the raw materials that lie underneath the African soil. Since 2005, China has become one of the major investors in Africa. When they are invited, the African presidents quickly rush to Beijing, to the dismay of London, Paris, and Washington. We are very far from an indigenous development project.

> The NEPAD strategy is not to raise issues of repatriation of the money embezzled by African potentates and deposited in foreign accounts, nor of cancellation of the external debt whose service swallows up the best part of the budget of certain countries. [...] In view of the difficult situation the African countries are in, undoubtedly the alternative is to demand the cancellation of the entire external debt, once and for all, and to make use of internal resources, especially by mobilizing savings. The NEPAD document does not give much importance to this issue and proposes no new actions which might end African dependence on external powers.
>
> ... It is scandalous that the African leaders broach neither the crucial question of the reform of the international financial institutions,

which impose policies with no regard for the social and economic
rights of their countries, nor the question of the modification of
unfair world trade rules, with their negative repercussions on people's food security and health. . . . NEPAD should have taken inspira-
tion from the experience of the African delegates' struggle at the
failed Seattle talks, and advocated joining forces with the otherThird
World countries to reverse the negative tendencies of corporate-
driven globalization.

—MOUSSA TCHANGARI, "Un projet néo-libéral pour l'Afrique,"
Alternative (Niger), July 24, 2002

On the pretext that it was time for action, not words, the populations
were not consulted. Africans' social, economic, and cultural rights, especially those of women, have not been taken into account. African civil
society, which cannot possibly be left out, has not been considered either
as a force for proposals (in defining alternatives) or as an opposition force
to be reckoned with in countering the tendencies toward authoritarianism
or neglect of the democratic process. In the opinion of most people,
NEPAD is already part of the past.

CHAPTER NINE

Debt Cancellations and Suspensions of Payment in the Past

Is it impossible to cancel debt?

There have already been debt cancellations in the past, some unilateral, some as a decision of justice, some conceded by the dominant powers. We will present here a few significant cases.

DEBT REPUDIATIONS

United States

In 1776 the thirteen British colonies of North America decided to form the United States, and to end their dependence on the British Crown. The new state freed itself from the burden of its debt by declaring null and void all debts due to London.

In the nineteenth century, after the election of Abraham Lincoln as president, the Southern states seceded and formed the Confederation of American States.[169] The War of Secession that followed (1861–65) saw the victory of the Northern states, which were opposed to slavery and in the process of industrialization. At this point, a further debt repudiation took place, this time to the detriment of the wealthy population of the Southern states. Loans had been contracted in the 1830s, mainly for the creation of banks (Planters' Bank in Mississippi and the Union Bank in North Carolina, in particular) or to underwrite the construction of the railways.

In Mississippi, for example, the initial repayments were made, but then in 1852 a law was passed that allowed for a referendum, giving the inhabitants the chance to vote for or against the repayment of the bonds of Planters' Bank. They voted against. After the War of Secession, in 1876, the Constitution was amended by a clause specifically forbidding the repayment of Planters' Bank bonds. The new regime thus legalized the decision to stop repayments. The amount in the eight states concerned came to $75 million.

USSR

In January 1918, the brand-new Communist government formed after the 1917 Revolution, refused to take responsibility for the loans made by Tsarist Russia and unconditionally canceled all such debts. The new state, fruit of a revolution whose aim was to end the war and give the land to the peasants, refused to honor loans that had been contracted mainly to pay for the carnage of the First World War. These notorious "Russian bonds" then became virtually worthless and the remaining beautifully engraved certificates were sold off in flea markets for years.

Mexico and Other
Latin American Countries

As long ago as 1867, Benito Juárez[170] refused to take on the loans that the preceding regime of Emperor Maximilian had contracted two years earlier with the French bank, the Société Générale de Paris, to finance the occupation of Mexico by the French army.

In 1914, in the middle of the revolution, when Emiliano Zapata[171] and Pancho Villa[172] were on the offensive, Mexico completely suspended its external debt payments. Thus, between 1914 and 1942, the most heavily indebted country on the continent reimbursed only symbolic amounts, to play for time. Between 1922 and 1942 (20 years!), lengthy negotiations took place with a consortium of creditors led by one of the directors of the JPMorgan Bank of the United States. Between 1934 and 1940, President Lázaro Cárdenas[173] nationalized without compensation the petroleum industry and the railways, which were in the hands of British and North-American companies. He also expropriated more than 18 million hectares of the great landed estates (*latifundias*) belonging to national and foreign owners and distributed them in the form of "communal property" (*ejido*). He also completely overhauled the public education system.

Naturally, the creditors (mostly from the United Kingdom and the United States) howled in protest at these radical, anti-imperialist, popular policies. But Mexico's tenacity paid off. In 1942 creditors renounced about 80 percent of the value of the debts (they also renounced the interest arrears) and made do with small compensation deals for the companies that had been expropriated. Other countries, like Brazil, Bolivia, and Ecuador, also suspended part or all of their repayments from 1931. In the case of Brazil, the selective suspension of repayments went on until 1943, when an agreement reduced the debt by 30 percent. Ecuador, too, stopped paying from 1931 until the 1950s.

In the 1930s, a total of fourteen countries suspended payments over a prolonged period. Only Argentina, one of the biggest debtors, maintained its payments without interruption. But it was also the Latin American country which had the worst economic results afterwards.

DEBT CANCELLATIONS THROUGH
FAVORABLE ARBITRATION

Cuba

Cuba was one of the first countries to successfully repudiate odious debt (in this case, a "subjugation" debt). In 1898, the United States had won the war against Spain and gained control of Cuba (until then, a Spanish colony). Cuba was separated from the Spanish Crown, as were Puerto Rico and the Philippines, and became a U.S. protectorate. After the war, Spain demanded that Cuba repay its debt but the United States rejected this demand.

The same year, a conference was held in Paris to deal with the problem; the United States contended that the debt was odious, since it had been imposed by Spain in its own interests, without the consent of the Cuban people. The conference agreed with the United States. Spain accepted the argument and Cuba did not have to pay.

Turkey

Between 1889 and 1902, Turkey experienced a serious financial crisis that made it incapable of honoring its debts to Tsarist Russia. In 1912 the International Court of Arbitration at The Hague agreed that the Turkish government's plea of force majeure was justified.

Costa Rica

In September 1919 the government of Frederico Tinoco in Costa Rica, considered illegitimate by the United States but recognized by other states including Great Britain, was overthrown. In August 1922 the new government terminated all contracts signed by its predecessor, especially those with its main creditor, the Royal Bank of Canada. Judge Taft, chief justice of the Supreme Court of the United States, which arbitrated in 1923, ruled in favor of annulment.

> The transaction in question was concluded at a time when the popularity of the Tinoco regime had disappeared, and the political and military movement to end that regime was gaining strength. The Royal Bank affair does not hinge on the form of transaction, but rather concerns the Bank's good faith. It lies with the Bank to prove that it provided the government with money for a truly legitimate purpose. This it has failed to do. We cannot consider that the Royal Bank of Canada has proved that the money paid was indeed destined for legitimate use by the government. Consequently, its claim must be rejected.
>
> —CHIEF JUSTICE, U.S. SUPREME COURT
> WILLIAM HOWARD TAFT, 1923

CANCELLATIONS CONCEDED BY THE DOMINANT POWERS

Poland

In 1919, the Treaty of Versailles at the end of the First World War considered that the debt contracted by Germany to colonize Poland could not be imputed to the newly constituted Polish state.[174] Article 255 of the

Treaty exonerated Poland from paying "that portion of the debt which, in the opinion of the Reparation Commission, is attributable to the measures taken by the German and Prussian Governments for the German colonization of Poland." A similar stand was taken in the peace treaty between Italy and France, which declared that it was "inconceivable that Ethiopia should take on the burden of debts contracted by Italy in order to dominate Ethiopia."

Germany

In 1953, the London Agreement canceled 51 percent of Germany's war debt. The idea was that the debt service should not exceed 3.5 percent of its export revenues, a percentage that is far exceeded nowadays by developing countries. In 2006 the average was more than 12 percent! And yet Germany did not fulfill any of the criteria required at present to qualify for a reduction and its dictatorship during the preceding decade had sown death and destruction in a large part of the world. The cancellation was very beneficial for Germany, which later became the leading economy in Europe and the driving force behind European reconstruction.[175]

Namibia and Mozambique

South Africa was acutely aware of the consequences that the long regime of apartheid had inflicted on southern Africa and in 1995 unilaterally and unconditionally canceled all its debt claims on Namibia and again in 1999 with Mozambique.

PROCEDURES UNDERTAKEN
BY THE DEVELOPING COUNTRIES SINCE 1985

Peru

In July 1985, the new president of Peru, Alan Garcia, decided to limit debt repayments to 10 percent of export revenues. This led to Peru's banishment from the international community by the IMF and the World Bank, under the impetus of the United States, causing isolation and destabilization. The experiment lasted only a few months and the arrears on the interest, estimated at some $5 billion ($1.27 billion of which was owed to France) were directly added to the debt stock (capitalization of interest).

Cuba (again!)

Also in July 1985, during a conference in Havana, Fidel Castro launched an appeal for non-payment of the debt and for Latin American and Caribbean countries to stand together and refuse to pay. This stance was under discussion but the governments of Mexico, Brazil, and Colombia, pressured by the United States behind the scenes, managed to put a stop to it.

From 1986, Cuba decided to suspend its debt repayments to the Paris Club. At this time, the amount concerned was more or less $2.5 billion. Twelve years later, in 1998, non-official contact was made between the Cuban government and the Club's representatives. Negotiations took place in Havana and ended in failure. Three factors prevented an agreement: the U.S. government was against any agreement being reached as long as Fidel Castro remained in power; Cuba was not a member of the IMF, which made it impossible to reach the kind of agreement the Club is used to; and the Russian government was opposed to concluding a deal, demanding that Cuba repay its debt to the former USSR. Cuba had refused to pay this debt because of a fundamental change in circumstances: the currency in which the debt was contracted (convertible roubles) no longer existed and the state that provided the loans no longer exists. Other non-official negotiations discreetly took place in 1999 in Paris: they remain fruitless.

Burkina Faso

In July 1987, during a speech given to the Organization for African Unity (OAU), Thomas Sankara, the young president of Burkina Faso, announced that he too was in favor of unilaterally canceling debt and creating an African movement of repudiation.

> The debt cannot be repaid, firstly because if we do not pay, the moneylenders will certainly not die of it; on the other hand, if we pay, we shall, with equal certainty, die. . . . Those who have led us into debt have gambled as though in a casino. When they were winning, there

was no debate. Now that they have lost through gambling, they
demand that we repay them. And there is talk of a crisis. They have
gambled, they have lost, those are the rules of the game. Life goes
on. . . . If Burkina Faso is alone in refusing to repay the debt, I will
not be present at the next conference.

—THOMAS SANKARA, speech to the OAU,

Addis-Ababa, Ethiopia, 1987

On October 15, 1987, Thomas Sankara was assassinated. Since then, no
African head of state has taken a stand to repudiate debt.

Argentina

Since December 2001, as far as debt is concerned, Argentina has been in
the headlines. After three years of economic recession, at the brink of disaster, Argentina was refused a loan which had been agreed to by the IMF.
And this despite the fact that Argentina's leaders had always implemented
the unpopular directives demanded by the IMF. This brought things to a
head and the country went into a serious economic crisis. President
Fernando de la Rua reacted by freezing savings accounts. It was thus
impossible for the holders of these accounts who had been patiently saving for many years, sometimes all their lives, to access their money.
Spontaneously, the middle class took to the streets, joined by the "have-
nots" (the unemployed, the slum dwellers, and a majority of the poor).[176]
During the night of December 19–20, 2001, the people protested against
the neoliberal policies of Fernando de la Rua's government and his sinister Minister of the Economy, Domingo Cavallo. This popular action succeeded in altering the course of history.

Three presidents followed in quick succession. De la Rua fled on
December 21, 2001, and his successsor, Adolfo Rodriguez Saa, was
replaced by Eduardo Duhalde on January 2, 2002. Duhalde announced
the biggest suspension of foreign debt in history, a total of more than $80
billion owed to private creditors and the countries of the Paris Club.

Hundreds of factories that had been abandoned by their owners were
occupied and production restarted under workers' control. The unemployed renewed their action in the "piqueteros" movement; the peso,
which had been linked to the dollar, was devalued; the people created

local currencies and shouted as one to the abhorred politicians, "Que se vayan todos!" (Down with the lot of you!).

After twenty-five years of uninterrupted agreement between the IMF and the Argentinean authorities (from the military dictatorship between 1976 and 1983 to the De la Rua government, including the corrupt regime of Carlos Menem), Argentina demonstrated that a country could stop debt repayments for a lengthy period of time and that its creditors would not be capable of organizing reprisals. The IMF, the World Bank, the governments of highly industrialized countries, the major media all had announced that chaos would ensue. But what happened? Instead of going under Argentina began to recover. The rate of growth over the next years was between 8 and 9 percent per year.

Nestor Kirchner, who was elected president in May 2003, challenged the private creditors by offering to exchange their bonds for new ones of a lower value. After lengthy negotiations which came to an end in February 2005, 76 percent of them agreed to waive more than 60 percent of the value of their securities. Once again, standing firm had paid off.

Unfortunately, the rest of the story is more disappointing. This agreement marked the resumption of repayments to private creditors. By the end of 2005 the government had paid back, in advance, the whole of its debt to the IMF: a total of $9.8 billion. It was possible to save $900 million on the interest, but the origin of the debt was never put on the table.

The dictatorship of General Videla, backed by the IMF and the superpowers, had used the debt to reinforce its hold on the country, to enrich its leaders and to firmly lock the economy into the dominant model. In order to repay this debt, subsequent governments sold off a large part of their national heritage and contracted new debts which are thus also odious. Furthermore, these new loans were subject to the implementation of massive liberalization, systematic privatization, and a decrease in social spending.

Consequently, Kirchner would have the right to end the agreements with the IMF and the World Bank, calling on the Olmos verdict (the name of the journalist who had filed a lawsuit against the dictatorship of Jorge Videla) of the Federal Court of Justice. This judgment gave solid legal reasons for pronouncing the debt odious and that it therefore did not have to be repaid.

Unfortunately, the agreement put to the private creditors in 2005 was more a Pyrrhic victory because to persuade the creditors to sign, the government offered to issue them new bonds with very favorable clauses involving a sort of automatic adjustment of the debt.

According to Eduardo Lucita, "These clauses are to a great extent responsible for the country's new debt. First of all, more than 40 percent of the debt is made up of bonds issued in pesos whose interest rate is fixed at 2 percent per year. But the capital is linked to the CER (a coefficient calculated with the rate of inflation). This adjustment means that for each point of inflation, the debt increases by about $600 million Also, many bonds issued in foreign currency are linked to the growth of GDP. This is a very important element in the calculation of interest because Argentina is experiencing a growth rate of more than 8 percent per year. It is estimated that each clause involves additional interest payments of about $1.2 billion. Finally, because 20 percent of the debt is issued in euros and in yen—currencies which are appreciating against the dollar—and because the Argentinean peso is fixed to the dollar and is losing value, there is a technical adjustment due to the difference of exchange which makes itself felt also on the increase of the debt."[177]

Argentina is back once again in a worrying situation with its debt. Its international funding is not good, but Venezuela is helping to refinance its debt. Future repayments are clearly on the increase. This is why the government of Cristina Fernandez de Kirchner, wife of Nestor Kirchner and elected president in October 2007, decided in March 2008 to increase export taxes on soya bean and other cereals. This gave rise to protest from farmers and a widespread political crisis. In July 2008, the president had to withdraw her proposal.

Even though renegotiating the debt is impressive, it can never solve the problems of debt once and for all. Debt leads to political crises and slows down national development. There are no possible alternatives. The only efficient solution is for our countries not to pay back these debts.

—EDUARDO LUCITA

Even though Fernando Solanas's film *The Dignity of the Nobodies* shows the situations of extreme poverty that Argentina is faced with, one event clearly symbolized that the time of standing firm to creditors is over: in September 2006 President Nestor Kirchner went to the New York Stock Exchange to ring the opening bell. There's no double about it— Argentina was back in line. And in 2008, Cristina Kirchner announced that she would pay back in advance the Paris Club—to whom Argentina owes $6.3 billion.

Paraguay

In 1986-87, Gustavo Gramont Berres, Paraguay consul in Geneva, contracted a debt of $85 million toward a bank in Geneva, the Overland Trust Bank, in the name of the Paraguayan State even though he did not have the authority to represent Paraguay.[178]

In the 1990s, Overland Trust Bank sold these debt bonds to nine other private banks that, in 1995, demanded that the loan and its interests be repaid. Paraguay refused and the banks went to the Swiss courts to have Paraguay convicted.

In May 2005, the Swiss Federal High Court ruled in their favor, but in the following August, the Paraguayan government decreed (Decree 6295) that it was making the repudiation of this contentious debt official and giving its reasons for doing so. Paraguay also officially communicated its decision through diplomatic channels to the Swiss government. In October 2005, at the General Assembly of the UN, the president of the Republic of Paraguay confirmed his country's unilateral action and their refusal to pay, stating: "This illegal action was carried out by the government employee of a corrupt dictatorship, who, in collusion with a group of international banks, wanted to rob our country of its desperately needed resources." Furthermore, Paraguay filed an action against Switzerland before the International Court of Justice at The Hague and demanded reparations. For thirteen years Paraguay has refused to pay but no sanction has been applied.

All these examples show that the rare cases of firmness have had very positive results for the indebted countries. What might happen if various democratically elected governments supported by citizens' movements together decreed a freeze on repayments? The Ecuadorian government could perhaps set the example. There is an urgent need for citizens to take in hand the problem of the debt everywhere they can, and to urge their governments to act accordingly.

Several "People's Tribunals Against the Debt" have been held in recent years. In December 2000 in Dakar, during the meeting "Africa: From Resistance to Alternatives," a group of women from the suburbs of Dakar wrote and performed *Le Procès de la dette* (The Debt on Trial) with the IMF, the World Bank, the G7, and the governments of the South standing accused. Women—victims in their daily life of structural adjustment policies—were questioned as witnesses. The involvement of the entire population—young people, women, athletes, trade unionists—was remarkable throughout the conference, and gave this particular event an impressive resonance. In February 2002, at the World Social Forum at Porto Alegre, the International People's Tribunal on Debt was held, at the initiative of the international network, Jubilee South, in collaboration with the CADTM. Various other tribunals were organized afterward. These examples show the need felt by the populations of the South, who endure the hardships caused by the debt, to see judged and condemned (symbolically for the moment) those responsible for the iniquitous system.

Furthermore, several attempts to allow the population to express their opinion democratically on the debt mechanism have been made. In Spain, during the general elections in March 2000, a "social consultation" was held calling for a vote on the abolition of the external debts owed by developing countries to the Spanish state. Despite the enormous difficulties made by the public authorities, who declared the consultation illegal, the referendum enabled over a million people to vote, of whom over 95 percent were in favor of abolition.

Then in Brazil, in September 2000, during the National Week which ends with National Independence Day and the "Grito de los excluidos" (Shouts of the Forsaken) with the march of the landless and the unemployed, six million people also took part, all over the country, in a similar kind of consultation, and 95 percent voted to stop the repayment of the Brazilian debt.

These initiatives are invaluable in popularizing the struggle against the debt and enabling the populations to express their anger and frustration.

QUESTION 39
Why do the governments of the South continue to repay the debt?

Since the debt crisis of the early eighties, the developing countries have become dependent on loans from the international financial institutions. The financial institutions thus have an efficient means of putting pressure on them to endlessly continue their repayments. This is why the Southern governments who try to oppose the Washington consensus are few and far between. For example, when East Timor became independent in May 2002, its leaders were immediately encouraged to take out debts but luckily, they refused to do so.

This pressure, as we have seen, is facilitated by a system of case-by-case negotiations which keeps the indebted state in a constant position of weakness—unlike the IMF, the World Bank, the Paris Club, and the London Club, which are extremely well organized. It is far more difficult for the government of a developing country to say no to all that than to simply accept the loans from these international institutions.

However, do the leaders of the developing countries really want to oppose the dominant model?

During the last twenty-five years, with a few rare exceptions, most governments have not been willing to act counter to neoliberal policy. The links between the leaders of these countries and the hub of decision making in most industrial countries are multifarious. Some of the ruling presidents, in particular in Africa, were brought to power during the Cold War, or owe their positions to it. Some are in power because they helped the elimination of or allowed the overthrow of heads of state who, like Thomas Sankara, the president of Burkina Faso and assassinated in 1987, wanted to commit their country to alternative, locally generated development and social justice. Others simply prefer to follow the neoliberal current for fear of being destabilized or overthrown.

Even among those who harshly criticize the domination of the G7 countries and who try to implement alternative policies, a large majority still believe that they have to remain credible to international finance, and that it is necessary for the development of their country to have recourse to large-scale debt, both internal and external debt.[179] Of

course, there are external pressures from the capitals of the most industrialized countries, from international financial institutions and from
private creditors of the North.

But there is another factor of conservatism that works in favor of large
debt and should not be underestimated. Most governments, both left and
right wing, try to gain the goodwill of the local capitalists who have every
interest in seeing the debt mechanism continue. This mechanism assures
them (as it does for capitalists in the North) a juicy profit because they
lend money to the state which then pays them back at very advantageous
rates of interest. It is extremely rare to find a recent case in which a state
has repudiated its public debt to local bankers. So most bankers prefer to
lend to the state and to other public institutions where their loans are
guaranteed by the government, rather than to local producers—especially
if they are small or medium-sized producers. Lending to the government
is far less risky and far more profitable. Several presidents in power today
have been elected promising to reduce social inequality. They promised
to put an end to the parasitic rent-collecting bankers and to free the country from the yoke of the international creditors. Brazil's experience is a
case in point. Today, bankers and the rest of the local capitalist class are
rubbing their hands in glee under the friendly governance of the party in
power—the Workers' Party!—and President Inacio Lula Da Silva.

If an older adult considers himself belonging to the left, it's because
he has problems. If a young person is right-wing, it's because he has
problems too. . . . I've shifted toward social democracy. When you're
61 you reach some kind of balance. . . . It's part of the human species'
evolution. Someone who was left-wing becomes more centrist,
more social-democratic and less left-wing. It depends on how much
gray hair you have. . . . For many years I criticized the former minister, Delfim Neto [in charge of the economy during the military dictatorship, 1964–85], and now he's my best friend.

—LULA, president of Brazil, December 2006

To complete the picture, many of the top leaders in the countries of
the South are graduates of the top business schools or universities of the
North (Harvard, Columbia, Princeton, Yale, Stanford, Oxford,

Cambridge, HEC Business School in Paris) and have been educated in the liberal mold.

Before becoming governor of the Central Bank of Brazil, Arminio Fraga Neto managed an investment fund for the speculator George Soros. The Ivorian Alassane Dramane Ouattara was director of the Africa Department of the IMF from 1984 to 1988 before becoming prime minister of Côte d'Ivoire from 1990 to 1993 and then assistant director-general of the IMF from 1994 to 1999. At the time of the crisis in Turkey in February 2001, the most symbolic gesture of the international financial institutions was to lend Turkey (along with money) Kemal Dervis, then vice president of the World Bank, who became Minister of Finance in his country (before managing UNDP). Vicente Fox, the Mexican president elected in 2000, was also manager of the Mexican subsidiary of Coca-Cola. Alejandro Toledo was a consultant employed by the World Bank before becoming president of Peru in 2001. Ellen Sirleaf-Johnson worked for the World Bank before becoming president of Liberia in January 2006. Is it any wonder that the policies followed conform perfectly to the wishes of Washington?

The populations in the South are never seriously consulted and are kept carefully out of the picture. However, it is perfectly possible for a democratic government to break the chain of debt. This can be done by repudiating illegitimate debt using the basis of a debt audit. International law provides efficient means for a Southern government to repudiate proceedings for odious or other illegitimate debt. However, Southern governments need to be ready to use these means.

QUESTION 40
What are vulture funds?

Emerging countries that contract debts may change the institution(s) they are dealing with, without having any say in the matter, because of the secondary debt market. This is a sort of secondhand market where debt bonds are bought and sold. A creditor can resell some of his bonds to an investor or an organization which then becomes the creditor. The value at which these debt bonds are sold varies from day to day, and the daily market rate depends only on the confidence—or lack of it—that the financial milieu has in the emerging country in question.

The phenomenon is growing: private institutions buy, at a low price, the debts of struggling countries from creditors who want to get rid of them in order to get back at least part of their money. Motivated solely by profit, these new unscrupulous creditors wait until the economic situation of their debtor country improves slightly (for example, when they reach the completion point of the HIPC initiative or renegotiate their Paris Club debt, or their exports benefit from a rise in the export price index); as soon as there is hope of a light on the horizon, the creditor brings a lawsuit against the indebted country, demanding total and immediate payment. The creditor thus makes an enormous profit, having bought the debt bonds at a ridiculously reduced price with no thought for the social and human consequences. This is the sinister activity of "vulture funds," which are well adapted to unstable situations where corruption is rife. The developing country sometimes has to pay a price higher than the small reductions they have struggled to obtain.

Let us see in detail how Peru was condemned to pay $58 million for debts that had been bought for $11 million.[180] In 1996 the American vulture fund Elliott Associates paid $11.4 million to buy Peruvian foreign debt bonds (bonds issued by the treasury of Peru). They had a face value of $20.7 million. Some time later, under the aegis of the Paris Club and the London Club and with the participation of the IMF and the U.S. government, a plan to reduce and to restructure the Peruvian debt was adopted.

Elliott Associates refused to take part. They did not want to concede any debt reduction. On the contrary, shortly afterward they sued Lima for full repayment (face value) plus capitalized interest—in all, a total of $35 million. Peru refused and Elliott Associates took the case to a New York court, which ruled against them. However, the Court of Appeals overturned this ruling in 2000 and Elliot Associates achieved "preferred creditor" status (that is, they were to be repaid first!). Peru was then ordered to pay the total amount of $58 million, since unpaid interest had continued to accumulate during the four years of the court case! Elliott had made a tidy profit of $38 million, with its lawyers sharing between them the modest sum of $9 million. Apparently Elliott Associates were old hands at the game, as they had already pulled off the same trick in Panama, Ecuador, and Paraguay, picking up $130 million in the process.

Let us look at another example. In 1979 Romania lent $15 million to Zambia to buy Romanian tractors. But because the price of copper (Zambia's principal export) fell, Zambia was accumulating delays in payment. In 1999 the value of the debt remaining was estimated at $30 million. At that moment, Donegal International, a vulture fund belonging to the Debt Advisory International group and registered in the British Virgin Islands—a notorious tax haven—came on the scene and offered to buy up Romania's debt for $3.3 million.

When Zambia reached the point when some of its debt was canceled as part of the HIPC initiative and then the MDRI (see chapter 7), Donegal International then sued Zambia for repayment of the total amount plus late interest payments—in all $55 million. This was seventeen times its initial investment and more than the reduction of debt received that year by Zambia ($40 million). To achieve its ends, Donegal International also demanded the freezing of Zambian assets in the United Kingdom.[181]

In April 2007 the High Court in London awarded a reluctant victory to Donegal International, ruling that Zambia was to pay them $15.4 million plus part of the legal costs—a total of about $17 million, which is a considerable amount in view of the initial $3.3 million paid out by Donegal. Even though the High Court criticized Donegal and its boss Michael Sheehan for their "dishonest" actions and even though it considered the amount to be exorbitant, nevertheless, the court ruled that the agreement was legal. Economics correspondent Ashley Seager, in an editorial in *The Guardian*, pointed out that the same Sheehan is also director of Walker International, a company that sued Congo-Brazzaville for $13 million.[182] It is actually impossible to establish how many vulture funds are currently active since they are often created on a one-off basis to prey on a specific indebted country.

Banks need to consider carefully the ethical implications of their decisions rather than simply clearing the debts off their balance sheets for the vultures to pick over. . . . Funds are incorporated in jurisdictions that preserve shareholder anonymity, which means it is impossible to access their backers. It is impossible to lobby share-

holders about the funds' policies in respect of poor country debt.
—RONNIE KING, Advocates for International Development, 2007

This brings us to a basic point: vulture funds are not simply a foreign body, totally alien to the system, resulting from the greed of a few unscrupulous speculators. Instead, they all too often do the dirty work of other creditors, for example the big banks, who cannot operate openly for fear of bad publicity.

The example of Congo-Brazzaville—another country under attack by vulture funds—is enlightening. Led by the dictator Denis Sassou Nguesso, dutifully subservient to the oil interest of the French oil company Elf (now part of Total), Congo reached the decision point of the HIPC in March 2006—which made it eligible to be considered for the relief of part of its debt (one of the biggest in the world per inhabitant; see Q 27). Even though international financial institutions were hesitating because they suspected embezzlement and concealment of funds, France applied pressure for the debt relief to go through. Vulture funds had been harassing the Congo for several years. Kensington International, which had paid $1.7 million to buy four debts (dating back to the 1980s) with a total face value of $32.6 million, won their lawsuit in a British court and Congo was ordered to pay them more than $121 million.

The story gets really juicy when the Congolese authorities clothe themselves in nationalistic righteousness and admit that although the SNPC—the Congolese National Oil Company—had to set up dummy corporations based in tax havens to conceal part of their oil revenue, it was not so that the ruling clique could embezzle the funds. Rather, it was to protect the revenue from vulture funds that were attempting to freeze Congolese assets abroad so that they would be available to be seized following legal decisions.

In January 2006, Isidore Mvouba, Congolese prime minister, even dared to say: "Our country is being harassed by vulture funds that are doing everything they can to prevent Congo from reaching decision point. They don't balk at organizing misinformation campaigns in the United States concerning the Congo. . . . We have had to protect the money of the Congolese people so that it does not fall into the greedy hands of these predators. . . . Nevertheless, the lawsuit which ruled

Lawsuits Filed by Private Creditors against

HIPC	CREDITOR	LOCATION OF CREDITOR
Cameroon	Winslow Bank	Bahamas
	Del Favaro	Italy
	Sconset	Virgin Isl. (UK)
	GraceChurch (Paris)	Cayman Isl.
	Antwerp	Virgin Isl. (UK)
Congo-B	GAT	Lebanon
	NUFI-AIG	United States
	FG Hemisphere	United States
	AF CAP Inc	Bermuda
	Berrebi	France
	Kensington Int	Cayman Isl.
	Walker International	Virgin Isl. (UK)
	Commissimpex	Congo-B
Congo-K (DRC)	FG Hemisphere	United States
	KHD Humboldt Wedag AG Koln	
Ethiopia	Kintel	Bulgaria
	Yugoimport	Serbia
Guyana	Citizens Bank	Guyana
	Booker	UK
	Export Services	United States
Honduras	Laboratoires Bago	Argentina
Nicaragua	LNC Investments	United States
	Hemisphere	United States
	Greylock Global Opp	Virgin Isl. (UK)
	Hamsah Investments	Virgin Isl. (UK)
	Inex, 14 Oct Krusevac, IMT AD, DP FAP, MFK Corp	Serbia
Uganda	Banco Arabe Espanol	Spain
	Transroad Ltd	UK
	Industry Machinery 14 Oktobar	Ex-Yugoslavia
	Sour Fap Famous	Ex-Yugoslavia
	Iraq Fund for Int Development	Iraq
	Shelter Afrique	Kenya
Sao Tomé & Prin.	Annadale Associates	UK
Sierra Leone	J&S Franklin Ltd	UK
	Umarco	France
	Executive Outcomes	Sierra Leone
	Chatelet Investment	Sierra Leone
	Scancem Int	Norway
Zambie	Connecticut Bank of Commerce	United States
	Donegal	Virgin Isl. (UK)
	TOTAL	

HIPC in August 2008 (in $ million)

LEGAL DECISION	INITIAL AMT. DEMANDED (w/o arrears)	TOTAL DEMANDED	FINAL DECISION
Adjudicated	9.0	46.3	46.3
Adjudicated	0.8	4.6	4.6
Arbitrage	18.2	53.9	
Pending	9.5	39.7	
Arbitrage	15.2	196.0	
Adjudicated	126.0	88.6	92.1
Adjudicated	11.2	24.3	8.3
Adjudicated	35.9	152.0	151.9
Adjudicated	9.6	20.8	10.9
Adjudicated	2.1	13.7	13.7
Adjudicated	29.6	118.6	118.6
Adjudicated	2038	47.8	47.8
Amicable agrmt.	292		
Adjudicated	55.8	81.7	81.7
Adjudicated		67.1	67.1
Arbitrage	8.7	8.7	
Arbitrage	122.8	178.0	
Amicable agrmt.	24.3	24.7	
Abandoned	4.1	7.5	
Adjudicated	14.1	14.1	5.3
Pending	1.5	1.5	
Adjudicated	26.3	87.1	87.1
Adjudicated	30.9	126.0	126.0
Adjudicated	10.5	50.9	50.9
Adjudicated	2.5	11.6	11.6
Pending	9.6	9.6	
Adjudicated	1.0	2.7	2.7
Adjudicated	4.0	16.7	16.7
Adjudicated	7.0	8.9	8.9
Adjudicated	0.3	1.4	1.4
Pending	6.0	6.4	
Amicable agrmt.	0.1	0.1	
Arbitrage	3.0	8.9	
Adjudicated	1.1	3.4	3.4
Pending	0.6	0.6	
Adjudicated	19.5	23.0	23.0
Pending	0.4	0.4	
Amicable agrmt.	3.7	3.7	
Adjudicated	0.9	0.3	0.3
Pending	15.4	55.0	15.4
	954.0	1606.3	995.7

against the Congo has at least resulted in attracting attention to the international financial predators who are ruining with impunity the developing countries."[183]

The Congolese people are thus powerlessly attending to the ferocious struggle for oil revenue fought between those close to power and the vulture funds. Whoever wins, the people know that unfortunately they will not benefit from the wealth that belongs to them. Asking the IMF not to grant debt relief would not be a step toward a just and lasting solution. Vulture funds are a catalyst, bringing to light that the economic model promoted by the IMF in the name of the principal creditors since the 1980s is structurally a creator of debt, of corruption, and of poverty.

The only way toward a solution inevitably calls for a fundamental change in the economic model itself and the refusal, firstly, of the domination imposed by the IMF and the World Bank through debt on the Congolese people to the benefit of rich creditors and multinationals; secondly, refusal of the HIPC initiative that propagates this model and aims at quelling all forms of opposition to the present economic model imposed from outside; and thirdly, the refusal that dictators (in this case Sassou and his entourage supported by France and Total—inheritors of the corrupt empire of Elf) can monopolize wealth. In the struggle between the Sassou clan, the vulture funds, and the Bretton Woods institutions it is not acceptable to criticize one in order to then defend the interests of the other. That would be a false opposition as they all contribute to the same logic. Vulture funds are visible evidence that the economic model based on debt is a runaway train.

More than forty legal proceedings have taken place or are still under way, and this only in the poorest and most heavily indebted countries. Court rulings have already granted nearly a billion dollars to vulture funds. This turns debt into a most profitable market.

In short, a country that "benefits" from an agreement with its creditors to reduce its debt may see its debt increase because, as its financial situation improves, its solvency increases and the commercial value of its remaining stock increases. On the other hand, if a country is late in paying back its debt, then its commercial value decreases. If we can draw a conclusion it should be this: in a market economy, it is better to cancel or repudiate the whole debt.

CHAPTER TEN

The Case for Canceling the Debt
of Developing Countries

QUESTION 41
What are the moral arguments in favor of canceling the debt of developing countries ?

Though countries of the South are often generously provided with human and natural resources, the burden of the debt has led to general impoverishment, made much worse by organized plunder.

Repaying the debt is an essential obstacle to satisfying basic human needs, such as access to clean water, decent food, basic health care, primary education, decent accommodation, and satisfactory infrastructures. Without any doubt, the satisfaction of basic human needs must take priority over all other considerations, be they geopolitical or financial. From a moral point of view, the rights of creditors, shareholders, or speculators are insignificant in comparison with the fundamental rights of five billion citizens.

It is immoral to demand that the developing countries devote what available resources they have to repaying well-heeled creditors (whether in the North or the South) rather than to satisfying fundamental needs.

The issue of the moral responsibility of the creditors was particularly apparent in the case of Cold War loans. When the IMF and the World Bank lent money to the Democratic Republic of the Congo's notorious ruler Mobutu, they knew (or should have known) that most of the money would not go to help that country's poor people, but rather would be used to enrich Mobutu. It was money paid to ensure

that this corrupt leader would keep his country aligned with the
West. To many, it doesn't seem fair for ordinary taxpayers in countries with corrupt governments to have to repay loans that were
made to leaders who did not represent them.

—JOSEPH STIGLITZ, *Globalization and Its Discontents*, 2002

Debt is one of the main mechanisms through which a new form of
economic colonization operates to the detriment of the developing countries. It is one more brick in the edifice of historic abuses, also carried out
by the rich countries: slavery, pillage of raw materials and cultural goods,
extermination of indigenous populations, and colonial servitude. The
time is overdue to replace the logic of domination by the logic of redistribution of wealth in the name of justice.

The G8, the IMF, the World Bank, and the Paris Club impose their
own truth, their own justice, where they call the tune. The time has come
to put an end to this phony justice of conquerors and oppressors.

The immorality of the debt is also a consequence of the fact that it was
frequently contracted by undemocratic regimes that did not use the
money received in the interests of their populations, and often organized
embezzlement on a massive scale, with the tacit or active agreement of the
states of the North, the World Bank, and the IMF. Creditors of the industrialized countries, who took advantage of the high interest rates in 1979
and the low prices of raw materials on the international market, know-
ingly lent money to often corrupt regimes. They have no right to demand
that the people repay such loans. Let them address the fallen dictators, or
those still in place, and their accomplices.

Let us risk a comparison. The activists who fought against slavery
were moved by an ideal of justice and were fiercely opposed to this abom-
inable practice. The time came when the balance of power shifted and the
abolition of slavery became unavoidable, despite the forecasts of economic disaster made by those who defended slavery. In the case of the
external public debt of the developing countries and the turn of events
since 1980, the situation is comparable (though not identical). The debt
has become a mighty mechanism of domination. The struggle of citizens
revolted by domination and its human ravages must be waged even more
intensely if this diktat is to be broken.

Demanding the total cancellation of the public external debt for all developing countries is central to today's abolitionist movement. Just as was the case for slavery, cancellation must be complete, for slavery cannot be amended, nor can it be reduced: it has to be abolished.

> The countries in the South must stop repaying their debt. That debt is illegitimate, since in most cases it was contracted by totalitarian and corrupt governments who embezzled the money for their own profit. It is also the result of the pillage of our wealth by the North during centuries of exploitation. The populations of the South no longer have to bear such a burden, which remains an instrument of domination and control by the rich countries over the poorest.
> —LIDY NAPCIL, international coordinator of Jubilee South, in *Le Monde*, "Jubilé Sud: les tribunaux de la dette" (Jubilee South: Debt on Trial), January 26, 2002

QUESTION 42

What are the political arguments in favor of canceling the debt of developing countries?

The mechanisms of the debt cycle have subjected the developing countries to the demands of Washington (where the IMF, the World Bank, and the U.S. Treasury all have their headquarters). For the countries concerned, the fundamentals of their economic policy are decided outside their territory. This means that the IMF and the World Bank have a hand in each economic decision a developing country makes. The debt enables creditors to exercise exorbitant power over the indebted countries.

The developing countries that have been subjected to the stranglehold of the creditors represented by the IMF and the World Bank have gradually been forced to abandon all sovereignty. Governments no longer have the power to implement the policies for which they were elected. In Guyana, for example, the government decided, in early 2000, to increase the salaries of the civil servants by 3.5 percent, after a fall in purchasing power of 30 percent in the previous five years. The IMF immediately threatened to remove it from the list of HIPCs. After a few months, the government had to backpedal.

In the summer of 2002 Brazil was shaken by particularly severe financial turbulence, due to the combined effects of the Argentinean crisis and the economic slowdown in the United States and the European Union. President Cardoso's government negotiated an agreement with the IMF that granted the country a loan on a scale never seen before: $30.4 billion by the end of 2003. Naturally, there was a catch: the IMF demanded that a strict austerity budget be adhered to until 2005. This loan, which was meant to calm the markets, was also a means of exerting control over Lula, who was subsequently elected head of state in October 2002. The IMF exacted an agreement in principle on this plan from the main presidential candidates before granting the loan. Magnanimously, it relented on its initial insistence on a written agreement. The IMF director at the time, the German Horst Köhler, was unequivocal: "By reducing vulnerability and incertitude, the new program . . . provides the new government with a bridge for after 2003." Conclusion: the IMF directly interfered in the internal politics of a country just months before a general election with a view to influencing the choice of its citizens. This is unacceptable because it flouts democracy.

> We have a flag, a national anthem, but everything else is decided upon by the West. It's all wrapped up in nice words, under cover of aid extended by such bodies as the WB and the IMF, that are nothing more than instruments of torture invented by the West to continue its domination.
>
> —AHMED BEN BELLA, president of the Algerian Republic, 1963 to 1965[184]

The citizens of the South know the IMF and the World Bank: they experience the destructive effects of Structural Adjustment Programs every day of their lives. Very often decisions are made in Washington or other capitals of the North, and leaders in the South are simply expected to implement them in their respective countries. However, people of the South are right to demonstrate in front of the presidential palace or the ministry of finance in their countries since popular pressure may prompt their leaders to shoulder their responsibilities and restore a little dignity. Protests in Bolivia in April 2000 and December 2004–January 2005 against water privatization ended in victory, like those against the privatization of natural gas in September–October 2003. In 2006, Evo Morales's new democratically elected government nationalized hydrocarbons. Popular mobilization in Niger in 2005 caused the government to repeal a budget law imposed by the IMF and the World Bank. Similarly successful were the large demonstrations in Conakry (Guinea) in December 2005–January 2006. Mobilization against the food crisis organized all over the globe in March–April 2008 also caused governments to distance themselves from neoliberal dogmas and resulted in a new global awareness, thus proving that united struggle can have positive results.

True sovereignty will remain an impossible dream for the developing countries as long as they remain under the yoke of the IMF/World Bank/WTO trio, and more generally of all the creditors of the North. Caught in the vise of debt repayment, most developing countries have been forced to sacrifice their financial, economic and political sovereignty.

> Globalization, as it has been advocated, often seems to replace the old dictatorships of national elites with new dictatorships of international finance. Countries are effectively told that if they don't follow certain conditions, the capital markets or the IMF will refuse to lend them money. They are basically forced to give up part of their sovereignty, to let capricious capital markets, including the speculators whose only concerns are short-term rather than the long-term growth of the country and the improvement of living standards, "discipline" them, telling them what they should and should not do.
> —JOSEPH STIGLITZ, *Globalization and Its Discontents*, 2002

After five centuries of pillage, slavery, and colonization, and after twenty-five years of structural adjustment policies, the populations of the South have a right to demand reparation for all the ills they have suffered, caused by an invisible mechanism set up by the creditors of the North with the support of the ruling classes of the South. Total cancellation of the debt should be the first act of reparation.

Too many inhabitants of the rich countries are unaware of the perverse mechanisms that drive inhabitants of developing countries to leave their land and their loved ones to try to survive in the North. Aid sent by the rich countries is far too meager and self-serving to even begin to compensate for this drain of natural and financial wealth from the South. The intolerable rise of self-interest, which can be commonly observed in Europe, in the United States and even in South Africa,[185] with its attendant racism and xenophobia, is a consequence of the ignorance of some and the bad faith of others. There is a pressing need to lift the veil and explain that it is in the common interest of the populations of North and South alike to unite in demanding total cancellation of the external public debt on the one hand, and an end to Structural Adjustment Programs on the other.

I must say yet again what I have not ceased to repeat since 1985. The debt has already been amply repaid, given the terms under which it was contracted, the arbitrary and vertiginous growth of interest rates on the dollar during the preceding decade and the fall in prices of the basic products which are the fundamental source of revenue for countries still needing to develop. The debt has become a self-perpetuating vicious circle where new debts are taken out to pay off the interest on standing ones.

It is clearer than ever that the debt is not an economic problem, but a political one, and it is as such that it must be resolved. The solution has to come mainly from those who have the resources and the power to do it: the rich countries. This can no longer be ignored.

—FIDEL CASTRO, Cuban head of state,
in a speech in Havana, April 12, 2000

QUESTION 43
What are the economic arguments in favor of canceling the debt of developing countries?

On the one hand, the figures given (see chapter 6) prove that the debt has already been repaid several times over: to date, the public authorities of developing countries have repaid their 1970 debt ninety-four times over, while at the same time the debt has multiplied by twenty-nine. Debt is no longer the reason for fair repayment of a loan obtained under regular conditions; instead it is a very clever instrument of domination behind which racketeering and pillage go unpunished.

On the other hand, the net transfers on the debt are strongly negative for the South. Between 1985 and 2007, public authorities of the various developing countries "gave" a total contribution of approximately $750 billion to capital holders in the North, derived from the work of local wage earners and producers. This financial hemorrhage that is bleeding dry the countries of the South and the East has to be stopped.

Instead, a cycle of ecologically sustainable and socially just development must be promoted. The iniquitous debt must be abolished, and mechanisms must be established for alternative funding of this development, together with effective restraints on the tendency to borrow.

The economies of the South have everything to gain from the cancellation of their public external and internal debt. Examples of actual cancellations carried out in the past have proved particularly beneficial for the economies of the countries concerned (see Q38).

The economies of the South would not be forced, as they are today, to export at all costs to repay their debt, leaving them dependent on external demand and on world market fluctuations.

The developing countries could also give priority to South-South relations instead of always seeking markets in the North in order to earn strong currencies, and set up a graduated form of protectionism. Since the San Jose agreements, this has been the case for petroleum products, which Venezuela provides to more than fifteen Latin American countries at preferential rates, through the Petrocaribe oil alliance.

Cartels could be created among countries that produce certain kinds of commodities so as to influence prices and world trade, rather like OPEC for petroleum. Developing countries would then be better able to preserve their nonrenewable resources (mines, oil, gas, fish stocks, and the like).

Furthermore, infrastructures and essential public services are powerful factors of endogenous growth. Private investment loses its efficacy when there is no appropriate public investment. Growth is an indispensable premise for attracting private capital. Yet any substantial public investment is made impossible by the weight of the debt and the obligatory budget austerity that goes with it. Canceling the debt, therefore, can play a powerful role in restarting the world economy.

> Following a rise in the price of oil decided by OPEC: A top Western official telephoned me from far away to say that he was concerned by the price of oil. I replied, "So am I!" But why don't we discuss the debt of the poor countries, too, and the unfairness of the terms of the exchange?
>
> —HUGO CHÁVEZ, president of Venezuela, in *Libération*,
> September 29, 2000

QUESTION 44
What are the legal arguments in favor of canceling the debt of developing countries?

Several arguments in international law can be invoked as legal justification for unilateral cancellation of the external debt. Three are outlined below, and a fourth one, which has no precise legal definition, is also discussed.:

• Force majeure *and a fundamental change in circumstances*

Force majeure can be invoked when a government or public body finds itself, due to external circumstances beyond its control, unable to fulfill its international obligations, including repayment of a debt. This is the legal translation of the fact that no one can be held to do the impossible—which is clear both in international law and from the point of view of common sense. These external and involuntary circumstances could, for example, be a fall in the prices of raw materials or an action on the part of the creditors—who are legally held co-responsible in the mechanism of indebtedness—or again the rise in interest rates in 1979. The developing countries contracted loans at reasonable rates in the 1970s, but the actions of the rich countries aimed at greatly increasing interest rates and maneuvering to lower the prices of raw materials on the world market radically changed the nature of the deal. This is indeed a case of *force majeure* and a radical change in circumstances brought about by the unilateral behavior of the industrialized countries.

- *The state of necessity*

The state of necessity is characterized by a situation that jeopardizes the existence of the state or its economic or political survival—such as severe social upheaval or the impossibility of fulfilling the needs of the population (health and education, for example). It is not a case of being absolutely prevented from fulfilling international obligations but of recognizing that to do so would necessitate sacrifices on the part of the population that go beyond what is reasonable. The *state of necessity* may justify repudiating the debt, since it implies establishing priorities among the different obligations of the state.

The United Nations Human Rights Commission has adopted numerous resolutions on the issue of the debt and structural adjustment. One such resolution, adopted in 1999, asserts: "The exercise of the basic rights of the people of debtor countries to food, housing, clothing, employment, education, health services and a healthy environment cannot be subordinated to the implementation of structural adjustment policies, growth programs and economic reforms arising from the debt."

The developing countries are no longer able to fulfill the fundamental human needs of their populations. This inability jeopardizes the very existence of all these states, which must invoke the state of necessity for the unilateral cessation of their repayments.

A state cannot be expected to close its schools, its universities, its courts of law, and to abandon its public services to the point of chaos and anarchy in the community, simply to have the money to repay its foreign or national creditors.

—DIRECTORY OF THE UN COMMISSION
ON INTERNATIONAL LAW, 1980, vol. 1

• *Odious debt*

International law recognizes the need to take into account the nature of the regime that contracted the debts and the use to which the funds raised were put. This implies the direct responsibility of creditors, whether private bodies or IFIs. If a dictatorial regime is replaced by a legitimate regime, the latter can demonstrate that the debts were not contracted in the interests of the nation or were contracted for odious ends. In this case, they are declared null and void, and the new government does not have to repay them. The creditors should pursue their case with the leaders of the dictatorship, on a personal basis. The IMF, the World Bank, or any other creditor is legally obligated to check that the loans they grant are put to legitimate use, especially when they cannot help but know that they are dealing with an illegitimate regime.

After the dictatorship that ended in 1984, Argentina had a perfect right to take this course. The Olmos verdict of July 13, 2000, pronounced before the Criminal and Correctional Court n°2, recognized that the policies carried out over seven years could be defined as legally organized pillage, with the active participation of the IMF and the World Bank.[186] But all this was to no avail. Enormous pressure was put on the Argentinean government until it finally agreed to take on the debt to the very last peso, until 2001 when, after more than three years of recession, it was completely unable to pay, following the refusal of the IMF to grant a further loan.

This doctrine could also have been used by many other governments that succeeded illegitimate regimes: in Latin America after the fall of the military dictatorships (Uruguay, Brazil, Chile), in the Philippines after the departure of Marcos in 1986, in Rwanda after the 1994 genocide, in South Africa at the end of the Apartheid regime, in Zaire after the overthrow of Mobutu in 1997, or in Indonesia after the fall of Suharto in 1998. It is a great pity that the governments that replaced the dictatorships capitulated before the creditors in taking on previous debts, however odious, and found themselves prisoners of repayments they could have avoided. In doing this, they have unduly burdened their people with the weight of odious debts. Their decision has had a negative impact on the daily lives of the generations that followed.

Yet the notion of odious debt has been invoked on occasion, as in Cuba in 1898, Costa Rica in 1922, Namibia in 1995, and Mozambique in 1999 (see Q38).

> If a despotic power incurs a debt, not for the needs or in the interest of the state, but to strengthen its despotic regime, to repress its population that fights against it, and so forth, this debt is odious for the population of the state. This debt is not an obligation for the nation; it is a regime's debt, a personal debt of the power that incurred it; consequently it falls with the fall of this power.
> —ALEXANDER NAHUM SACK, "Les effets des transformations des états sur leurs dettes publiques et autres obligations financières" (*The effects of the transformations of states on their public debts and other financial obligations*), Recueil Sirey, 1927

A debt can be defined as odious if it meets one of the three following conditions:

1. It has been incurred by a dictatorial and despotic regime, with a view to strengthening its rule.
2. It has been incurred not in the interests of the people but against its interests and/or in the personal interests of the rulers or persons close to the regime.
3. The creditors knew (or were in a position to know) the odious use of the loans.

These three conditions—absence of consent, absence of benefits, creditors' knowledge—need to be further developed.

The democratic (or non-democratic) nature of a regime is not only determined by the way the government is appointed. A loan granted to an elected government that does not abide by the principles of international law must be considered odious. In the case of well-known dictatorships, creditors cannot plead ignorance and cannot claim payment. In this case, the use a loan is put to is not fundamental for characterizing the debt as odious. Financial support for a criminal regime, even if it happens to build a school or a hospital, amounts to consolidating the said regime.

The nature of regimes aside, the use of funds should suffice to qualify debts as odious whenever these funds are used against the population's major interests or when they directly enrich the regime's inner circle. Thus, debts incurred within the framework of structural adjustments (see Q17 and Q18) fall into the category of odious debts, since the destructive character of the SAP has been clearly shown, including by UN agencies.[187]

Consequently, all debts incurred by the Apartheid regime in South Africa are odious, since this regime violated the UN Charter, which defines the legal framework of international relations. In a resolution adopted in 1964, the United Nations asked its specialized agencies, including the World Bank, to discontinue their financial support of South Africa. In contempt of international law, the World Bank ignored this resolution and continued to lend to the Apartheid regime.[188]

International law also stipulates that debts resulting from colonization are not transferable to newly independent states, in conformity with article 16 of the 1978 Vienna Convention, which stipulates: "A newly independent state is not bound to maintain in force, or to become a party to, any treaty by reason only of the fact that at the date of the succession of states the treaty was in force in respect of the territory to which the succession of states relates." Article 38 of the 1983 Vienna Convention on the succession of states in respect of states' property, archives, and debts (not yet in force) is quite explicit in this respect: "1. When the successor state is a newly independent state, no state debt of the predecessor state shall pass to the newly independent state, unless an agreement between them provides otherwise in view of the link between the state debt of the predecessor state connected with its activity in the territory to which the succession of states relates and the property, rights and interests which pass to the newly independent state. 2. The agreement referred to in paragraph 1 shall not infringe the principle of the permanent sovereignty of every people over its wealth and natural resources, nor shall its implementation endanger the fundamental economic equilibrium of the newly independent state."

It should be kept in mind that the World Bank is directly involved in some colonial debts, since in the 1950s and 1960s it generously loaned money to colonial countries to maximize the profits derived from colonial exploitation. It must also be noted that the debts granted by the World

Bank to the Belgian, French, and English authorities to serve their colonial policies were later transferred to the newly independent states without their consent.[189] Moreover, the World Bank refused to implement a 1965 UN resolution ordering it to stop giving financial support to Portugal as long as that country pursued its colonial policy.

We must also define as odious all debts incurred in order to pay back odious debts, which can rightly be considered a laundering operation.

The definition of odious debts is still debated; it still has to be modeled and placed at the service of international justice. But creditors are already rushing to defuse the potential bomb it represents. The World Bank, for instance, attempted a sort of counterattack with its September 2007 report titled "Odious Debt: Some Considerations." A biased and botched document at best, it clearly has no other purpose but to get rid of this sensitive issue. This is evidenced by the last part of the WB's report, which consists of proposals for alternatives to repudiation of odious debts by the countries of the South. Yet these alternatives include no convincing means of breaking the current spiral: improving good governance, negotiating with creditors and possibly joining the HIPC initiative (see Q31) so as to benefit from debt relief aimed at making the debt sustainable.

The World Bank claims that unilateral repudiation of odious debts would make it impossible for the countries concerned to access capital markets. But we have already shown (see Q38) that Paraguay's unilateral decision to repudiate debts claimed by a Swiss bank consortium in 2005 did not lead to the country's isolation. In any case, if a coalition of developing countries against the repayment of odious debts should emerge, it could only have beneficial effects, since globally the developing countries are exporters of capital (the net transfer on the debt being negative; see chapter 6). An end to repayments, even if it meant an end to loans, would be globally positive for the developing countries. If the World Bank incites governments to repay rather than to repudiate odious debts, it is to preserve its domination. But despite all the World Bank's insistence in this regard, the notion of odious debt is unlikely to go away.

Recall that George W. Bush ventured into odious debt territory in 2003, just after the military aggression he launched against Iraq. Once he had gained control of the country, he was unwilling to take over the debts contracted by Saddam Hussein and pronounced them odious, in which

DEBT, THE IMF, AND THE WORLD BANK

regard he was not wrong. But the creditors stopped him short, afraid that this argument would be taken up elsewhere with equal justification. The United States then pulled strings in the Paris Club to obtain an exceptional cancellation of Iraq's debt. And Bush never mentioned the subject of odious debt again.

To conclude, international law abounds in doctrines and jurisprudence that could provide grounds, and indeed have already provided grounds, for the cancellation or repudiation of debts. Social movements as well as democratic and progressive governments must insist that international law, and especially the Universal Declaration of Human Rights and the Covenant on Economic, Social, and Cultural Rights, take precedence over the rights of creditors and usurers. These fundamental texts can in no way be compatible with the repayment of an immoral, and often odious, debt.[190]

• *Illegitimate debt*

An "illegitimate debt" has, strictly speaking, no definition in law, yet a definition emerges from various cases encountered in the history of indebtedness.[191] It is reasonable to classify as illegitimate a debt that goes counter to law or public policy; a debt that is unjust, inappropriate, or abusive; a debt that an indebted country should not be forced to repay because the loan or the conditions attached to the loan violate a country's sovereignty and infringe human rights. The debts of the countries of the South frequently come under this definition. The loans granted by the IMF and the World Bank, conditioned by the enforcement of structural adjustment policies, can thus be considered illegitimate.

Joseph Hanlon sets out four criteria for classifying a loan as illegitimate: a loan granted for the purpose of reinforcing a dictatorial regime (unacceptable loan); a loan contracted at excessive interest rates (unacceptable conditions); a loan granted to a country while being aware of its incapacity to repay (inappropriate loan); a loan dependent on IMF-imposed conditions, creating an economic situation that makes repayment more difficult still (inappropriate conditions).

It is clear, therefore, that the notion of illegitimate debt is based first and foremost on a moral judgment. The concept of "illegitimate debt" was first mentioned in an official verdict in 2000, the Olmos verdict[192] (see Q38), which served to reveal the illegitimate nature of the external debt contracted during the Argentinean dictatorship (1976–83) and the liability of the creditors and debtors.

Norway first invoked this concept at the end of 2006 to allow a number of its debtor countries to forgo repayment of certain debts. At the end of the 1970s, the Norwegian shipbuilding industry was ailing, with shipyards standing idle for want of clients. To remedy the situation, the government decided in 1976 to launch a Ship Export Campaign which granted cheap credit to countries of the South in exchange for the purchase of Norwegian ships. In all, thirty-six such projects were agreed with twenty-one countries, but in 1987 only three had been successfully completed and only two countries managed to honor their debt.

One of the countries that failed to honor its debt was Ecuador. The state-owned Flota Bananera Ecuatoriana (FBE) bought four ships from Norway between 1978 and 1981 for a sum of $56.9 million. In 1985, the FBE went bankrupt, and another state-owned company, Transnave, took over the ships. The debt was then divided into two parts: one part, worth $17.5 million, remained the responsibility of Transnave and the state of Ecuador, and the other part, worth $13.6 million, was renegotiated within the Paris Club. The first part was fully repaid, but the second increased substantially in the years that followed. In March 2001, it stood at $49.6 million, and the total payments made by FBE, Transnave and the government already amounted to $51.9 million.

Due to international pressure, the Norwegian parliament and government eventually recognized that this situation was inadmissible. In October 2006, the Norwegian Minister of International Development, Erik Solheim, admitted his country's shared responsibility in the failure of development assistance projects organized in the framework of the Ship Export Campaign. He announced the cancellation of the resulting debt for countries that remained debtors, such as Ecuador, whose campaign-related debt amounted to $36 million.

Norway led the way. Not only did it do partial justice to the injured countries, but it also started a major international debate on the responsibility of creditors with regard to borrowers. This cancellation is entirely unilateral and is not the result of a negotiation with other Paris Club creditors. It proves, therefore, that it is possible for a creditor to break with the creditor bloc if there is the desire and determination to do so. Moreover, Norway made a commitment not to include this cancellation in its official development assistance account, as opposed to what so many other countries have done.

Norway took care to announce that its decision in no way involved the Paris Club and that it would take no further initiatives of this kind on a unilateral basis. Only a strong popular movement can ensure that other initiatives will follow.

> People are like underground rivers which, at a given moment, rise to the surface. People are ceasing to be spectators and are ready to be the protagonists of their own lives and their own history. That's what's wonderful about life.
>
> —ADOLFO PEREZ ESQUIVEL,
> Nobel Peace Prize Laureate, 1980

QUESTION 45
What are the environmental arguments in favor of canceling the debt of developing countries?

The two basic causes of the destruction of our environment are well known: at one extreme is the accumulation of wealth, which leads to the exhaustion of natural resources with total disregard for ecosystems, and at the other is the poverty that forces populations to sell off their resources to the highest bidder.

Overproduction and overconsumption prevail in rich countries. Natural resources are overexploited beyond their capacity for renewal. And so mankind in general consumes more than can be produced on a sustainable basis.

The side effects of this overconsumption are also well known: air and water pollution, accumulation of toxic waste, and the disappearance of green spaces. The governments and multinationals of the North, which are responsible for the destruction in the first place, try to offload the consequences onto developing countries whenever they can. For example, the United States sends industrial waste containing heavy metals to India to be reprocessed, and the stranglehold of the debt forces developing countries to accept highly polluting industries from the North. While the pollution-friendly global economic model creates pollution in the South, the spiraling debt has created a subservience such that the South has also been turned into the dustbin for the North.

Let us look at a concrete example. On August 19, 2006, the chemical tanker *Probo Koala* docked in Abidjan (Côte d'Ivoire). More than five hundred tons of toxic products (basically sludge from oil refineries) were unloaded and then dumped at at least fourteen sites without the slightest precaution. Very serious consequences ensued. Thousands of inhabitants of the Ivorian capital complained of nausea, vomiting, and respiratory problems. More than ten people died and thousands went to authorized health centers. The flora and fauna of the surrounding area were seriously affected. Fish were found dead in fish farms, and market gardens had to be closed. The government was forced to resign, but then the same prime minister, Charles Konan Banny, was asked to form a new one. In so doing, Côte d'Ivoire recognized that it was incapable of preventing such a tragic situation or of providing a satisfactory solution.

This was not merely an unfortunate accident. In the wake of various restructuring plans, the means that states had for regulating their economy had been dismantled. Structures of prevention, control, and emergency action were either abandoned or rendered incapable of functioning efficiently, particularly in Sub-Saharan Africa.

Deprived of the wealth it produces—because it has to repay debt and because of the misappropriation of funds carried out with the complicity of the superpowers—black Africa has become the favorite dumping ground for toxic waste. And when a catastrophe happens, the damage is even worse. This is what happened at Abidjan. Far from being unpredictable, what happened was the culmination of the logical process of financial globalization, and the instigators of financial globalization were well aware of its consequences.

The underpopulated countries of Africa are in general underpolluted. The quality of the air is unnecessarily good compared with Los Angeles or Mexico. Polluting industries should be encouraged to move to the less-developed countries. A certain amount of pollution

should exist in countries where salaries are low. I think that the economic logic whereby tons of toxic waste can be dumped in places
where salaries are low is irrefutable. . . . Any concern [about toxic
products] will anyway be much greater in a country where people
live long enough to develop cancer than in a country where the
infant mortality rate is 200 in 1,000 by the age of five.

    —LAWRENCE SUMMERS, internal memo of the World Bank,
    December 13, 1991[193]

Let us look at another example. The tidal wave caused by the tsunami
in December 2004 off the coast of Indonesia caused a lot of damage to
some containers of hazardous waste (uranium, lead, cadmium, mercury)
stored on the coast of Somalia, a very poor country that has lost any structure since the beginning of the 1990s. According to the United Nations
Environment Program, "Containers of hazardous radioactive waste, of
chemical and other waste which had been dumped along the Somali
coastline, were damaged by the tsunami. . . . Many people have complained of numerous health problems, for example bleeding from the
mouth, abdominal haemorrhages and unusual skin and respiratory problems."[194] Like in Côte d'Ivoire, and no doubt elsewhere.

To sum up, "the economic logic whereby tons of toxic waste can be
dumped in places where salaries are low," so dear to Lawrence Summers,
is at work. The example of the waste in Abidjan is a compendium worthy
of caricature: the *Probo Koala* is registered in Panama, has a Russian crew,
is run by a Greek company, Prime Marine, and is chartered by a company
registered in the Netherlands.

In order to get the currency necessary to repay their debt or to stay in
power, governments are prepared to overexploit and sell off their natural
resources (minerals, oil, fishing), endanger their biodiversity (numerous
animal and plant species are becoming extinct), and encourage deforestation, soil erosion, and desertification. In Africa 65 percent of agricultural
land has been damaged in the last fifty years—five hundred million
hectares.

The lack of health infrastructures, drinking water, and fuel is a serious
hazard. Rubbish is often dumped into the sea or rivers without any treat-

ment. Hazardous products such as mercury or cyanide used, for example, when processing minerals in gold mines, are thrown away without any caution, poisoning water supplies and groundwater.

> It is sometimes said: "Emerging countries will soon emit more CO_2 than industrialized countries and responsibility will change radically." This analysis is false because CO_2 remains in the atmosphere for hundreds of years. Much of the CO_2 emitted since the industrial revolution, that is to say, for about 200 years, is still there. About 80 percent of the accumulated total, the additional CO_2 in the atmosphere today, comes from industrialized countries. Even if tomorrow emerging countries should emit the same amount, the ratio 80/20 (which is an indication of the historical responsibility of developed countries) will vary only slightly over the next 40 years. Which is why the climate debt subsists.
>
> —JEAN-PASCAL VAN YPERSELE,
> Belgian climatologist, 2008[195]

Because of this irreversible damage caused to the environment, the question of ecological debt (which includes climate debt) can no longer be evaded. Only when creditors of the present financial debt recognize this ecological debt and make reparation, when there is massive investment in energy efficiency and in new technologies and an unconditional transfer of these technologies to emerging countries, will it be possible to integrate the ecological issue.

QUESTION 46

What are the religious arguments in favor of canceling the debt of developing countries?

The various religions have all addressed the problem of debt in their teachings.

The Bible

The Bible contains the notion of Jubilee, which consists of an exceptional year every fifty years when debts are annulled or "forgiven."

> And let seven Sabbaths of years be numbered to you, seven times seven years; even the days of seven Sabbaths of years, that is forty-nine years. Then let the loud horn be sounded far and wide on the tenth day of the seventh month; on the day of taking away sin let the horn be sounded through all your land. And let this fiftieth year be kept holy, and say publicly that everyone in the land is free from debt: it is the Jubilee, and every man may go back to his heritage and to his family.
>
> —LEVITICUS 25: 8–10

A Jubilee year is marked by social and environmental measures such as letting the land lie fallow, freeing slaves, and remitting debts.

Thus moneylending is legitimate for reasons of subsistence, on condition that there is no interest charged and that the loan does not exceed seven years. At the end of this period, the debt is remitted. If someone's situation deteriorates so much that he has to sell himself into bondage to survive, and become a slave, he must be freed after seven years.

The Koran

According to the founding text of Islam, the domain of trade and exchange must be marked by a moral, social, and therefore a religious dimension. Usury, that is, the practice of lending for interest, called *riba*, is thus rejected.

Islam considers it to be an unfair practice, since the difficulties of the borrower can enable the lender to get rich without any effort.

> Allah has allowed trading and forbidden usury.
>
> —KORAN II, v. 275

> And if (the debtor) is in straits, then let there be postponement until he is in ease; and that you remit it as alms is better for you, if you knew.
>
> —KORAN II, v. 280

Do not devour usury, making it double and redouble.

—KORAN III, v. 130

This is why, in theory, Muslim banks are based on different principles, excluding the use of interest.

Elsewhere . . .
In Ancient Greece and Rome, in the Jewish culture, debt cancellation is commonplace.

> Indeed, in Ancient Greece, even in Christ's time, debt cancellation was a political act, defined, intelligent, fairly frequent, destined to prevent civil war and reestablish harmony between social classes. In fact, there was a vicious circle in motion, whereby the inequalities between rich and poor grew, so that the only way the poor could survive was by getting in debt to the rich, which led directly to internal enslavement, or to civil war and the destruction of the city. It was not enough to seek the cause of this effect, which would have been fatal for the city, but it had to be eradicated, in order to start anew on a good basis. Debt cancellation was therefore a political commonplace of Greek culture, as it is in Jewish culture. In the Jewish tradition, the Jubilee year is precisely the year of remission of all debts, which occurs every hundred years, leading the majority of the population, who are poor and therefore indebted, to "jubilate," and freeing the people from the threat of enslavement.
>
> —ALAIN JOXE, *L'empire du chaos. Les Républiques face à la domination américaine dans l'après-guerre froide* (*The Empire of Disorder : The Republics versus American domination in the post-Cold War period*), 2002

Recent Initiatives
The Jubilee 2000 campaign for the abolition of the debt was set up from 1996 onward in many countries North and South. It consisted of a vast international campaign for the abolition of the debts of the poor countries, mainly at the instigation of churches from all over the world—

Europe, America, Africa, and Asia—together with social movements and NGOs. The campaign collected twenty-four million signatures thanks to an unprecedented mobilization of public opinion.

> One sign of the mercy of God which is especially necessary today is the sign of charity. . . . The human race is facing forms of slavery which are new and more subtle than those of the past. . . . Some nations, especially the poorer ones, are oppressed by a debt so huge that repayment is practically impossible.
>
> —JOHN PAUL II, *Bull of Indiction of the Great Jubilee of the Year* 2000

In the North, especially in Great Britain and Germany, the request for cancellation only concerned the debt of the poorest countries. In the South, demands were often more radical and aimed at complete cancellation of the Third World debt. The social forces engaged in this combat joined up in November 1999 to form Jubilee South, composed of eighty-five movements from forty-two countries. At the end of 2000, as the Jubilee year drew to a close, the conclusion was as clear as daylight: there had not been any debt cancellation to speak of. Nevertheless, the Catholic and Protestant churches considered that the Jubilee Campaign was over. The big British campaign, Jubilee 2000, was considerably weakened by the withdrawal of the support of the church leaders. In France, the platform "Dette et Développement" led by the Comité catholique contre la faim et pour le développement (CCFD) (Catholic committee against hunger and for development) and composed of about thirty trade unions and associations (including CADTM France), took up the theme and has gained a recognized status in discussions with government authorities. As for Jubilee South, it has decided to carry on the fight for total, immediate and unconditional cancellation of the external and internal public debt of the Third World, just like CADTM.

QUESTION 47
Who owes what to whom?

For several centuries, the domination of the North over the South and the seizure of its wealth have mainly resulted from plundering the resources of the South, the slave trade, and colonization. The tons of minerals and natural resources extracted from Latin America, Asia, and Africa since the sixeenth century have never been paid for. The dominant European powers of the time used force to help themselves, for their own exclusive benefit. The civilizing and evangelizing missions, with which they justified their presence, were never decided with the consent of the local populations, nor did they do them much good!

Furthermore, the large-scale pillage was accompanied by the destruction of the local economic and social fabric. The territories of the South did not have the means of developing structures to promote their own development; they just served to provide the mother country or dominant power with easy resources. The Indian textile industry, for example, was destroyed by the British Empire. It is, then, perfectly legitimate to ask for financial reparation for this illegitimate exploitation. There exists a historic debt owed by the wealthy classes of the North to the populations of the South, which must be taken into consideration.

Cultural treasures were also commandeered by the rich countries, especially Western Europe. The peoples of the developing countries have thus been deprived of the legacy of their ancestors. The richest pickings of their heritage are now seen in the Louvre (Paris), the British Museum (London), at the Royal Museum for Central Africa (Tervuren in Belgium), and in the museums of Vienna, Rome, Madrid, Berlin, and New York. When it was not straightforward pillage as such, representatives of the colonial powers did not hesitate to undervalue what was found in archaeological digs to enable them to take advantage of the local authorities and get the lion's share.

The considerable deficit in human development in the South on the one hand, and the grave ecological consequences of the present system for the populations of the indebted countries on the other, and lastly, the legal, political, and economic arguments mentioned above, clearly demonstrate that the present financial debt is largely odious and that the debt the ruling classes of the North owe to the South is at once historical, human, cultural, social, moral, and ecological.

Nevertheless, most of the governments of the South adopt a singular position. They embrace the neoliberal logic that is at the origin of the iniquitous system of indebtedness, despite the fact that they are supposed to work for the good of their countries. It is on these grounds that we ask the governments of the South to repudiate the financial debt toward the North, but we consider that most of those presently in power are accomplices of the system and that they benefit from it on a personal level. Thus they too are accountable for having run up this multifaceted debt.

Consequently, the populations of the South have a right to demand immediate reparation from the ruling classes of both North and South.

> The external debt of the countries of the South has been repaid several times over. Illegitimate, unjust and fraudulent, debt functions are an instrument of domination, depriving people of their fundamental human rights with the sole aim of increasing international usury. We demand unconditional cancellation of debt and the reparation of historical, social, and ecological debts.
> —APPEAL BY THE SOCIAL MOVEMENTS,
> World Social Forum, Porto Alegre, 2002

QUESTION 48
Who has the right to impose conditions on debt cancellation?

The term "conditionality" designates the strong constraints imposed on the developing countries by the IMF and the World Bank, by means of Structural Adjustment Programs. If the system of domination created by the debt is to be ended, there has to be a definitive break with the logic of structural adjustment and its conditionalities.

Certain countries, widely trumpeted by NGOs, are now proposing to subject debt cancellation to positive "conditionalities." Reductions could take place if a democratic process is instigated, if projects promoting human development are set up (building schools, health centers). However tempting they may appear, such positive conditionalities raise the unavoidable question of who has a right to impose them.

Certain institutions (the IMF, World Bank, G8, and even some very active NGOs of the North) believe they have the right to determine what is "good" and what is "bad." But since the whole situation is so different from one country to another, the populations concerned may not have the same aspirations as the institutions and the NGOs of the North. There is only one possible way forward—the populations concerned and their democratically elected representatives, and they alone, must be the ones to decide.

They must be the only ones to establish development priorities, to select which projects are to be given priority, to control the use of the funds made available, and to be responsible for monitoring the projects. They must have full control of the entire process from start to finish. Some decisions may be made after consulting an NGO or a specialized institution that is able to make a useful contribution at the level of planning. Dialogue with movements of North and South may be fruitful, of course. But it is fundamental that decisions concerning the South are made by the people of the South for the people of the South (unlike the present system where the decisions are made in the North to promote the interests of international finance and the multinationals of the North).

It is up to the populations of the developing countries to dictate the conditionalities, and no one else. To make sure that this principle of decision by the South and for the South is implemented with complete transparency, it is crucial that the debt be canceled and solid safeguards set up. For populations to be able to influence the decision making process on the use of the funds, they must be able to get actively involved.

How the funds made available from debt cancellation, and other innovative measures taken to finance development (see Q54) are allocated would be decided by the people themselves, using a participative process like the one that has been working in Porto Alegre. The participative process is already bearing fruit in this Brazilian town, which is at the cutting edge of this very struggle, and it can be adopted by the different developing countries liberated from debt.

In Porto Alegre, Brazil, citizen participation in preparing municipal budgets has helped reallocate spending to critical human development priorities. During the first seven years of this experiment the share of households with access to water services increased (from 80 percent to 98 percent), and the percentage of the population with access to sanitation almost doubled (from 46 percent to 85 percent).

—UNDP, *Global Human Development Report*, 2002

Any decisions on major borrowing must be decided by parliament after a thorough and broad public debate. This participative democracy, in conjunction with the cancellation of the debt and the renunciation of Structural Adjustment Programs, is the only way to give back to the peoples of the developing countries the power of decision over their lives. The only acceptable conditionalities are those emanating from the populations of the South.

To do something for other people without them is to do it against them.

—TOUAREG PROVERB, quoted by Daniel Mermet,
in *Agenda*, 2001

QUESTION 49
Can the development of emerging countries be ensured simply by repudiating their debt?

First of all, it is important to state that repaying a debt that has been contracted reasonably and legally is morally binding. But the situation is totally different in the present debt crisis seriously affecting developing countries. The usual moral obligation to repay a debt fell away as the trap closed on developing countries at the beginning of the 1980s, destroying all hope of development. The issue is not about rejecting a legitimate obligation illegally or immorally; it is instead about taking into consideration the mechanisms of domination, pillage, and hardship that developing countries experience when demanding some kind of justice.

The peoples of theThird World have to repay a debt from which they
have not had the slightest benefit and whose profits they have never
received.

—ADOLFO PEREZ ESQUIVEL,
Nobel Peace Prize Laureate, 1980

The system put in place by the industrialized countries, the IMF, and
the World Bank has ensured their domination of developing countries.
Debt is the volatile center of this system. For more than twenty-five years,
developing countries have been repaying debts in amounts bearing no
relation to what has actually been injected into their economies. It is no
longer a reasonable agreement between creditor and borrower but rather
a new kind of colonial relationship between the oppressor and the
oppressed. Populations in developing countries have not benefited from
the money they are being forced to repay. Under these conditions, there
is de facto no moral obligation of repayment. Jubilee South is right when
they say: "We owe nothing, we pay nothing."

But we must be wary of being on the wrong track: it is not enough to
put the clocks back to zero. The system that has led to the impasse must
be modified in order to provide a fair and lasting solution. Canceling debt
is a necessary but not sufficient condition. From now on, debt cancellation must be accompanied by alternative financial mechanisms that do
not lead to further subjugation by debt and by complementary measures
in numerous fields (see Q54).

There has been a lot said recently about debt cancellation and
rightly so. If debts are not cancelled, many emerging countries will
simply not be able to develop. A huge proportion of their present
export revenue goes straight to paying back their loans from developed countries.

—JOSEPH STIGLITZ, *Globalization and Its Discontents*, 2002

CHAPTER ELEVEN

Issues Raised by Canceling the Debt of the Developing Countries

Would canceling the debt of developing countries cause a global financial crisis?

The external public debt of all the developing countries, estimated at $1.35 trillion, is an unbearable burden for the weak public finances of the countries of the South. However, this debt represents very little indeed in comparison to the enormous indebtedness of the North.

At the end of 2007, the public debt of the Triad countries was over $30 trillion, which is more than twenty-two times the external public debt of the developing countries.[196]

The total debts of the United States (government, household, and business) came to $49 trillion, or thirty-six times the debt we are demanding should be canceled.

It is an established fact that the total public external debt of developing countries is less than 2 percent of the world's global lending. Canceling it would in no way endanger global finance.

It is interesting to compare the external public debt of a group of developing countries with the public debt of certain rich countries that have managed to maintain strong economic links with them (see page 271).

The 2007 property crisis in the United States also provides some interesting figures that back up the argument in favor of cancellation. In order to dampen the simmering crisis and to help out the banks, on August 9, 2007, the European central bank decided to restore confidence by becoming Lender of Last Resort: in two days it injected the astronom-

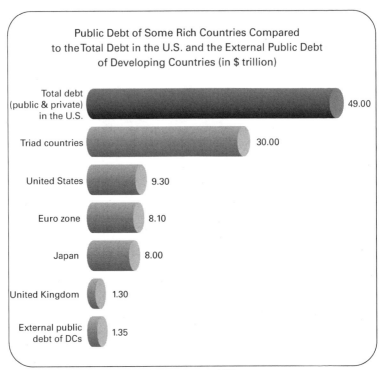

Public Debt of Some Rich Countries Compared
to the Total Debt in the U.S. and the External Public Debt
of Developing Countries (in $ trillion)

Total debt (public & private) in the U.S.	49.00
Triad countries	30.00
United States	9.30
Euro zone	8.10
Japan	8.00
United Kingdom	1.30
External public debt of DCs	1.35

Source: U.S. Federal Reserve; Banque de France[197]

ical sum of 156 billion euros, the equivalent of. more than $200 billion. This is similar to the external debt of a very highly indebted country such as Brazil or Turkey. Since August 2007, the banks have wiped out about $1 trillion of "bad" loans (ongoing at date of publication). By doing so, they have clearly shown the world that canceling the whole of the external public debt owed to all the banks by all the developing countries is not only possible but can be easily done. The amount owed to them by the governments of developing countries totals exactly $200 billion, which is five times the amount they wiped off their books in 2007–9.

The creditors of the external public debt of the developing countries are big private organizations, states, and multilateral institutions. Even though it amounts to billions of dollars, the developing countries' debt does not play in the same division as the gigantic sums manipulated by international finance. They have made a lot of money from the debt of

Public Debt of Some Rich Countires Compared to External Public
Debt of Developing Countries (in $ trillion)

COUNTRY	PUBLIC DEBT	REGION	EXTERNAL PUBLIC DEBT
United States	9.30	Latin America	.40
Japan	8.00	E. Asia and the Pacific	.26
United Kingdom	1.30		
		South Asia	.16
EURO ZONE:	8.70	Sub-Saharan Africa	.13
France	1.80		
Germany	2.30		
Italy	2.35		
Belgium	.41		

Source: Banque de France; World Bank

developing countries, from privatizations in all four corners of the world, and from the neoliberal offensive against salary earners and small producers over the last twenty years. They have more than been repaid for the sums lent and the risks taken. It is now time to say, Stop!

The argument that debt cancellation would set a bad example to all present and future borrowers by increasing the moral hazard of loans (the borrowers might believe that the debts will be canceled and will therefore take them on regardless of the need for them) is hypocritical and erroneous. Hypocritical, because financial markets, where there is nonstop speculation, have never been models of virtue, and now less than ever with all the scandals over the last few years, from Enron to Parmalat, EADS, or the whole subprime crisis. Erroneous, because if the potential creditors knew that an illegitimate debt carried the risk of being canceled, they would think twice in the future before lending money. They would verify that their loans really were going to be used for legitimate aims and that they were dealing with democratic regimes. Surely that would be a good thing.

Furthermore, the IMF and the World Bank hold resources that they rarely mention. The IMF has long hoarded one of the largest holdings of gold on the planet totaling 3,200 tons.[198] According to its 2007 annual report, the IBRD, the largest of the Bank's five institutions, has made a profit of about $1.7 billion every year since 2004, and in its 2007 report lists its "capital and reserves available" at $33.7 billion.

If cancellation, such as we demand, prevents them from carrying out their present functions, these institutions will disappear. Would that really harm humankind? How many financial crises and human disasters is it going to take before the World Bank and the IMF are finally stopped from doing further harm? Since the world needs multilateral institutions, they will have to be replaced by new bodies—bodies that are truly democratic and respect their international obligations to respect human rights.

The international debt bubble is enormous. Japan had a similar debt bubble that burst at the end of the 1980s, and the country is only just about getting over it now. In 2002, we wrote, "It is not impossible that the United States, which managed to scrape through in the 1980s and 1990s by getting others to bear the brunt of their deficit and their military operations, will fall foul of the household and business debt crisis as well as the present simmering crisis on the stock exchange and the permanent war they are waging against Third World countries. The cost of rescue there is likely to be far higher than that of cancellation of the developing countries' debt. Between the beginning of the fall in stock values in 2000 and summer 2002, over $15 trillion went up in smoke. That is almost ten times the total external public debt of the developing countries." And sure enough, we have indeed seen the predicted crisis in the form of the subprime crisis that broke out in summer 2007 (see Q15).

Canceling the external public debt of the developing countries requires a sum that is far too small to cause an international financial crisis. On the other hand, maintaining the debt could very well cause one.

The rich nations could eliminate the debt of Africa without even noticing it economically.
—Jesse Jackson, president of the RainbowPUSH Coalition

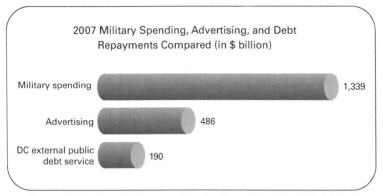

Source: SIPRI Yearbook 2008; www.zenithoptimedia.com; World Bank, *Global Development Finance 2008*

QUESTION 51
If developing countries' debts were canceled, would the citizens of the North end up paying the bill?

Developing countries repay their debts to Northern countries, to multilateral institutions (of which the same Northern countries are the main shareholders), and to private banks in the North. We have shown that wealth is transferred from the South to the North (with the ruling classes in the South skimming off their commission), despite the generous speeches and declarations made in the industrialized countries. Would the North miss this wealth and suffer impoverishment if the debt were cancelled?

It would be advantageous to all humanity to reconsider some of this phenomenal expenditure.

The creditors have already been repaid several times the actual amount initially lent to the developing countries. The creditors have thus already been amply rewarded for the loan of their capital. It is therefore legitimate and perfectly reasonable to consider putting an end to all further repayment. This would free up the budget for the social spending that would make it possible to really tackle the root causes of poverty. This being said, what would happen from the point of view of the creditors if the debt was totally canceled?

As far as private creditors are concerned, their revenues would fall, so the dividends paid out to their shareholders would have to be reduced accordingly, which would primarily affect the better-off classes. Private creditors would simply have to erase from their accounts the money coming in from the developing countries and shed a tear for the time when they were making easy money from the world's poor.

For bilateral creditors, the developing country debts they hold ($280 billion; see Q24) have a lower-than-nominal value that varies depending on the country, but is on average about 75 percent of its nominal value.[199] Thus the real value of bilateral credits is less than $70 billion, which is less than one-tenth of the yearly military spending of the G7 countries ($790 billion, out of the $1.339 trillion spent on defense and arms worldwide).[200] The $70 billion is only 0.26 percent of the total GDP of the United States plus the twelve Euro zone countries plus the United Kingdom and Japan, which together makes $27.3 trillion (see Q50). For the G7 countries, a loss of income on this scale could easily be assimilated without the populations of the countries having to suffer. A more equitable distribution of national wealth would make such a sum—and more—available without affecting living conditions in the least.

Moreover, in line with our analysis throughout this book, it is logical to propose that the North should be obliged to pay compensation for the human, moral, ecological, social, and cultural debt it owes the populations of developing countries. Canceling the debt would be a first step, before considering compensation.

Transfer of technology could also be usefully organized. Why not decide on a lump sum for the inventors of techniques that can improve the lives of humankind as a whole, so that they can be placed in the public domain as quickly as possible, and thus made available to the populations of the South? In the essential domain of medicine, why not decide to make research a public service, entirely financed by governments, without patents, and with all results going directly into the public domain, worldwide? There are plenty of possibilities, but the political will is not there.

Coming back to the comparison with slavery (see Q41), the activists who battled against slavery throughout history did not stop to ask themselves whether or not the abolition of slavery would deprive the North of resources, or whether it would impoverish the rich countries. They were motivated by high ideals of justice, stronger than all else. Finally, the scales tipped in their favor and slavery was abolished. The North did not become poorer; it rapidly adapted to the new international situation. This time, society must be vigilant so that after debt has been abolished, the system of domination by means of the debt is not replaced by a new, more subtle mechanism of domination.

It is essential to set up a new system of international law and order, based on justice, so as to guarantee the universal respect of human rights and ecological sustainability.

> We are trying to find a way of making a self-reliant Argentina, which does not take money from American plumbers and carpenters who earn $50,000 a year, and wonder what their money is being used for.
> —PAUL O'NEILL, U.S. Secretary of the Treasury,
> CNN, August 18, 2001

> The US Treasury Secretary Paul O'Neill has tried to give the impression that it is the American taxpayers, its plumbers and carpenters, who pay for the multi-billion dollar bail-outs—and because they pay the costs, they ought to have the vote. But that is wrong. The money comes ultimately from workers and taxpayers in the developing countries, for the IMF almost always gets repaid.
> —JOSEPH STIGLITZ, *Globalization and Its Discontents*, 2002

Basically, the same procedure is at work in the North, where the public debt is enormous—on the order of $30 trillion—and where taxpayers' money is used to repay private banks and other institutional investors that in turn make tremendous profits from the citizens of the countries of the North. Here, too, the mechanism is very subtle: a growing portion of taxes is used to repay the debt, and at the same time the state is withdrawing from sectors where its role has been central for a long time (social security, education, culture) and is privatizing these services.

It can be seen that there is good reason for the citizens of the North and of the South to present a united front since they are both victims of systems of a very similar nature. Were this to happen, the international balance of power would change radically.

Is it not time to reconsider the lifestyle in the North?

Using data available from international institutions, the website www.worldometers.info compares annual spending in various countries. The population of the United States spends around $130 billion a year on alcohol and tobacco, and almost $5 billion on perfume. The world spends some $1 trillion on illegal drugs every year. Surely all this implies that it would not be unreasonable for the citizens of the North to change their lifestyles to waste less and free up more resources. Does consuming large quantities of cosmetics and cigarettes matter, when the other half of humankind is surviving on less than $2 a day? It is time to wake up. Better allocation of resources would enable everyone to live better, while consuming less at the same time. In this way, cancelling the debt would also be a source of hope for the North, leading to some hard thinking about a real redistribution of wealth and a great public debate about development and about the quality of life in the North, both currently and in the future.

QUESTION 52
Will canceling the debt help reinforce existing dictatorial regimes?

The IMF and the World Bank use debt reduction as a means of maintaining the mechanisms of dependence of indebted nations, whereas social movements such as the CADTM see the total cancellation of the debt of developing countries as only a first step. If the debt is totally canceled, this would completely change the balance of power in favor of the people. It would then become possible to adopt a fundamentally different approach, in the light of which the situation after debt cancellation would not be seen in the same terms as the present situation. For example, the argument that existing dictatorial regimes would be reinforced by canceling the debt would be invalidated.

How is it that dictators manage to get into power and stay there for so long? Why does their existence make it so hard for democratic forces to consolidate and take over? Why were dictators like Suharto in Indonesia,

Mobutu Sese Seko in Zaire, Omar Bongo Ondimba in Gabon, Gnassingbe Eyadema in Togo, and the apartheid regime in South Africa able to remain in place for more than thirty years? Because they serve the interests of the system and therefore have the backing of the creditors. Why have so many coups d'état overthrown democratically elected governments like that of Salvador Allende in Chile or Patrice Lumumba in the former Belgian Congo when it first became independent? Because these governments tried to break away from the system.

In the 1970s and 1980s, the neoliberal leaders realized it was easier to keep a country subservient and to have easy access to its natural resources when the leader of the country was a corrupt dictator rather than when it was ruled by a democratically elected government that would be influenced by the opinions of their electors. By the middle of the 1980s, democratic protests within dictatorial regimes and the pressure of international public opinion were such that it became more difficult to openly support the world's dictators. Unfortunately, many of the democratically elected governments that have replaced such dictators have continued to serve the same economic policies. Sometimes, it has even been the dictator himself who has managed to get himself "elected" by means of very opaque elections backed by the international donors, such as Idriss Déby Itno in Chad, Zine el-Abidine Ben Ali in Tunisia, and Paul Biya in Cameroon.

Suggesting that the fight against dictators precludes cancelling the debt just doesn't hold water. On the contrary, dictatorial regimes are actually reinforced by the debt. The backing of the creditors makes their position stronger and also makes it easier for them to skim off some of the funds for themselves. It is common knowledge that several dictators use the debt both for their own personal gain and also to set up mechanisms to counter any opposition within the country. Since global neoliberalism has become the norm, we have seen the debt grow, corruption grow, and the poor get poorer. This is not just a coincidence. All three advance in lockstep.

Let us consider the following example. Angola, one of the most promising countries for the coming decades in terms of oil resources, was ravaged by civil war for over twenty-five years. The war finally ended in 2002 with the death of the leader of one of the two sides (Jonas Savimbi, of UNITA) and a famine that devastated the population. Elf, the multinational petroleum company, helped to arm both camps, as did others, which obviously increased the violence of the fighting. The adversaries, UNITA and the government of Eduardo Dos Santos, both sold off oil very cheaply in order to procure arms. A government that cares about its population would obviously ask for the oil contracts to be renegotiated and the part reserved for the state to be reevaluated. Angola has become heavily indebted for having forfeited its oil in exchange for arms.

In Angola as elsewhere, as long as this debt exists, the fight against corruption and authoritarianism has little chance of success, whereas the fight to end the debt is, in itself, a means of opposing corruption and dictatorship with considerable hope of success.

Cancelling the debt would be a preventive therapy to protect against the risk of future dictatorships. If an odious debt had been signed with a dictator, and the creditors were not repaid because the debt was canceled once its origin had been proven by a scrupulous audit, then potential creditors would not be so willing in the future to provide loans to dictators. Once bitten, twice shy. This would become a built-in deterrent against dictatorships and corruption, since the creditors would provide their own screening of regimes to which they loan funds.

The expropriation of ill-gotten gains is another indispensable measure to be taken. To topple existing dictators thorough judicial inquiries into cases of embezzlement and into assets deposited by the moneyed classes of the developing countries in tax havens and Northern banks must be made. We have estimated that, in 2007, these assets were greater than the external public debt of the developing countries since a total of $2.38 trillion has been deposited by the rich of developing countries in the banks of the industrialized countries.

A significant percentage of this money (20 percent? 30 percent? more?) has been accumulated illegally. If it is proved that embezzlement has taken place, the ill-gotten gains must be expropriated, followed by their restitution to the populations from which they were extorted by unscrupulous leaders. Sources of hidden funding would thus be cut off, the war booty of dictators confiscated, and nepotism—deprived of means—would no longer be so easy. This would also be a strong signal to all the democracies in developing countries, since it would be an abrupt change in the present geopolitical system. Obviously, legal action

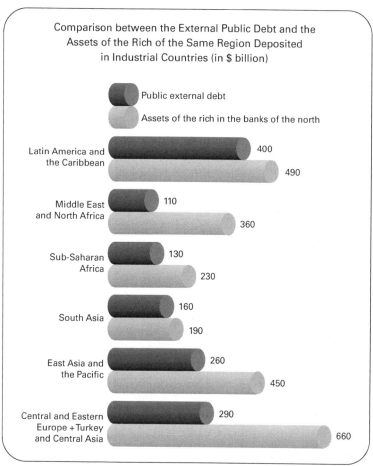

Source: Calculated by the authors from World Bank data; Bank for International Settlements

can be taken on this independently, without the debt having to be canceled first. How strange it is that this question is never raised by governments, either of the North or of the South.

Once the ill-gotten goods have been legally recovered, they should be restored to the population to improve their standard of living, providing conditions in accord with fundamental human rights. Although confiscated funds were finally returned, for example, to the Chilean dictator Augusto Pinochet or the corrupt Argentinean president Carlos Menem, it has also been the case in the last few years that some ill-gotten funds have been returned to the population to which they belong. Money deposited by dictators in Swiss banks, where a lot of the world's dirty money is deposited, has been returned to the governments of the developing countries it had been embezzled from. This was only possible after a lot of hard work by honest Swiss judges, social movements (especially some Swiss-based North-South solidarity groups), and the governments of the developing country determined to recuperate the money stolen by former dictators, or corrupt former governments. All together, a total $1.6 billion has been returned to the rightful countries, from frozen accounts belonging to the ex-dictators Ferdinand Marcos (Philippines) and Sani Abacha (Nigeria) of about half a billion each, and the rest being returned from accounts opened by Alberto Fujimori (Peru) and Vladimiro Montesinos Torres, the former head of the Peruvian secret service, not forgetting Saddam Hussein (Iraq), Nursultan Nasarbáyev (Kazakhstan), and Moussa Traoré (Mali).[201] In June 2008, it was agreed that $74 million of illicit assets deposited by Raul Salinas, the brother of the former Mexican president Carlos Salinas de Gortari, would be returned, after legal proceedings that lasted more than thirteen years. Great Britain also gave back to Nigeria money that Sani Abacha had deposited in a bank in Jersey. Other legal battles are being fought, and it cannot stop there. People must be aware and vigilant so that the money embezzled by the Duvalier family (Haiti) and the Mobutu clan (ex-Zaire) is not given back to them, which would of course be totally unacceptable. In all cases, it is essential that the social movements in the developing countries manage to ensure that the retroceded money really is used to improve the living conditions of the population.

There is a crisis because the masses no longer accept that wealth is concentrated in the hands of the few. There is a crisis because a small number of people are putting enormous amounts of money in foreign banks, amounts of money which would be sufficient for the development of Africa. There is a crisis because in view of the wealth enjoyed by a very small number of individuals which it is easy to name, the masses are no longer willing to live in the ghettos and slums. There is a crisis because people everywhere are refusing to live in Soweto when Johannesburg is so close by. That is why the

fight has begun, and as the fight gets stronger, those holding the
purse strings are starting to get worried.
                    —THOMAS SANKARA, president of Burkina Faso,
                                                        1983 to 1987

Indebtedness, corruption, and cut-price selling of resources are three
sides of the same problem. Corruption (especially by means of debt) is
the instrument used to make leaders place their country's economy under
the "protection" of the IMF and the U.S. Treasury, of the finance and the
multinationals of the North, giving them cheap access to natural
resources. Thus, though the debt has consistently benefited dictatorships, canceling it would lead to a fundamental change.

QUESTION 53
Should borrowing be avoided at all cost?

We aim to eradicate usury, not borrowing per se. Borrowing is not a problem in itself, and it is important to understand how our arguments are the
result of a meticulous analysis of the present debt crisis.

To prevent a repetition of the present situation of massive overindebtedness, borrowing needs to be limited as much as possible. We are suggesting alternative means of financing that, if implemented, would mean
that borrowing could once again be acceptable, without the accompany-
ing oppression, domination, and misappropriation of public goods that
goes on at present. Any decision to contract a major loan should be made
under the supervision of the populations concerned, and be debated in
parliament (or whatever legislative body is in place), before being voted
on in a constitutional manner.

It is also essential that the conditions of the loan should be acceptable.
The government's signature on a loan contract should not mean giving up
the sovereignty of the country and accepting that an eventual litigation
with the creditors be submitted to the jurisdiction of New York or
London. It is not acceptable to hand the house keys to the creditors, as is
often the case. This is why the present system needs to be reformed, since
the creditors have taken good care to build multilateral institutions tai-

lored to their needs (IMF, World Bank, Paris Club, London Club) and to take on each debtor individually, thus putting the debtors at their mercy. Two new principles need to be respected. First, the obligation to repay and to pay interest on these loans will only be valid if it is proven that the debt did indeed enable creation of sufficient wealth in the countries concerned. Second, strong and efficient protection of debtor countries needs to be organized on a world scale, so that the countries can defend themselves against all forms of abuse and spoliation by the banks, international private investors, and international financial institutions.

Ecuador's new constitution, which was voted by the Assembly in September 2008, enables the country to carefully control recourse to borrowing and protects it against the excesses that have been far too numerous for several decades.

Article 290. Public debt is subject to the following principles:

1. The government will have recourse to public debt only in cases when tax revenues and resources from cooperation and international exchanges are insufficient.

2. It will be ensured that public borrowing does not affect national sovereignty, human rights, well-being, or the protection of the environment.

3. Public debt will be used exclusively to finance programs and investment projects in the field of infrastructure and projects that will generate the resources needed to reimburse the loans. An existing public debt could also be financed provided that the new conditions are advantageous to Ecuador.

4. Renegotiation agreements will not include, explicitly or tacitly, any kind of anatocism[202] or usury.

5. Debts that are declared illegitimate by a competent entity will be repudiated. In cases when a debt is declared void, the state will exercise its right to restitution.

6. Administrative responsibility for public debt contracting and management, including eventual tort proceedings, is imprescriptible

7. The nationalization of private debts is forbidden.

8. The granting of debt guarantees by the state will be regulated by law of the National Development Plan.

9. The Executive has no constitutional obligation to assume debts contracted by the autonomous regions or local governments.

—CONSTITUTION OF ECUADOR, 2008[203]

The Bolivian Constituent Assembly also adopted a new draft constitution in December 2007 that strictly defines the conditions under which the country may borrow.

Article 322

I. The Multinational Legislative Assembly shall authorize recourse to public borrowing when the capacity to generate revenue to cover the capital and interest has been proven, and when the most advantageous conditions relating to taxes, payback periods, amounts, and other circumstances have been technically justified.

II. Public debt shall not include loan stock that has not been authorized and expressly guaranteed by the Multinational Legislative Assembly.

Article 324

Debt toward the state and economic prejudice caused to the state shall not be subject to prescription.

Article 325

Illicit economic acts, speculation, monopolization, usury, smuggling, tax evasion and other related economic offences shall be punished by law.

Article 330

IV. The Central Bank of Bolivia and public bodies and institutions shall not incur the debts of the bank or private financial bodies. The latter must constitute and maintain a financial restructuring fund to be used in case of bank insolvency.

—BOLIVIAN DRAFT CONSTITUTION, 2008

CHAPTER TWELVE

Constructing Radical Alternatives

QUESTION 54
What are the alternatives for human development in the developing countries?

It is useless to expect market economy logic to meet essential needs. The 2.8 billion people living on less than $2 a day do not have enough purchasing power to interest the markets. Only government policies can guarantee the fulfillment of basic human needs for all. This is why it is necessary for political leaders to dispose of the political and financial means that will enable them to honor their commitments and duties to their fellow citizens.

The Universal Declaration of Human Rights and the International Covenant for Economic, Social and Cultural Rights can only be effectively implemented through the concerted action of a powerful social and citizens' movement. The first step is to stop the drain of resources engendered by the repayment of the debt. It would be foolish to wait for international institutions to decide to cancel the debts of developing countries. Only the determined action of one or several states can result in such a measure. The jurists who met in Quito in July 2008 are perfectly right when they claim: "We support the sovereign acts of states that, founded in law, declare as null and void the illicit and illegitimate instruments of the public debt, including the suspension of payments."[204]

Once this first step has been taken, the present economy of international indebtedness must be replaced by a socially just and environmentally sustainable model of development that is independent of financial market fluctuations and loan conditionalities imposed by the IMF and the World Bank.

For debt cancellation to benefit human development, the money that would have been used to repay loans must be used for human development. The modalities must be decided upon in a democratic manner by all countries concerned.

PUTTING AN END TO
STRUCTURAL ADJUSTMENT PROGRAMS

Structural Adjustment Programs (SAPs), whether they are known by this label or the new one—Poverty Reduction Strategy Papers (PRSPs), adopted recently by the international financial institutions that encourage total liberalization of the economies of the South—have succeeded in weakening the states. They have made them more dependent on external fluctuations (evolution of world markets, speculative attacks, and the like) and subjected them to unacceptable conditionalities imposed by the IMF and the World Bank, backed by the governments of the creditor countries grouped in the Paris Club. The human consequences of SAPs are tragic. They must be eradicated and replaced by policies whose absolute priority is to meet basic human needs, giving first priority to food sovereignty and security, and seeking to create regional complementarity.

Structural adjustment goes beyond the simple imposition of a set of macroeconomic policies at the domestic level. It represents a political project, a conscious strategy of social transformation at the global level, primarily to make the world safe for transnational corporations. In short, Structural Adjustment Programs (SAPs) serve as "a transmission belt" to facilitate the process of globalization, through liberalization, deregulation, and reducing the role of the state in national development.

—UN COMMISSION ON HUMAN RIGHTS (UNCHR),
Effects of Structural Adjustment Policies on the Full Enjoyment of Human Rights, report by independent expert Fantu Cheru ,
E/CN.4/1999/50, February 24, 1999

The UN Commission on Human Rights (UNCHR) adopted several resolutions on the issue of the debt and structural adjustment.[205] In one, Article 5, adopted in 1999, the CHR states: "The exercise of the basic rights of the people of debtor countries to food, housing, clothing, employment, education, health services and a healthy environment cannot be subordinated to the implementation of structural adjustment policies, growth programs and economic reforms arising from the debt."

GIVING BACK TO THE CITIZENS OF DEVELOPING COUNTRIES WHAT WAS STOLEN FROM THEM

Considerable wealth, illicitly accumulated by government officials and local capitalists, was safely placed in industrialized countries, with the complicity of private financial institutions and the acquiescence of the governments of the North. Restitution requires the completion of judicial procedures conducted both in the Third World and the industrialized countries. A further advantage of such investigations would be that corrupters and corrupted would no longer get away with their crimes. It is the only hope, if democracy and transparency are ever to overcome corruption.

We must also demand reparation for the pillage to which the Third World has been subjected over the last five centuries. This implies the restitution of economic and cultural assets stolen from the Asian, African, and Latin American continents.

States shall provide redress through effective mechanisms, which may include restitution, developed in conjunction with indigenous peoples, with respect to their cultural, intellectual, religious and spiritual property taken without their free, prior and informed consent or in violation of their laws, traditions and customs.

—UN DECLARATION ON THE RIGHTS
OF INDIGENOUS PEOPLE, 2007[206]

LEVYING AN EXCEPTIONAL TAX
ON THE ASSETS OF THE VERY WEALTHY

In its 1995 report, UNCTAD suggests raising a "one-shot" tax on the assets of the very wealthy. Such a tax, levied worldwide, would free up considerable funds. This tax (different from recurrent taxes on the estates of the very wealthy, which exist in some parts of the planet) could be levied on a national basis. Such an exceptional solidarity tax—of about 10 percent of the assets of the wealthiest of each country—could generate considerable resources.

According to the *2008 World Wealth Report*[207] published by Merrill Lynch and Capgemini, 10.1 million people in the world own over $1 million of assets, and their cumulative wealth amounts to $40.7 trillion, which is thirty times the external public debt of all developing countries. So, for example, a one-shot 10 percent tax on these assets would bring in over $4 trillion without reducing their owners to poverty.

> The dominant economic model began to impose itself when the majority of developing countries were still dependent and consequently could not participate in its creation; it was thus inevitable that, from its origin, the odds would be stacked against them and contrary to their interests. . . . The current international economy is undoubtedly unjust, mainly because the "developing" countries did not participate in its creation and today they are subjected to most of its negative effects. As such, it is important, in the interests of human rights, to repair the current situation.
>
> —RAÚL FERRERO, Special Rapporteur to the UN
> on the New International Economic Order
> and the Promotion of Human Rights, 1983[208]

A number of questions remain. What taxation rate should be imposed? A single rate? A progressive rate? What proportion of the funds should be allocated to global projects? To continental projects? Should there be a fund for reforestation? Should there be a fund for complete denuclearization? How should projects be prioritized? By whom? By the UN General Assembly after national referendums? Or continental ones? What proportion would go toward local projects? In any case, one thing is certain: this path must be pursued, and a truly redistributive system must be put in place, granting governments the means to fulfill their obligations toward citizens in terms of economic, social, and cultural rights.

EQUAL REDISTRIBUTION OF WEALTH
ON A GLOBAL SCALE

Never has wealth been so unequally distributed on a global scale. To fight against this rampant inequality, it is imperative to implement international taxes that could take multiple forms: a Tobin-type tax (see Glossary) on short-term, usually speculative, financial transactions (one of the demands of ATTAC), a tax on the profits of transnational companies (in 2006, Total made the highest profit in the history of the French economy: €2.58 billion, of which a third was given to shareholders as dividends), a tax on polluting industries, and so on. These revenues must go toward education, public health, food security, the promotion of public goods, and the protection of the environment.

RAISING OFFICIAL DEVELOPMENT AID
TO A MINIMUM 0.7 PERCENT OF GDP

Official development aid is not fulfilling its role. It is given not according to the needs of the South, but rather to the geopolitical, commercial, and publicity interests of the donors. Headline effects are what matter, and only visible and profitable projects are selected; the companies involved are usually from the donor countries; and statistics are manipulated. The definition of development aid is blurry (see Q34). It includes low-interest loans repayable down to the last cent, loan reduction, student bursaries (subsidies for tuition fees for students from the South who study in donor countries), refugee programs (and too often the forceful deportation of refugees), fees for consultancy and expertise of doubtful value, the salaries of technical assistants from overseas, who usually contribute very little to the poorest sectors of the population, and others. The portion of development aid that actually reaches the country and benefits the poorest is often ludicrously small. The trebling of development aid would make substantial sums available. Finally, as an act of goodwill, development aid should be freely given, and instead of calling it aid or donation, it should be termed *reparation*. For it is really a matter of repairing the damage caused by centuries of pillage and unequal exchange.

In this context, the Charter of Economic Rights and Duties of States adopted by the United Nations 1974 is an important tool.[209] Chapter 1, principle (i), states that relations between states must be governed by a series of principles, including that of "remedying of injustices which have been brought about by force and which deprive a nation of the natural means necessary for its normal development." Article 17 stipulates the general obligation of states to "cooperate with the efforts of developing countries to accelerate their economic and social development by providing favorable external conditions and by extending active assistance to them, consistent with their development needs and objectives, with strict respect for the sovereign equality of States and free of any conditions derogating from their sovereignty." Article 22 lays down a similar obligation to all states to "respond to the generally recognized or mutually agreed development needs and objectives of developing countries."[210]

ENSURING THE RETURN OF PREVIOUSLY PRIVATIZED STRATEGIC SECTORS INTO THE PUBLIC DOMAIN

The reserves and distribution of water, the production and the distribution of electricity, telecommunications, postal services, the railways, companies extracting and processing raw materials, the credit system, and some sectors of education and health have been or are being systematically privatized. It is important to ensure that these companies and services are brought back under public control.

Article 2/2: "Each state has the *right to nationalize, expropriate or transfer ownership of foreign property*, in which case appropriate compensation should be paid by the state adopting such measures, taking into account its relevant laws and regulations and all circumstances that the State considers pertinent.[211] In any case where the question of compensation gives rise to a controversy, it shall be settled under the domestic law of the nationalizing State and by its tribunals."

—UN, Charter of Economic Rights and Duties of States, 1974

ADOPTING REGIONALLY CENTERED
DEVELOPMENT MODELS

This type of development implies the creation of integrated political and economic zones, the emergence of endogenous development models, a strengthening of domestic markets, the creation of local savings banks for local financing (in many countries, the sums placed in foreign banks by the richest are greater than the external debt of the country), the development of free public health and education, the installation of progressive taxation and mechanisms of wealth redistribution, diversification of exports, agrarian reform that guarantees universal access to land for peasants, and urban reform that guarantees universal access to housing.

The current global architecture must be replaced by regional economic groupings. Only such a development, at least partly centered in the regions themselves, can enable the emergence of coherent South-South relations, a sine qua non for the economic advancement of developing countries.

REFORM OF TRADE

Trade regulations must be radically reformed. Concerning agriculture, as the small farmers' movement Via Campesina puts it, the right of each country (or group of countries) to food sovereignty, and especially to self-sufficiency in staples, must be recognized.

Global trade regulations must be subordinated to strict environmental, social, and cultural criteria. Health, education, water, or culture must be excluded from the arena of international trade. Public services must be the means of ensuring this and must therefore be excluded from the

General Agreement on Trade in Services (GATS), which envisages total liberalization of public services. Moreover, the Trade-Related Intellectual Property Rights (TRIPS) agreement must be banned. It prevents countries of the South from freely producing goods (for example, medicines) that could satisfy the needs of their populations.

> Article 5. All states have the right to associate in organizations of primary commodity producers in order to develop their national economies.
> —UN, Charter of Economic Rights and Duties of States, 1974

There is clearly a need for mechanisms that guarantee better prices for a basket of products exported on the world market by developing countries: stabilizing the prices of raw materials at a satisfactory level for producer countries, guaranteeing export revenues, and building up regulatory reserves—which implies abandoning the policy of zero reserves.

To bring about such concerted mechanisms, efforts by developing countries to create cartels of producer countries must be supported. The Organization of Petroleum Exporting Countries (OPEC) is too often denigrated, although it plays a positive role in many respects.[212] The creation of such cartels could ensure a decrease in the volumes exported (which, on the one hand, would prevent the depletion of natural resources, and on the other, increase the areas reserved for subsistence crops) and an increase in export revenues, which could be reinvested in the development projects of exporting countries. Why should there not be a cartel of copper producers? Not so long ago, Chile alone accounted for 30 percent of world exports. Why not a coffee cartel? Or a tea cartel? The possibilities abound.

Furthermore, the developing countries must be able to resort to protectionist measures to protect local production, namely, as Via Campesina demands: "the abolition of all direct or indirect export support or subsidies," "the prohibition of production and commercialization of genetically modified seeds and products," and "a prohibition on patenting living organisms as well as the private appropriation of knowledge relating to agriculture and food."

To guarantee the independence and food sovereignty of all the peoples of the world, it is crucial that food is produced in the framework
of diversified production by peasants. Food sovereignty is the right
of each people to define its own agricultural policies and, in the case
of food, to protect and regulate national agricultural production and
the domestic market in order to reach sustainable objectives, and to
decide how to attain self-sufficiency without getting rid of their surpluses in third countries through the practice of dumping. . . . We
must not favor international trade over other social, environmental,
cultural and development criteria.[213]

—VIA CAMPESINA

ADOPTING A NEW FINANCIAL DISCIPLINE

The recurrent financial crises of the 1990s demonstrated that no sustainable development can be attained without strict control of capital flows
and tax evasion. Several measures are therefore needed to subordinate the
financial markets to the fulfillment of fundamental human needs: re-regu-
lation of financial markets; control of capital movements; abolition of tax
havens and the lifting of banking secrecy to effectively fight against tax
evasion, embezzlement of public funds, and corruption; and the adoption
of regulations to ensure the protection of countries that contract external
debt. Clearly, a completely new financial architecture is required. The setting up in December 2007 of a Bank of the South is a step in this direction (see Q57).

ABOLISHING TAX HAVENS
AND OFFSHORE CENTERS

Tax—and legal—havens have the effect of inflating financial bubbles and
weakening legal economies (between $500 billion and $1.5 trillion are
laundered each year).[214]

The offshore center of the City of London alone represents 40 percent of tax haven revenues. Next on the list of tax havens are Switzerland,

the Netherlands, Ireland, and Luxembourg, accounting for about 30 percent. The remaining 30 percent are held in some sixty exotic destinations, such as the Virgin Islands, Cayman Islands, and Bermuda. It is necessary to abolish these tax havens and offshore centers and lift banking secrecy to effectively eradicate tax evasion, misappropriation of public funds, and corruption.

ENSURING DEMOCRATIC CONTROL
OF DEBT POLICIES

The decision of a state to contract loans, and the terms on which they are negotiated, must be submitted for popular approval (parliamentary debate and vote, citizen control). In this respect, the new Bolivian draft constitution provides for the Multinational Legislative Assembly to authorize the country's recourse to loans.[215] Similarly, the Ecuadorian constitution, in a transparent manner, places debt decisions in the hands of the people's elected representatives.

> Art. 9: The orientations and limits on public loans will be known and approved by the National Assembly together with the drawing up of the budget, in accordance with the law.
> —CONSTITUTION OF ECUADOR, 2008

ENSURING PEOPLE'S RIGHT
TO MIGRATE AND SETTLE

Apart from the fact that freedom to travel and settle is a basic human right, migrants' remittances to their families living in developing countries represent a significant revenue for millions of families. In 2007 alone, remittances totaled $251 billion, which is four times more than the "donation" portion of the development aid package. Obviously, the measures elaborated on above would greatly remove migratory pressures. It is from this angle that the problem must be tackled, and not by closing borders to men and women.

Eight out of ten Haitians and Jamaicans who have college degrees live outside their country. In Sierra Leone and Ghana, the same ratio is five out of ten. Many countries in Central America and Sub-Saharan Africa, as well as some island nations in the Caribbean and the Pacific, show rates of migration among professionals over 50 percent.

—WORLD BANK, *International Migration, Remittances and the Brain Drain*, October 24, 2005

ESTABLISHING GENDER EQUALITY

More than a buzzword, gender equality is absolutely indispensable for any real alternative. It is important to emphasize, in this era of ambiguous words, that it is a question of "equality" and not "equity." These two words are often employed interchangeably but they do not mean the same thing, nor do they have the same urgency. If a person has six apples and decides to give them to two people, he might consider it equitable to give two to one and four to the other, according to his own criteria. This is the best kind of "equity" women can hope for—according to objective possibilities, according to the parties that hold power, according to the order of priorities. It cannot be overstated that many ideologies, even progressive ones, have abandoned the cause of women's emancipation. Women are not human beings at a lower echelon of humanity; they should benefit from the same privileges as men in all spheres. First, in the public domain, this means the same civil and political rights, the same economic, social, and cultural rights. In other words, three apples for him and three for her. Second, and more important, in the private sphere, there must be equality in the family, the household, and the community. For it is the private sphere that becomes the last refuge of patriarchy when societal advances are won. This is where the desire for power subsists, the place where revenge for external injustices can be enacted. Patriarchy enables the exploited slave of the workplace to become a tyrant in his home! Feminism, as an instrument of gender emancipation and struggle against patriarchy, is an integral part of the alternative, and this is non-negotiable.

States should undertake, at the national level, all necessary measures for the realization of the right to development and shall ensure,
inter alia, equality of opportunity for all in their access to basic
resources, education, health services, food, housing, employment
and the fair distribution of income. Effective measures should be
undertaken to ensure that women have an active role in the development process. Appropriate economic and social reforms should
be carried out with a view to eradicating all social injustices.

—UN, Declaration on the Right to Development[216]

GUARANTEEING INDIGENOUS PEOPLES' RIGHT
TO SELF-DETERMINATION

The hierarchical world history view often produces a racist vision of social
relations. It is with much condescension that even the best-intentioned
texts broach the issue of "indigenous rights." Native peoples who have
acquired minority status in their own countries as a result of historical
events such as colonial massacres and pillage must be in a state of permanent resistance to protect their rights. Even in cases where native groups
are in the majority in relation to the descendants of white colonists, as they
are in many Andean countries, racism reverses the hierarchy of values and
gives all the rights to the dominant minorities. Autonomy is thus a political means of enforcing claims to those rights. Here again, autonomy can
only be won by creating a balance of power. This is how during recent
decades, everywhere in the world, indigenous populations have rejected
submission to the dominant model and have risen up against multinationals, against governments, and against international institutions, to demand
their rights and self-determination for their societies. New constitutions in
Bolivia, Venezuela, and Ecuador embody these struggles and open the way
to a just autonomy for indigenous peoples, allowing them to maintain or
rehabilitate the traditions, customs, rights, and the political and democratic conceptions that are theirs. Is this the best way? Is it the only way?
That is a question to be reflected on and debated within the social movements. What is clear is that autonomy will enable people to test their
choices and to meet other communities as equals.

In September 2007, after more than twenty years of negotiations, the UN General Assembly adopted a Declaration on the Rights of Indigenous Peoples, recognizing for some 370 million people the "right to self-determination" and the "right to determine and develop priorities and strategies for exercising their right to development" in order to protect their cultures and the integrity of their lands, free from any form of discrimination.[217] Furthermore, reparations are envisaged for the damages suffered: "Indigenous peoples deprived of their means of subsistence and development are entitled to just and fair redress." Even if this declaration does not the have the legal and binding character of a treaty, it is a laudable step forward. It should be noted that eleven countries, including Russia and Colombia, abstained while four others (the United States, Canada, Australia, and New Zealand) voted against it.[218]

PROTECTING THE COMMON GOODS
OF MANKIND

Reflection on the common goods of mankind is at the heart of debates in the global justice movement. The notion has acquired various names (public goods, common resources) and covers an increasingly broad range of items. Thus the classification of common goods can only be established after a vast democratic consultation reflecting different histories and cultures.

The notion of "common goods" covers the notion of "right" in many respects. Defending common goods means guaranteeing the right and access for all to water, pure air, energy, food, transport, and basic education (though it also encompasses knowledge in the larger sense of the term), development rights, equality, liberty, pleasure—in other words, the right to life. All these rights have been magnificently enunciated in the charters and treaties of the United Nations.

On the global scale, other rights must be guaranteed: the universal right to decent jobs through radically reduced working hours—as opposed to the current logic where unemployed people coexist with stressed and overworked employees; the universal right to an income for all citizens; the defense of pension schemes based on defined benefit rather than defined contribution (creating a defined benefit plan where it does not exist); free education (including higher level) and health; programs of socially useful public works and the protection of the environment (for example, housing construction and urban renewal, renovation of existing habitats, and public rail transport systems); free public transport; literacy and vaccination campaigns; primary health care on the successful Nicaraguan model of the period from 1980 to 1983 or that of Venezuela between 2003 and 2005.

The issue of *political democracy* is obviously crucial. Without the active intervention of citizens at all decision-making levels, the proposals elaborated above have little meaning.

BUILDING A NEW INTERNATIONAL ARCHITECTURE

Proposals are needed that radically redefine the foundations of the international architecture. Let us review the case of the WTO, the IMF, and the World Bank.

A major aim of a new WTO should be, in the area of trade, to guarantee the implementation of a series of existing fundamental international treaties, beginning with the Universal Declaration on Human Rights, and then all the fundamental treaties concerning human rights (individual or collective) and protection of the environment. Its function would be to supervise and regulate trade in a way that strictly conforms to environmental and social norms in accordance with the conventions of the International Labor Organization (ILO). This definition is in direct opposition to the current objectives of the WTO (see Q23). It obviously entails a strict separation of powers: it is out of question for the WTO, or any other organization, to have its own tribunal. The Dispute Settlement Body of the WTO must be abolished.

The organization that would replace the World Bank ought to be largely regionalized (the banks of the South could be interconnected). It would grant donations or loans at very low or zero interest rates on condition that the money be used in strict respect of social and environmental norms, and more broadly, of fundamental human rights. Contrary to the current World Bank (see Q8), the new bank that the world needs will not seek to represent the interests of the donors, nor will it force debtors to bow to market domination. Its first mission would be to defend the interests of the populations that receive the loans and donations.

As for the new IMF, it would retrieve part of its original mandate, which was to guarantee currency stability, fight speculation, control capital movements, and put an end to tax havens and tax fraud. To achieve this aim, it could act together with national authorities and regional monetary funds to collect various forms of international taxes.

All these avenues require the elaboration of a new global architecture that is coherent, multilevel, and consistent with a healthy separation of powers. Its cornerstone must be the United Nations, provided its General Assembly becomes the true decision-making body—which implies abolishing permanent membership of the Security Council and related veto rights. The General Assembly could delegate specific missions to bodies on an ad hoc basis.

We believe in the necessity and the feasibility of UN reform for three reasons. First, its charter is largely progressive and democratic. Second, its constitutive principle is democratic (one state = one vote)—even if it needs to be complemented by a system of direct proportional representation, as suggested above. Finally, in the 1960s and 1970s, the General Assembly adopted a number of resolutions and declarations that were clearly progressive (and that in principle remain applicable) and it established some useful institutions (ILO, UNCTAD, WHO).

Another question, yet to be fully explored, is the setting up of an international legal body, an international judiciary (independent of other international powers), to complement the current structure that includes the International Tribunal of The Hague and the recently founded International Criminal Court. Under the neoliberal offensive of the last twenty years, commercial law has gradually overshadowed public law. Non-democratic institutions such as the WTO and the World Bank operate with their own juridical system: the Dispute Settlement Body of the WTO and the ICSID (see Q8), whose role has increased disproportionately. The UN Charter is regularly violated by the permanent members of the Security Council. New spaces outside the rule of law are created, namely "enemy combatants" held in custody in Guantánamo Bay by the United States. The United States, having challenged the International

Tribunal of The Hague (it was found guilty in 1985 of aggression against Nicaragua), refuses to recognize the International Criminal Court. All this is very worrying and urgently calls for initiatives to complement an international legal system.

Meanwhile, institutions such as the World Bank and the IMF must be brought to account. In reality, though in principle they fall under the jurisdiction of the international judicial system and are bound by the human rights treaties, these two institutions (together with regional development banks) ignore them.

> Increasing malnutrition, falling school enrolments and rising unemployment have been attributed to the policies of structural adjustment. Yet these same institutions continue to prescribe the same medicine as a condition for debt relief, dismissing the overwhelming evidence that Structural Adjustment Programs have increased poverty.
>
> —FANTU CHERU,
> UN Independent Expert[219]

Furthermore, these institutions have actively supported (and still support) dictatorial regimes and have destabilized (and continue to destabilize) democratic governments whose politics displease Washington and other capitals. The list of their misdeeds is long and the crimes they have committed and still commit are serious. Legal proceedings against them must be initiated before the various competent institutions, starting with the national jurisdictions.[220]

QUESTION 55

If and when the debt is canceled, how can a new round of indebtedness be avoided?

Contrary to the IMF and the WB, which agree to debt relief in order to make the debt sustainable while retaining the related mechanism of structural overindebtedness, the total debt cancellation we demand must go hand in hand with a radical change of logic and new types of funding.

These new sources of money, which should be managed with the active participation of the local populations, do not imply fresh borrowing.

- After debt cancellation, the developing countries would no longer have to pay debt service. Even if they were refused credit access (since creditors would probably refuse to lend to countries that had obtained total debt cancellation), the amounts saved (see Q28) could be redeployed for their domestic needs.
- The expropriation of ill-gotten gains, after inquiries into embezzlement and corruption among the ruling classes of the South, would funnel considerable sums back to the developing countries—on the order of tens of billions of dollars a year for several years.
- A reevaluated and redefined ODA exclusively in the form of donations, as reparation for a historical, human, moral, social, ecological, and cultural debt, this time owed to the South, would bring in several hundred billion dollars a year.
- A Tobin-type tax on financial speculation linked to the foreign exchange markets and a tax on profits made by transnational corporations would also bring in significant amounts. Indeed, according to the BIS figures, daily currency transactions reached over $3.2 trillion in April 2007, not counting derivatives estimated at $2.4 trillion.[221] Even supposing that a tax would result in reducing the total by half, the amount concerned would still be $2.8 trillion. A 0.1 percent tax on such an amount would bring in $2.8 billion . . . per day!
- Developing countries, now no longer under the obligation to procure hard currency for their debt repayments, could consolidate their export revenues and at the same time ensure a reallocation of land, favoring food crops, reducing the areas cultivated for export produce and better preserving resources, forests, and land.
- Redistributive tax policies, on a global scale as well as within the developing countries, could do away with the inequalities brought about by the dual logic of the debt and structural adjustments. A "one-shot" tax on the estates of the richest 10 percent of families in each country would generate substantial fiscal revenues.

All these initiatives are suitable for financing an "alternative development" within the context of "alternative globalization." In any case, they place strong limits on the need for borrowing.

> We cannot repay the debt because we do not have enough to pay. We cannot repay the debt because we are not responsible for the debt. We cannot repay the debt because conversely others owe us what the greatest wealth will never pay for, the debt of blood. Our blood was shed.
>
> —THOMAS SANKARA, president of Burkina Faso, 1983–87, Addis Ababa, July 1987

QUESTION 56
What is debt auditing?

A debt audit consists of analyzing each loan, determining the circumstances in which it was contracted, examining how the money was used, what results were reached and who profited by them. It thus gives an in-depth insight into the amount of the debt and the payments it incurs, who contracted it and in what conditions. In this respect, debt auditing makes it possible to allocate responsibilities, and in the case of illegitimate debt, it opens the way to a claim for reparations against domestic state bodies that overstepped their competence, as well as against creditors who acted in full knowledge of the facts. Lastly, debt auditing makes it possible to find out which debts are odious and must therefore be considered void.

In international law, public auditing is the primary instrument through which the competence of public authorities can best be tested. As a tool, it gives governments the possibility to decide on the licit or illicit nature of the external public debt. This is so true that in the case of Brazil, public auditing of the debt has constitutional status. Finally, it is for the government of the concerned state to decide, on the basis of internal competence and after analyzing the legitimacy of the debt, whether or not it must be repaid.

From the standpoint of the international community, an odious debt could be taken to mean any debt contracted for purposes that are not in conformity with contemporary international law and, in particular, the principles of international law embodied in the Charter of the United Nations.

—MOHAMMED BEDJAOUI, Special Rapporteur
of the International Law Commission, 1977[222]

Similarly, when a government refuses to make an audit, citizens have a right to demand it. A citizen audit places the issue of law at the heart of considerations about the debt and citizens at the heart of their country's democratic and political life. The audit thus provides social and financial protection for citizens as well as being a legal argument for debt cancellation.[223]

By giving people the right to see how public money is used, the citizen audit also allows for the setting up of democratic structures through which they can manage the restitution of ill-gotten gains and their use for the benefit of the more deprived sections of the population. It is then possible for a constitutional government wishing to improve the living conditions of the population to put an end to serious human rights infringements resulting from the spiral of indebtedness, and to decide that the debt must be repudiated. Furthermore, the citizens' structure that has either carried out or accompanied the auditing process will also be in a position to demand the restitution of money misappropriated by corrupt leaders, which is an efficient way of fighting corruption, whether practiced by public or by private creditors.

During the audit process, a government has the right to freeze repayment of public debts. At the same time, Structural Adjustment Programs must be stopped and replaced by policies that give priority to fundamental human needs and ensure that cultural, social, and economic rights are effectively respected.

The debt audit tool thus makes it possible to identify responsibilities and to expose illegal, void, or odious debts, opening the way to debt repudiation and a claim for reparation both from state bodies that went beyond their authority and from creditors who acted in full possession of the facts.

The origins of the debt date back to the origins of colonialism. Those
who lent us the money, they are the ones who colonized us. They are
the same people who managed our states and our economies. It was
the colonizers who led Africa to contract loans with creditors of the
North, their brothers and cousins. We are strangers to this debt.
Therefore we cannot repay it.
—THOMAS SANKARA, president of Burkina Faso, 1983–87

The audit principle has already been applied in Brazil, Argentina, and
Peru, and since 2005 the dynamics around the process have been inten-
sifying. For instance, in July 2007 Rafael Correa, president of Ecuador,
signed a presidential decree instituting a commission for a full audit of the
public debt (CAIC). Consisting of representatives of the state but also of
Ecuador's social movements and of international networks working on
the debt issue (including CADTM), the commission's mandate is to identify illegitimate debts that could ultimately be eligible for cancellation. In
2005, the country spent more than 40 percent of its budget on servicing
the debt, while expenditures for health and education amounted to 15
percent of the budget, so the stakes are enormous.

Article 10: Competent bodies, determined by the Constitution and
the Law, shall first carry out financial, social and environmental
analyses of the impact of projects so as to establish financing possibilities. *These institutions shall also be in charge of financial,
social and environmental monitoring and auditing all through the
cycle of internal and external public indebtedness: terms of loan,
follow-up and renegotiation.*
—CONSTITUTION OF ECUADOR, 2008[224]

It is also encouraging to note that in the North, too, some countries
are beginning to acknowledge their responsibilities in the indebtedness of the Third World. For instance, the Norwegian government
decided in 2006 to unilaterally and unconditionally cancel part of its
bilateral debts considered as illegitimate with five debtor countries (see
Q44). Similarly, in March 2007 the Belgian senate adopted a resolution asking the government to cancel the debt of the least advanced

countries and to organize an audit on the odious nature of the debts in other developing countries.

Wishing to capitalize on such victories in which social and citizens' movements have often played a vital part, CADTM works toward reinforcing its partners' capacity for action all over the world. For instance, a workshop with various social movements in Central Africa was held in the Democratic Republic of the Congo in November 2007, just before a meeting of the West African CADTM network in Côte d'Ivoire. These two workshops aimed at establishing bases for a citizens' audit of the debt in the two sub-regions. Citizens' audits are not an end in themselves but should be used as a tool to allow, or if need be, force governments to meet the interests of the population, repudiate their debts, regain control over natural resources, and set up initiatives to recover assets embezzled by former dictatorships.

A project for an audit of international financial institutions was also launched by CADTM, Jubilee South, and other anti-debt campaigns. Here, too, auditing is a positive measure for exposing the way international indebtedness works, and for fighting it more effectively.

The audit is a particularly effective tool that can lead to promising actions in the future if populations learn to use it effectively.

QUESTION 57
Are China, sovereign funds, or the Bank of the South valid alternatives?

Over the last several years new players have appeared as providers of capital: China, sovereign funds or more recently the Bank of the South. Traditional creditors frown on these newcomers for rocking the boat, but are they a real alternative?

Since 2004, a significant rise in the price of staple products has tripled the currency reserves of most developing countries. In June 2008, China alone held the equivalent of $1.7 trillion in reserve currency and the reserves of the developing countries totaled more than $3.5 trillion, an amount three times the reserves of Japan, Western Europe, and North America together. This is without historical precedent. Some countries used part of these reserves to anticipate on repayments to the WB, the IMF, and the Paris Club, thus reducing their dependence on these institutions. IMF loans, which still amounted to $107 billion in 2003, just before the price of staple goods started rising, were down to $16 billion in 2007.

CHINA

China's loans to developing countries are a less costly alternative that is also free of the conditionalities enforced by the Bretton Woods institutions. African countries rich in natural resources already use them, and others will follow suit or wish to access the Chinese treasure trove. However, this is in no way an alternative for countries of the South. China massively invests in countries with natural resources that are not available on its own territory but is careful not to share any of the power thus gained, and populations no more benefit from those exports than they did before. Local ruling classes are satisfied, since money flows in without the lender meddling in the management of the country. China does not shy away from lending money to countries where financial resources are appropriated by the ruling class and where human rights are regularly violated, such as Gabon or Sudan. On the other hand, China does not encourage development in countries where it invests; it sends its own workers for the required infrastructure without calling on local manpower, and it demands that loans be paid back down to the last cent. The borrowing country's foreign debt thus significantly increases.

The case of the Democratic Republic of the Congo is enlightening in this respect. In September 2007, when the Congolese people were expecting the government to publish a report by the commission appointed to audit mining contracts and expose those that did not comply with legal requirements, the government signed a mining contract with a consortium of Chinese companies for a duration of thirty years. This contract took the form of a joint venture with 68 percent of capital held by Chinese and 32 percent by Congolese companies. While Chinese money will only be available after the feasibility studies, the Congolese government has already turned over mineral deposits to the tune of at least 10.6 million tons of copper and 600,000 tons of cobalt. The Chinese investments will be paid back in three phases: during the first phase all profits will be used to pay back the mining investments, including interest; during the second, 66 percent of profits will be used in this way, and the remaining 34 percent will go to shareholders; during the third phase all profits will go to the shareholders according to their shares in the capital stock. During the first two phases (the duration of which is not specified), the DRC will grant special privileges to the joint venture, such as "complete exoneration of all taxes, rights, tariffs, charges, direct or indirect royalties, whether at home or in import-export, payable within the DRC and those related to mining activities and the development of infrastructures." No money will be allotted to the state budget. It means finally that the Congolese people are being deceived, with the complicity of their own ruling class, which has sold out national resources for their own gains and to the greater profit of Chinese companies. It is a rerun of the same detrimental policy previously pursued with Western transnational companies and with loans from traditional creditors, whose position has been weakened since 2005 by the emergence of new players.

Let us note, too, that in East Asia the thirteen main economic powers (ASEAN, China, Japan, and South Korea) signed the Chiang Mai agreements that will make collaboration between central banks of these countries possible, with a view to creating a united front against a possible monetary or financial crisis. It is this kind of agreement that Washington prevented in the middle of the 1997–98 Asian crisis.

SOVEREIGN FUNDS

To invest part of their currency reserves, a number of governments of the South have created sovereign wealth funds. The first of these were created in the second half of the twentieth century by governments that wished to set aside part of their export revenues from oil and manufactured goods. In order of importance are the Abu Dhabi Emirate, Kuwait, China, Singapore, and Russia. The fund in the Abu Dhabi Investment Agency (ADIA) is estimated at $875 billion. Libya recently announced the creation of a $40 billion fund. Venezuela created Fonden, a national development fund, in early 2007. Algeria and Brazil are also considering creating one. All in all, sovereign funds control nearly $3 trillion.

These sovereign funds, which are a public source of capital for local companies in developing countries, compete with the International Finance Corporation (IFC), the WB agency in charge of loans or capital inflow for private companies in the South. These sovereign funds are also used by the developing countries that seek to acquire companies in industrialized countries. In November 2007, ADIA invested $7.6 billion in Citigroup, the world's leading bank. Between August 2007 and July 2008, sovereign funds contributed over $90 billion to the capital of private financial corporations that had been hard hit by unwise investments in the U.S. mortgage market. Although some elected officials voiced misgivings in the name of economic patriotism, Western CEOs and heads of states generally welcomed them. To have a privileged foothold in big financial corporations, some sovereign funds made considerable financial efforts. For instance, the Singapore fund Temasek lost over half of the amount it had invested in Merrill Lynch in December 2007 after a 55 percent fall in share price over seven months. Smarting from this costly experience it then refused to help Bear Stearns, which was finally bought by JPMorgan with the help of the Federal Reserve. At the end of July 2008, in order to get a new capital boost from Temasek, Merrill Lynch promised to pay $2.5 billion as compensation for the loss in share value.

The sovereign fund policy developed by some governments in developing countries is different from the policy implemented in the years after the oil boom in 1973. At that time, developing country governments recycled petrodollars by lending them to private banks in the North, from which they later borrowed. The current policy of governments that acquire capital in companies in the North and South is definitely sounder but still follows the dominant capitalist logic. Investments are not used to promote an alternative non-capitalist project, whereas potentially they could be powerful levers for implementing policies that strengthen the public sector, for breaking the hold of private corporations over major means of production, for developing a solidarity economy, and for redistributing wealth on principles of justice and equality.

NEW INITIATIVES IN LATIN AMERICA
AND THE CARIBBEAN

In Latin America several regional initiatives are also worrying the governments of industrialized countries, but here the context is very different. Among these initiatives are Petrocaribe, Alba, and the Bank of the South. Thanks to the creation of Petrocaribe by Venezuela and some fifteen countries in the area, Caracas sells its oil below the world market price and signs agreements to finance projects for improving the refining processes in countries that need them most. The Alba agreement, jointly launched by Venezuela, Cuba, Bolivia, and Nicaragua, and relying on Venezuela's oil revenues, operates partly on a barter basis: over 20,000 Cuban doctors provide free health care to the Venezuelan population in exchange for oil. Over 50,000 eye operations have been carried out free of charge for Venezuelan patients in Cuba under the same agreement. Other countries, whether they are members of Alba or not, also benefit from the agreement. A Bank of Alba was launched in 2008.

Finally, in 2007, seven Latin American countries (Argentina, Bolivia, Brazil, Ecuador, Paraguay, Uruguay, and Venezuela) created the Bank of the South. Divergences between governments of the member countries have delayed the actual launching of the new institution. Brazil, a country that does not really feel the need of another multilateral bank for Latin America since it can rely on a major public development bank (BNDES), pays lip service to the project and tries, along with Argentina, to use the Bank of the South for the benefit of Brazilian and Argentinean companies so as to ensure they have contracts and investments in the area. Setting aside details of the divergences between negotiating governments, there are two options to be considered:[225] Either set up a bank that will support a neo-developmental project (support for the regional expansion of capitalist ventures such as the Argentinean Techint, Brazilian civil engineering companies, or Petrobras) modeled on the European Union, dominated as it is by the interests of big capital. Or develop an instrument to finance economic, social, and cultural policies that break away from the logic of maximum profit and give priority to economic, social, and cultural integration by implementing the various agreements and conventions that guarantee civil, political, economic, social, and cultural rights.

In spite of declarations of good intention and the signing, at the end of September 2009, of a constitutive agreement by the seven presidents concerned, the Bank will not enter into force until 2012 when the parliaments of the member countries have all ratified the agreement. The founding charter designates Caracas as the Bank's main headquarters. Member countries have agreed on the principle of "one country = one vote" (whereas for the World Bank and the IMF, voting rights are linked to economic weight and political influence), and on an initial capital of $7 billion (which could be increased to $20 million if other countries join the new institution).

This being said, there has been a negative development during the long months of negotiations following the signing of the founding charter: Brazil has managed to soften the principle of "one country = one vote" by restricting its scope to certain specific decisions.

It is vital that social movements in the concerned countries call upon their governments to implement genuine financing alternatives and demand that their actions measure up to the historical opportunities.

[SIDEBAR]
The June 2009 Inter-ministerial Agreement
Concerning the Bank of the South

According to the latest information received, the governments of the seven countries committed to the creation of the Bank of the South have agreed on the following points:

- The Bank will be able to finance private, public or mixed companies, cooperatives, etc. for development projects in key economic and social sectors, in order, particularly, to improve regional infrastructures and reduce regional imbalance. The agreement mentions sovereignty in terms of food and energy, natural resources, knowledge and health care (financed projects must contribute to do this), which is a positive step. On the other hand, the agreement states the need to improve competitivity, which tends to fit a model influenced by social-liberal continuity.

- The country concerned by a project financed by the Bank must give its agreement on the eligibility of the project.   .

- The Bank can issue bonds and finance itself by every means.
- Eligible to be shareholders are: the countries of UNASUR (category A shareholders); other countries (category B); central banks, public or mixed financial entities (at least 50% held by the state) and multilateral credit organizations (category C).
- If countries increase their share, this will not affect their voting rights as stipulated in the agreement.

The different management bodies of the Bank of the South are as follows:

- The Board of Ministers: responsible for mid- and long- term general policy, it meets annually and among other functions appoints the members of the Board of Directors (*consejo de administración*) and the Executive Board (*directorio ejecutivo*) and admits new shareholders. It is composed of the ministers of the member countries. Decisions are taken on the basis of a ¾ majority, following the rule of "one country = one vote";
- The Board of Directors (*consejo de administración*): meets once every quarter and ensures economic, financial, and credit supervision and management. The directors (one per member country) will be appointed for a 3-year term. The rule "one country = one vote" is also applicable. For decisions to be valid, there must be a quorum of three-quarters of the members, and these decisions must be approved by an absolute majority of members present.
- The Executive Board (*directorio ejecutivo*): meets every week and includes one director for each of the UNASUR member countries of the Bank (category A shareholders), one director for the whole group of category B shareholders and one director for the whole group of category C shareholders. Category A shareholders have greater weight. Directors are appointed for 3 years.
- The Executive Committee, which comprises the president of the Executive Board (*directorio ejecutivo*) and three directors.
- The Board of Audit.

*

- Brazil, Venezuela and Argentina (the "big three" of the 7 countries) will be able to borrow up to four times the capital they

hold; Bolivia, Ecuador, Paraguay and Uruguay (the smaller 4) up
to eight times. For the remaining UNASUR countries, the
amount will be determined later, as required.

• In case of disputes, the competent court of law will be that of a
member country or another court of law, in compliance with the
decision of the Executive Board (*directorio ejecutivo*).

• The staff of the Bank will enjoy immunity and tax exemptions (as
for the World Bank, the IMF, the IDB, etc.).

Among new initiatives we must also mention the achievement of
Venezuela, Bolivia, and Ecuador in regaining control of some of their natural resources: Bolivia leaving the International Center for Settlement of
Investment Disputes (see Q8), a kind of tribunal set up by the WB; the
start of discussions for an ICSID of the South.

Although these various new initiatives change the situation, they do
not radically change the rules of the game. Agreements signed between
China and its partners are favorable to Beijing. The central banks of the
countries that signed the Chiang Mai agreement still lend a large part of
their currency reserves to the U.S. government in the form of Treasury
bonds. Several countries that are members of the Bank of the South do
the same, though in a qualified way. Though currency-rich developing
countries have reduced their foreign debts, they are still indebted since
they have sharply increased their internal public debt, which is now three
times the external public debt. Private companies' external debts in developing countries also sharply increased. In the 1990s, with each big financial crisis, private debts were socialized and led to an increase in the public debt. If a new international architecture (based on the International
Covenant on Economic, Social and Cultural rights and on the Charter of
Economic Rights and Duties of States) is not adopted by a sufficient
number of progressive governments in the South, the WB and the IMF
will be able to make it through the current crisis and capitalize on future
external shocks brought about by a possible fall in the prices of staple
goods and a rise in interest rates.

QUESTION 58
Can the developing countries' external public debt be compared to the public debt of the North?

Although the difference in amounts is enormous, the first similarity is in the way they evolve through time. The external public debt of the developing countries and the public debt of the North both exploded in the 1970s. In the North, the general recession of the years 1973–75 obliged governments to borrow in order to restart their economic activity: the creation of jobs in the public sector; state-sponsored projects (for example, Ariane, Airbus, and the Minitel in France); and a policy of major industrial or military works. Thus states and local collectivities were ensnared by the rise in interest rates at the beginning of the 1980s. Their public debt (mainly internal) grew very fast as they had to take out further loans to repay, as did the South. So here, too, there was a snowballing effect.

The second similarity concerns the credit holders and the financial flows they impose. The portion of the North's public debt held by citizens of modest means is marginal. When, in the North, a government issues a loan offer through treasury bonds, the big private financial institutions (banks, insurance companies, mutual funds, pension funds) grab almost everything in a few days. Here, too, it is these institutions and very affluent individuals who hold the major part of the public debt in the North. The main difference with the developing countries resides in the fact that their external public debt obliges the developing countries to procure hard currency for their repayments, leading to excessive exporting.

From the point of view of the debtors, the state repays creditors with money taken from tax revenues. Workers' income is more highly taxed than capital income. Furthermore, indirect taxation, such as VAT, tends to increase, which is relatively more costly for the middle and popular classes. Thus the state mainly repays the rich private financial institutions with money raised by the heavy taxation of those with modest incomes. Again, there is a transfer of wealth, here in the North, from the people to the capital-holders. Therefore, there are objective grounds for deep solidarity between the victims of the public debt in the developing countries and victims of the public debt in the North.

Lastly, a third point of similarity is that in the North, as in the South, heavy indebtedness is the ideal pretext for imposing austerity policies and modifying the social balance in the interests of the capital-holders. Introduced in the 1980s, in parallel with the Structural Adjustment Programs in the South, these policies found themselves a general framework in the European Union with the Maastricht Treaty. The priority was placed on stringent reduction of the public deficit, which means rigor and austerity, and in particular privatizations, the overhaul of the social security and pension systems, and spending cuts in health and education. In France, it is highly symbolic that the governments appointed by Jacques Chirac and Nicolas Sarkozy adopted two typical measures: an income-tax cut benefiting few low-income households and the partial privatization of several public companies such as Air France, Aéroports de France, France Telecom, Electricité de France, Gaz de France, Crédit Lyonnais, Dassault Systèmes, and various motorway companies. Thus the economic consequences of the debt for the common people—structural adjustment in the South, austerity in the North—have a great deal in common.

Consequently, we can say that the debt strikes the North and the South with frightening and comparable vigor, in its origins, in its very mechanisms, and in its consequences. What specific perimeter can we give for developing countries? Can China be included? Can Russia? Or those East European countries that recently joined the EU? We cannot be consistent and decide on an arbitrary limit, as the IMF and the WB do, and then suggest different solutions for populations that are affected by mechanisms triggered by the same underlying logic. We must demand the same solutions, namely the cancellation of the public debt contracted in the North toward major private financial institutions. An original idea to implement this could be a one-shot tax on the assets of creditors in countries of the North (such as the institutional investors, consisting mainly of banks, insurance companies, and pension funds)—a tax equal to the amount of debts owed to them. The tax would be used to anticipate repayment of the debt owed by the state. And this would bring a swift solution to the debt issue! For the citizens of the North, the effect would be considerable: the government, freed of the debt burden, would be able to afford to finance social projects, job creation, reparations to peoples in the South, and to work effectively in the interests of the greatest number.

The public debt holdings markets (government bond markets), set up by the main beneficiary countries of financial globalization and then imposed on the other countries (usually without much trouble) are, in the very words of the IMF, the "cornerstone" of financial globalization. What this means is that it is quite simply the most solid mechanism instigated by financial liberalization for transferring wealth from certain social classes and strata and from certain countries, to others. Tackling the powerbase of finance implies dismantling these mechanisms and therefore canceling the public debt— not only that of the poorest countries, but also that of any country whose vital social forces refuse to let their government continue to impose austerity budgets on citizens in the name of repaying the interest on the public debt.

—FRANÇOIS CHESNAIS, Tobin or not Tobin?

CHAPTER THIRTEEN

International Campaign
for Debt Cancellation

QUESTION 59
How did the international campaign
for debt cancellation start?

The international campaign for the cancellation of the debt is now central in the movement for an alternative globalization. Although the debt issue is not new, it has taken several years to form an international network of such far-reaching proportions.

In the Third World, the campaign for the nonpayment of the external debt became massive and popular between 1982 and 1990 in Latin America, the continent most affected by the crisis. Numerous Latin American trade union and peasant farmer organizations tried to promote continental solidarity. Cuba played an active role in trying to federate the Latin American countries in favor of stopping debt repayments.

In the North, some organizations pioneered the campaign, such as the Association internationale des techniciens, experts et chercheurs (AITEC: International association of technicians, experts and researchers) in Paris, which first broached the subject in 1983, or the CADTM in Belgium from 1990 on. Several books by Susan George had a non-negligible influence in reinforcing the movement in its early stages.[226] The international campaign found new fervor in the late 1990s, with the launch of the Jubilee 2000 campaign (with the support of the Catholic and Protestant churches). In May 1998, at the G8 Summit in Birmingham (UK), 70,000 Britons demonstrated for the cancellation of the debt of the poor countries under the banner of Jubilee 2000 Great

Britain. The year 1999 saw the largest ever petition (24 million signatures collected between 1998 and 2000) brought to the G8 summit in Cologne. The Jubilee 2000 movement would then split: some large NGOs in the North decided to no longer demand debt cancellation because of pressure from the Vatican while some campaigns in the South created Jubilee South. This network brings together organizations from all continents in the South (Asia, Africa, Latin America), coordinated by country and by continent. The CADTM network, which was starting to become truly international, decided to enter into a strategic alliance with Jubilee South and thus to contribute to boost the anti-debt movement beyond 2000.

The *consulta* (referendum on a popular initiative) carried out in Spain by the Citizens' Network for the Cancellation of External Debt (RCADE) in March 2000 and the referendum organized in Brazil in September were big steps forward.

Several networks carried out a systematic effort toward convergence. Debates divided the movement. Some, like RCADE, CADTM, and Jubilee South, consider that fighting for debt cancellation necessarily leads to questioning the capitalist system. Others think this system must not or cannot be changed and that their task is to help liberate countries from the burden of the debt, thereby supporting, albeit critically, the IMF and WB strategies but without challenging the system.

From 1999 onward, the weight of movements in the South has gradually increased. Large mobilizations occurred in Peru (1999), in Ecuador (1999–2001), in Brazil (September 2000), and in South Africa (1999–2000). The World Social Forum, which also developed at a continental and local level, represented a turn in approach. Initially organized in Porto Alegre (Brazil), the WSF moved to Mumbai, Bamako, Caracas, Karachi, Nairobi, and Belem in 2009, yet it managed to retain its life force.

In the above-mentioned debate, a huge step forward was taken in June 2005 and confirmed in September of the same year during the second North-South Dialogue organized in Havana (after Dakar in 2000). The moderate and radical sides agreed to refuse all conditionalities imposed by the North. Moreover, Jubilee South contributes to the collective development of the anti-debt movements the notion of historical, social, cultural, and environmental debt.

Links between the various approaches were also woven by the activist movements: between debt and migrations; between food sovereignty and rejection of the debt and Structural Adjustment Programs; among common struggles against IMF/WB/WTO; between anti-debt movements and movements against big dams and other energy-related mega-projects; and among movements against deforestation.

A new major topic has been introduced, notably by CADTM: contrary to a commonly accepted notion, countries of the South do not inevitably have to contract loans with the North if they wish to develop. Alternative policies, which do not generate debts, are perfectly applicable both nationally and internationally.

In 2006–7, there seemed to be a lull on the debt front. Anticipated repayments to the IMF gave the wrong impression that the debt was a thing of the past. In reality, the conditions for new financial inequalities and for a new debt crisis are taking shape, and the issue is still central.

Within a few years, despite many obstacles, much ground has been covered on the road toward convergence between the various movements fighting to liberate peoples of the burden of the debt. Furthermore, social movements and large global campaigns have moved toward better coordination, particularly thanks to common days of action all over the world. Action has steadily increased.

No doubt the issue of the debt will come back to the fore in the coming years. Let us hope that governments of the South, under the pressure of their populations, will challenge the need to repay, and that alternative proposals will be effectively implemented.

The present crisis is a mirror showing citizens of the world what the future globalized capitalism has in store for them. In this respect the Argentinean uprisings are a laboratory of counter-powers, the significance of which is too often ignored. . . . Rebellious Argentina shows us that other worlds are indeed possible, that they are already among us.

—CÉCILE RAIMBEAU, DANIEL HÉRARD, *Argentine rebelle,*
un laboratoire de contre-pouvoirs

QUESTION 60
What is CADTM and How was it Born?

Seeing the ravages of neoliberal corporate-driven policies in the 1980s, more and more citizens identified the debt as the main instrument of subordination of the South. In France, when the G7 met in July 1989, at the time of the Bicentenary of the French Revolution, a campaign called "Ça suffa comme ci" (Enough's enough), launched under the impetus of the writer Gilles Perrault and the singer Renaud, ended by drawing up L'Appel de La Bastille (the Bastille Appeal), demanding immediate and unconditional cancellation of the Third World debt. Although there was no immediate follow-up in France, the campaign was carried on in Belgium, with the founding of the Committee for the Abolition of the Third World Debt (Comité pour l'annulation de la dette du Tiers-Monde), or CADTM.

The international network based in Liège promotes radical alternatives to the different forms of oppression in the world. The Third World debt and structural adjustment are at the heart of its preoccupations, to put an end to the dictate of the G8, the transnational firms, and the World Bank/IMF/WTO trio. Working in an internationalist perspective, CADTM has been pluralist from the start. It attracts activists, trade union organizations, parties, parliamentarians, solidarity campaign committees, and NGOs. The ball is rolling!

The first major turn of events came in 1994. On January 1, in the Chiapas region of Mexico, the Zapatistas and the deputy commander, Marcos, caused a stir at the time of the implementation of the North American Free Trade Agreement (NAFTA) between Canada, the United States, and Mexico. Based on the claims of the indigenous peoples, their struggle also found its place within the general context of the struggle against all oppression in the world and against corporate-driven globalization. The year 1994 also marked the fiftieth anniversary of the Bretton Woods institutions (IMF, World Bank), which was being commemorated in Madrid. On this occasion, CADTM took part in the campaign "Les Autres Voix de la Planète" (The Planet's Other Voices), which organized a counter-summit and a street demonstration (15,000 demonstrators) destined to draw attention to an alternative point of view. The campaign gave its name to CADTM's journal, published every three months.

Next, the petition "Banque mondiale, FMI, OMC: ça suffit!" (World Bank, IMF, WTO: Enough!) launched by CADTM brought to the surface a broad network of sympathizers, opposed to the international financial institutions' logic. In 1996, the G7 Summit in Lyon was the scene of a huge international mobilization, still using the theme "The Planet's Other Voices," followed by the "Intergalactic Meeting of Zapatistas" in La Realidad (Mexico).

In 1998, the Jubilee 2000 Campaign on the one hand and the birth of ATTAC on the other relaunched the theme of the debt in France, and more generally, in Europe. CADTM has been working on it from the outset.

Since then, the CADTM network has developed both in the North (Belgium, Switzerland, France, Japan) and in the South (particularly in Latin America, the Caribbean, Africa, Syria, Lebanon, India, and Pakistan).[227] In 2008, CADTM was present in twenty-five countries, and its message has been relayed by various partners on every continent.

CADTM could thus enlarge its field of action with:

- international meetings—seminars on law, training workshops, meetings of the CADTM network;
- multiple publications on the debt (books, DVDs, CDs);
- continuous series of lectures, often supported by films that opened debates such as *Bamako, Life and Debt, Darwin's Nightmare, The End of Poverty?*
- increasing media coverage (press, radio, television, Internet);
- variety of consciousness-raising actions (popular theater, concerts, comics).

CADTM does not limit its actions to the central demand of total and unconditional cancellation of the external public debt of the developing countries and the abolition of the Structural Adjustment Programs imposed on Third World countries. It also puts forward numerous proposals for constructing sustainable alternatives to the present financial logic, which appear throughout this book.

As a recognized authority on the debt issue and a popular movement mobilizing in both North and South, CADTM is well equipped to bring its influence to bear on the struggle to construct another world.

Appendix

The 145 Developing Countries in 2008

The list drawn up in 2009 comprised 144 countries. The countries no longer in the Developing Country category are Croatia, Equatorial Guinea, Hungary, Oman and Slovakia. However, American Samoa, Gaza and the West Bank, Kosovo and Mayotte have now entered this category.[228]

Sub-Saharan Africa

Angola, Benin, Botswana, Burkina Faso, Burundi, Cameroon, Cap-Verde, Central African Republic, Chad, Comoros Islands, Congo, Democratic Republic of the Congo, Equatorial Guinea, Eritrea, Ethiopia, Gabon, Gambia, Ghana, Guinea, Guinea-Bissau, Côte d'Ivoire, Kenya, Lesotho, Liberia, Madagascar, Malawi, Mali, Mauritania, Mauritius, Mozambique, Namibia, Niger, Nigeria, Rwanda, São Tomé and Príncipe, Senegal, Seychelles, Sierra Leone, Somalia, South Africa, Sudan, Swaziland, Tanzania, Togo, Uganda, Zambia, Zimbabwe.

Latin America and the Caribbean

Argentina, Belize, Bolivia, Brazil, Chile, Colombia, Costa Rica, Cuba, Dominican Republic, Dominica, Ecuador, Grenada, Guatemala, Guyana, Haiti, Honduras, Jamaica, Mexico, Nicaragua, Panama, Paraguay, Peru, St-Kitts-and-Nevis, St-Lucia, St-Vincent and Grenadines, Salvador, Suriname, Uruguay, Venezuela.

East Asia and the Pacific
Cambodia, China, Fiji, Indonesia, Kiribati, Laos, Malaysia, Marshall
Islands, Micronesia (Federal States), Mongolia, Myanmar, North Korea,
Palau, Papua-New Guinea, Philippines, Solomon Islands, Samoa,
Thailand, East Timor, Tonga, Vanuatu, Vietnam.

South Asia
Afghanistan, Bangladesh, Bhutan, India, the Maldives, Nepal, Pakistan,
Sri Lanka.

Eastern and Central Europe, Turkey, Central Asia
Albania, Armenia, Azerbaijan, Belarus, Bosnia Herzegovina, Bulgaria,
Croatia, Georgia, Hungary, Kazakhstan, Kyrgyzstan, Latvia, Lithuania,
Macedonia, Moldavia, Montenegro, Poland, Romania, Russia, Serbia,
Slovakia, Tajikistan, Turkey, Turkmenistan, Ukraine, Uzbekistan.

Middle East and North Africa
Algeria, Djibouti, Egypt, Iraq, Iran, Jordan, Lebanon, Libya, Morocco,
Oman, Syria, Tunisia, Yemen.

Triad
Andorra, Antigua-and-Barbuda, Australia, Austria, Bahamas, Bahrain,
Barbados, Belgium, Brunei, Canada, Cyprus, Czech Rep., Denmark,
Estonia, Finland, France, Germany, Greece, Iceland, Ireland, Israel, Italy,
Japan, Kuwait, Liechtenstein, Luxembourg, Malta, Monaco,
Netherlands, New Zealand, Norway, Portugal, Qatar, San Marino, Saudi
Arabia, Singapore, Slovenia, South Korea, Spain, Sweden, Switzerland,
Taiwan, Trinidad-and-Tobago, United Arab Emirates, United Kingdom,
United States.

Highly Indebted Poor Countries in 2008
Afghanistan, Benin, Bolivia, Burkina Faso, Burundi, Cameroon, Central
African Republic, Chad, Comoros, Congo, Côte d'Ivoire, Democratic
Republic of the Congo, Erythrea, Ethiopia, Gambia, Ghana, Guinea,
Guinea-Bissau, Guyana, Haiti, Honduras, Kenya, Kyrgyzstan, Liberia,
Madagascar, Malawi, Mali, Mauritania, Mozambique, Nepal, Nicaragua,

Niger, Rwanda, São Tomé and Príncipe, Senegal, Sierra Leone, Somalia, Sudan, Tanzania, Togo, Uganda, Zambia.

Glossary

BALANCE OF PAYMENTS — A country's balance of current payments is the result of its commercial transactions (imported and exported goods and services) and financial exchanges with foreign countries. The balance of payments is a measure of the financial position of a country in the world. A country with a surplus in its current payments is a lending country for the rest of the world. On the other hand, if a country's balance is in the red, that country will typically have to turn to the international lenders to borrow what funding it needs.

CENTRAL BANK — A country's central bank runs its monetary policy and holds the monopoly on minting the national currency. Commercial banks must get their currency from it, at a supply price fixed according to the main rates of the central bank.

CHICAGO BOYS — The phrase refers to a team of neoliberal economists at the University of Chicago who, following the teachings of Milton Friedman (d. 2007), had a deep influence on the economic policy of the Pinochet regime, then Margaret Thatcher's in Britain, and Ronald Reagan's in the United States.

DEVELOPING COUNTRY (DC) — Developing countries, according to World Bank terminology, are countries having a low or middle income, as defined by the criterion of gross national income per capita. The list of developing countries is reviewed each year on 1 July, and comprised 144 countries in 2009 (the statistics used in this book are based on the 2008 list provided in the Appendix). Concerning the limitations and the ideological character of such terminology, see Q1 and Q2.

DEBT RESCHEDULING — Modification of the terms of a debt, for example, by modifying the due dates or by postponing repayments of the principal and/or the interest. The aim is usually to give a little breathing space to a country in difficulty by extending the period of repayment and reducing the amount of each installment or by granting a grace period during which no repayments will be made.

DEBT SERVICE — The sum of the interests and the amortization of the capital borrowed.

DEBT STOCK — The total amount of debt.

DEVALUATION — A public-policy- or market-driven reduction in the exchange rate of a currency.

EXPORT CREDIT AGENCY — When private businesses of the North obtain a market in a developing country, there is a risk that economic or political problems may prevent payment of bills. To protect against that, the business can take out insurance with an export credit agency, such as COFACE in France or Ducroire in Belgium. If there is a problem, the agency pays instead of the insolvent client, and the Northern business is sure of getting what is owed. One of the main criticisms lodged against these agencies is that they are not very fussy about the nature of the contracts insured (arms, infrastructure and huge energy projects such as the gigantic Three Gorges Dam project in China) nor about their social or environmental consequences. They often give their support to repressive and corrupt regimes (like Total in Myanmar, formerly Burma), which means implicitly supporting fundamental human rights violations.

G7/G8 — Group meeting regularly since 1975 composed of the most powerful countries on the planet: Canada, France, Germany, Italy, Japan, the United Kingdom, and the United States. It became the G8 after admitting Russia in June 2002. G7 finance ministers still meet on financial issues without Russia. Their heads of state meet every year, generally in June or July. The G8 is challenged by emergent countries, particularly China, and by the movement for an alternative globalization that sets up a counter-summit for each of those annual meetings.

GROSS DOMESTIC PRODUCT (GDP) — The GDP represents the market value of the total output of final goods and services (excluding intermediate goods such as the window glass in an automobile) produced inside a country in one year.

GROSS NATIONAL PRODUCT (GNP) — The GNP represents the wealth produced by a nation, as opposed to a given territory. It includes the revenue of citizens of the nation living abroad.

HIGHLY INDEBTED POOR COUNTRIES (HIPC) INITIATIVE — An initiative designed to relieve the debt burden of certain very poor and over-indebted countries, but which aims above all to reinforce the logic of structural adjustment. Introduced in 1996 and "enhanced" in 1999, it has fallen way behind schedule and has quickly proved inadequate in terms of debt reduction. In 2010, only thirty or so countries have managed to obtain a reduction of their debt via this program, after implementing the economic reforms urged upon them by their creditors. The conditions imposed are very severe and very often the final debt relief is meager. See Q31 and Q32.

HUMAN DEVELOPMENT RATING (HDR) — Instrument used by the United Nations to estimate a country's degree of development based on per capita income, the level of education, and the average life expectancy of the population.

IMF — The IMF was created in 1944 at the Bretton Woods Conference, for the purpose of managing the stability of the international financial system. Over the years, the IMF has gradually deviated from its initial mandate to engage, together with the World Bank, in the management of the wolrd's various debt crises. In practical terms, it has been, and remains, one of the world's main promoters of neoliberalism, particularly since the early 1980s and during the financial crises of emerging countries in the 1990s. Since the crisis that erupted in 2007, its mandate and its lending capacity have again been extended. The IMF now concerns itself not only with the countries of the South, but has become very active in certain European countries. See Q 16. Website: www.imf.org.

INFLATION — The cumulated (normally on a yearly basis) rise of prices as a whole. Inflation implies a fall in the value of money since, as time goes by, larger sums are required to purchase particular items. This is the reason why corporate-driven policies seek to keep inflation down.

INTEREST RATES — When A lends money to B, B repays the amount lent by A (the capital) as well as a supplementary sum known as interest, so that A gains by agreeing to this financial operation. The interest is determined by the interest rate, which may be high or low. To take a very simple example: if A borrows $100 million for ten years at a fixed interest rate of 5 percent, the first year he will repay a tenth of the capital initially borrowed ($10 million) plus 5 percent of the capital owed, that is, $5 million, for a total of $15 million. In the second year, he will again repay 10 percent of the capital borrowed, but the 5 percent now only applies to the remaining $90 million still due, that is, $4.5 million, or a total of $14.5 million. And so on, until the tenth year when he will repay the last $10 million, plus 5 percent of that remaining $10 million, that is, $0.5 million, for a total of $10.5 million. Over ten years, the total amount repaid will come to $127.5 million. The repayment of the capital is not usually made in equal installments. In the initial years, the repayment concerns mainly the interest, and the proportion of capital repaid increases over the years. In this case, if repayments are stopped, the capital still due is higher. The nominal interest rate is the rate at which the loan is contracted. The real interest rate is the nominal rate reduced by the rate of inflation.

LEAST DEVELOPED COUNTRIES (LDC) – A notion defined by the United Nations in 1971 on the following criteria: low per capita income, poor human resources, and little diversification in the economy. In 2010, the list included forty-nine countries where thirty years ago there were only twenty-five LDCs. Only two countries were successful in leaving the group: Botswana in 1984 and Cap Verde in 2008.

LONDON CLUB – The members are the private banks that lend to Third World states and companies. The Club first met in 1976 to try to solve Zaire's repayment problems. During the 1970s, deposit banks had become the main source of credit for countries in difficulty. By the end of the decade, these banks were granting over 50 percent of total credit allocated, all lenders combined. At the time of the debt crisis in 1982, the London Club had an interest in working with the IMF to manage the crisis.

Groups of deposit banks, known as advisory commissions, meet to coordinate debt rescheduling for borrower countries. The meetings, unlike those of the Paris Club that always meets in Paris, are held in New York, London, Paris, Frankfurt, or elsewhere at the convenience of the country concerned and the banks. The advisory commissions, started in the 1980s, have always advised debtor countries immediately to adopt a policy of stabilization and ask for IMF support before applying for rescheduling or fresh loans from the deposit banks. Only on rare occasions do advisory commissions pass a project without IMF approval, if the banks are convinced that the country's policies are adequate.

Here is the definition given by the IMF: "A committee of bankers representing a debtor country's commercial bank lenders—often called the London Club—was typically set up in parallel with the Paris Club when countries faced debt service problems. The aim of the London Club was to ensure that equal treatment was provided to all bank lenders while providing rescheduling terms to help the country return to creditworthiness."[229]

MARSHALL PLAN – The European Recovery Program, better known as the Marshall Plan, was set up in 1947 by the U.S. administration to rebuild European economies after the Second World War, with a double objective: help European countries get back to a position in which they could again be trade partners, and prevent a deteriorating economic situation that might have led to a shift by these countries to the Soviet bloc. The aid essentially consisted of gifts ($11 billion out of a total $13 billion). Sixteen West European countries benefited from it. See Q6.

MONOCULTURE – The cultivation of one crop. Many countries of the South have been induced to specialize in the production of one commodity for export (cotton, coffee, cocoa, groundnuts, tobacco) to procure hard currency for debt repayments.

MORAL HAZARD – An argument often used by opponents of debt-cancellation. It is based on the existence of assymetrical information with respect to a borrower and a lender. Only the borrower knows whether he really intends to repay the lender. By canceling the debt today, there would be a risk that the same facility might be extended to future debtors, which would increase the reticence of creditors to commit capital. They would have no other solution than to demand a higher interest rate including a risk premium. Clearly the term "moral" here is applied only to the creditors, whereas the debtors are automatically suspected of "amorality." Yet it is easily demonstrated that this "moral hazard" is a direct result of the total liberty of capital flows. It has accompanied the opening of financial markets, as this is what multiplies the potentiality of the market contracts that are supposed to increase the welfare of humankind but actually bring an increase in risky contracts. So financiers would like to multiply the opportunities to make money without risk in a society which, we are unceasingly told, is and has to be a high-risk society. A fine contradiction.

MUTUAL FUND – Common investment funds in the United States.

NET TRANSFERS ON DEBT – The difference between the amounts received as new loans and the amounts repaid (both capital and interest) over the same period. The net transfer is positive when the concerned country or continent receives more than it repays. It is negative when the repaid amounts are higher than the received amounts.

NORTH ATLANTIC TREATY ORGANIZATION (NATO) – Based in Brussels, NATO was supposed to ensure U.S. military protection for the Europeans in case of aggression, but above all it gives the United States supremacy over the Western bloc. Western European countries agreed to place their armed forces within a defense system under U.S. command, and thus recognize the preponderance of the United States. NATO was founded in 1949 in Washington. In 2008 it had twenty-six members: Belgium, Canada, Denmark, France, Iceland, Italy, Luxembourg, the Netherlands, Norway, Portugal, the United Kingdom, and the United States, to which were added Greece and Turkey in 1952; the Federal Republic of Germany in 1955 (replaced by Unified Germany in 1990); Spain in 1982; Hungary, Poland, and the Czech Republic in 1999; Bulgaria, Estonia, Latvia, Lithuania, Romania, Slovakia, Slovenia in 2004. Instead of dissolving with the end of the Cold War, NATO rallied and launched several military interventions beyond its initial field of action which was officially limited to the North Atlantic. NATO troops are directly involved in the occupation of and war in Afghanistan, which serves the geostrategic interests of the EU and United States. Website: www.nato.int.

OECD (ORGANIZATION FOR ECONOMIC COOPERATION AND DEVELOPMENT) – The OECD was established in 1961 and is based in Château de la Muette (Paris). It includes the fifteen countries that made up the European Union until 2005 plus Switzerland, Norway, Iceland; in North America, the United States and Canada; and in Asia and the Pacific: Japan, Australia and New Zealand. Between 1994 and 1996, three Third World countries entered the OECD: Turkey, also a candidate for the EU; Mexico, also part of NAFTA with its two North American neighbors; and South Korea (December 1996). Since 1995, three countries of the former Eastern bloc have joined: the Czech Republic, Poland, and Hungary. In 2000, the Slovak Republic became the thirtieth member.

The OECD member countries in alphabetical order: Australia, Austria, Belgium, Canada, Czech Republic, Denmark, Finland, France, Germany, Greece, Hungary, Iceland, Ireland, Italy, Japan, Luxembourg, Mexico, Netherlands, New Zealand, Norway, Poland, Portugal, South

Korea, Slovakia, Spain, Sweden, Switzerland, Turkey, United Kingdom, United States.Website: www.oecd.org.

OFFICIAL DEVELOPMENT ASSISTANCE (ODA) – Official Development Assistance is the name given to loans granted in financially favorable conditions by the public bodies of the industrialized countries. A loan has only to be agreed at a lower rate of interest than going market rates (a concessionary loan) to be considered as aid, even if it is then repaid to the last cent by the borrowing country. Tied bilateral loans (which oblige the borrowing country to buy products or services from the lending country) and debt cancellation are also counted as part of ODA. Apart from food aid, there are three main ways of using these funds: rural development, infrastructures, and non-project aid (financing budget deficits or the balance of payments). The latter increases continually. This aid is made "conditional" upon reduction of the public deficit, privatization, environmental "good behavior," care of the very poor, democratization, and so forth. The main governments of the North, the World Bank, and the IMF establish these conditions. The aid goes through three channels: multilateral aid, bilateral aid, and the NGOs.

ORGANIZATION OF PETROLEUM-EXPORTING COUNTRIES (OPEC) – Founded in September 1960 and based in Vienna (Austria) since 1965, OPEC is in charge of coordinating and unifying the petroleum-related policies of its members, with the aim of guaranteeing them all stable revenues. To this end, production is organized on a quota system. The organization consists of twelve petroleum-producing countries: the five founding countries, Saudi Arabia, Iraq, Iran, Kuwait and Venezuela, joined by Qatar in 1961, Libya in 1962, the United Arab Emirates in 1967, Algeria in 1969, Nigeria in 1971, Ecuador in 1972 (though it suspended its membership from December 1992 to October 2007), and Angola in 2007. Gabon was a member from 1975 to 1994, Indonesia from 1962 to 2008 (and withdrew when it became a net importer of petroleum).

In 2005 OPEC member states owned 78.4 percent of the estimated oil reserves and supplied 43 percent of the global production in crude oil. Each country, represented by its minister of energy and petroleum, chairs the organization in turn. Since 2007 Libyan Abdalla El-Badri has been General Secretary of OPEC.

PARIS CLUB — This group of lender states was founded in 1956 and specializes in dealing with non-payment by developing countries. Website: www.clubdeparis.org; see also and particularly www.clubde-paris.fr.

PENSION FUNDS — Pension funds collect part of their clients' monthly salary and speculate on the financial markets to lay out this capital to advantage. There is a dual objective: to provide a pension for their clients when they retire at the end of their working lives and to make extra profits for themselves. Both objectives depend on contingencies and their fulfillment is uncertain. On many occasions, workers have found themselves with neither savings nor a pension after crashing bankruptcies, such as that of Enron in 2001 in the United States. The system of pensions by capitalization has become generalized in the Anglo-Saxon world. In 2008, some countries in continental Europe, such as France, retained despite everything a distributive pension system based on solidarity between generations.

POVERTY REDUCTION STRATEGY PAPER (PRSP) — Set up by the World Bank and the IMF in 1999, the PRSP was officially designed to fight poverty. But it turns out to be an even more virulent version of the Structural Adjustment Programs in disguise, as it tries to win the approval and legitimization of the social participants. It is sometimes called Poverty Reduction Strategy Framework (PRSF).

RISK PREMIUM — When loans are granted, the creditors take account of the economic situation of the debtor country in fixing the interest rate. If there seems to be a risk that the debtor country may not be able to honor its repayments then that will lead to an increase in the rates charged. Thus the creditors receive more interest, which is supposed to compensate for the risk taken in granting the loan. This means that the cost to the borrower country is much higher, accentuating the financial pressure it has to bear. For example, in 2002, Argentina was faced with risk premiums of more than 4,000 points, meaning that for a hypothetical market interest rate of 5 percent, Argentina would have to borrow at a rate of 45 percent. This cuts it off de facto from access to credit, forcing it even deeper into crisis. For Brazil in August 2002, the risk premium was at 2,500 points.

SEPARATE FUNDS — Funds owned that do not come from indebtedness, particularly social capital and reserves.

SOVEREIGN WEALTH FUNDS — Financial investment funds—through shares or bonds or other financial products—owned by a state. Sovereign funds are often fed by export revenues, particularly oil revenues. The funds dispose of part of the country's currency reserves and invest it in various ways (shares, bonds, real estate, and so forth). See Q57.

STRUCTURAL ADJUSTMENT PROGRAM (SAP) — Economic policy imposed by the IMF in exchange for new loans or the rescheduling of old loans. See Q17 and Q18.

SUBSISTENCE AGRICULTURE — Crops destined to feed the local population (millet, manioc, sorghum, and the like), as opposed to those crops intended for exportation (coffee, cocoa, tea, nuts, sugar, and the like).

TAX HAVENS AND OFFSHORE CENTERS — These are essentially notional spaces in corporation accounting (institutional investors, transnational companies), making it possible for a transaction at a specific location to escape any kind of control and taxation related to that location because the transaction is regarded as occurring elsewhere.

For more information from the point of view of those who wish to profit from tax havens, see www.escapeartist.com/Offshore/Tax_Havens, www.paradisfiscaux.com, www.easyentrepreneur.co.uk.

For information on fighting tax havens, see www.taxjustice.net/cms/front_content.php?idcat=2.

For the French text of the platform against tax and legal havens, see www.cadtm.org/article.php3?id_article=2582.

TOBIN TAX — A tax on exchange transactions (all transactions involving conversion of currency), originally proposed in 1972 by the U.S. economist James Tobin as a means of stabilizing the international financial system. The idea was taken up by the association ATTAC and other movements for an alternative globalization, including CADTM. Their aim is to reduce financial speculation (which was on the order of $1.2 trillion a day in 2002) and redistribute the money raised by this tax to those who need it most. International speculators who spend their time changing dollars for yens, then for euros, then dollars again and so on as they calculate which currency will appreciate and which depreciate, will have to pay a small tax, somewhere between 0.1 percent and 1 percent, on each transaction. According to ATTAC, this could raise $100 billion on a global scale. Considered unrealistic by the ruling classes to justify their refusal to adopt it, the meticulous analyses of globalized finance carried out by ATTAC and others have, on the contrary, demonstrated how simple and appropriate such a tax would be.

TRADE BALANCE — The trade balance of a country is the difference between merchandise sold (exports) and merchandise bought (imports). The resulting trade balance either shows a deficit or a credit.

UNCTAD (UNITED NATIONS CONFERENCE ON TRADE AND DEVELOPMENT) — Established in 1964, after pressure from the developing countries, to offset the GATT effects. Website: www.unctad.org.

UNDP (UNITED NATIONS DEVELOPMENT PROGRAM) — The UNDP, founded in 1965 and based in New York, is the UN's main agency of technical assistance. It helps the developing country, without any political restrictions, to set up basic administrative and technical services, trains managerial staff, tries to respond to some of the essential needs of populations, takes the initiative in regional cooperation programs, and coordinates, theoretically at least, the local activities of all the UN operations. The UNDP generally relies on Western expertise and techniques, but a third of its contingent of experts comes from the Third World. The UNDP publishes an annual Human Development Report which, among

344 DEBT, THE IMF, AND THE WORLD BANK

other things, classifies countries by their Human Development Rating (HDR). Website: www.undp.org.

WARSAW PACT — A military pact between the countries of the former Soviet Bloc (USSR, Albania, Bulgaria, Hungary, Poland, the German Democratic Republic, Romania, Czechoslovakia). It was signed in Warsaw in May 1955, as a reaction to the Federal German Republic joining NATO. Albania withdrew in 1968 after Soviet intervention in Czechoslovakia. After the dislocation of the USSR, the Pact's military organization was dissolved in April 1991.

WORLD BANK — The initial aim of this institution, created at Bretton Woods in 1944, was to aid the financing and reconstruction of Europe at the end of the Second World War, and the financing and development of the countries of the South. However, its role is far from neutral and it is rightly criticized for its anti-democratic mode of operation, for its active role, together with the IMF, in enforcing the dominance of the most industrialized economies and of transnational corporations over developing countries, and for its support of projects that destroy the environment and infringe human rights. The World Bank Group is comprised of five bodies: the International Bank for Reconstruction and Development (IBRD), the International Development Association (IDA), the International Finance Corporation (IFC), the Multilateral Investment Guarantee Agency (MIGA), and the ICSID (International Center for the Settlement of Investment Disputes). See Q8; www.worldbank.org.

WORLD TRADE ORGANIZATION (WTO) — The WTO, founded on 1 January 1995, replaced the General Agreement on Tariffs and Trade (GATT). The main innovation is that the WTO enjoys the status of an international organization. Its role is to ensure that no member states adopt any kind of protectionism whatsoever, in order to accelerate the liberalization of global trading and to facilitate the strategies of the transnational corporations. It has an international court (the Organ for the Settlement of Differences) that judges any alleged violations of its founding text drawn up in Marrakesh. See Q23; www.wto.org.

Notes

1. Since our book *Who Owes Who? 50 Questions About World Debt* was published, the World Bank has modified these country groupings. For example, South Korea has been taken from the developing countries category and placed with the developed countries. Although this decision is debatable, we abide by the new classification so that our calculations will be on the same basis as the World Bank's. There have been similar changes regarding the Czech Republic and Estonia.
2. For the whole of this book, the sources *World Development Indicators 2008* and *Global Development Finance 2008* were consulted on the World Bank website in August 2008.
3. UNDP, *Human Development Report 2006*.
4. See www.iucnredlist.org.
5. See www.elysee.fr section "Archives."
6. See World Bank, *Global Development Finance, 2008*. We include in this the repayments to the IMF, which the World Bank enters in a separate category.
7. Authors' calculation. The World Bank and the various international institutions provide no precise data on repayment of the internal public debt.
8. Net transfer is the difference between the amount of loans received over a period of time and the amount of repayments over the same period. The net transfer is positive when the country or the continent concerned receives more than it repays in the form of debt servicing. It is negative if the amounts repaid are higher than the amounts entering the country.
9. For example, the figures of 1990 were used as a basis for calculation in 2000 to create a smokescreen, since the target is easier to achieve when one takes demographic and monetary evolution into account. If, for example,

the number of poor people remains stationary, the proportion of poor people decreases mechanically from year to year.

10. Unless otherwise indicated, quotations from the World Bank concerning this question are taken from this publication.

11. UNDP, *Human Development Report, 2006, Economica*, p. 5.

12. Thomas Pogge, "Un dollar par jour. Que savons-nous de la pauvreté dans le monde?" January 2006, www.mondialisations.org/php/public/art.php? id=22324&lan=FR.

13. See http://go.worldbank.org/MLVZFZTMS0.

14. FAO, bBriefing paper,"Hunger on the rise," www.fao.org/newsroom/common/ecg/1000923/fr/hungerfigs.pdf.

15. Ibid.; FAO, "Soaring prices add 75 million people to global hunger rolls," press release, September 18, 2008.

16. FAO, *The State of Food and Agriculture* 2007, www.fao.org/docrep/010/a1200e/a1200e00.htm.

17. UNESCO, *Education for All, Global Monitoring Report, 2006,* http://unesdoc.unesco.org/images/0014/001416/141639e.pdf. Unless otherwise indicated, the quotations from UNESCO on this question are taken from this publication.

18. UN Millennium Project, Overview 2005: *Investing in Development: A Practical Plan to Achieve the Millennium Development Goals,* directed by Jeffrey Sachs, www.unmillenniumproject.org/reports/index_overview.htm. Unless otherwise indicated, the quotations concerning this question are taken from this publication.

19. UNESCO has systematically been marginalized by the World Bank and the U.S. government. The United States withdrew from UNESCO between 1984 and 2003 to protest against the directions being taken by this organization.

20. UNDP, *Human Development Report, 2002.*

21. Jeffrey Trewhitt, spokesman for IFPMA (International Federation of Pharmaceutical Manufacturers), denounced these South African laws as creating "a very, very bad precedent that could undermine the legitimate protection given by patents in the world. We can expect to see this potential danger spreading to a lot of developing countries." Quoted by Mike McKee, "Tripping Over Trips," *IP Magazine* (September 1999); www.ipmag.com. For a more detailed presentation of the context of this complaint, see Martine Bulard, "Les firmes pharmaceutiques organizent l'apartheid sanitaire," *Le Monde diplomatique,* January 2000.

22. At the time, Al Gore was U.S. vice president under President Bill Clinton. In 2000 he was the Democratic nominee for president in the U.S. presidential election but ultimately lost to George W. Bush. A few years later, Al Gore repositioned himself as an advocate of climate protection.

23. See Julie Castro and Damien Millet, "Malaria and Structural Adjustment: Proof by Contradiction," in Christophe Boëte, *Genetically Modified*

Mosquitoes for Malaria Control (Eurekah/Landes Bioscience, 2005).

24. See www.who.int/mediacentre/factsheets/fs094/fr/ et www.rollback-malaria.org.

25. However, the nature of the insecticide is itself problematic, since it can cause irritation to the eyes and skin. For this reason installation of the mosquito nets is limited. Moreover, the product evaporates over time and the nets are seldom retreated.

26. UN, *Millennium Development Goals Report, 2007*, www.un.org/millenniumgoals/reports.shtml. Unless otherwise indicated, the quotations from the UN on this question are taken from this publication.

27. FAO, *The State of World Fisheries and Aquaculture 2006*, www.fao.org/docrep/009/a0699e/a0699e00.htm.

28. FAO, *State of the World's Forests 2007*, www.fao.org/docrep/009/a0773e/a0773e00.htm.

29. See Éric Toussaint, *Your Money [or] Your Life: The Tyranny of Global Finance* (Mumbai: Vikas Adhyayan Kendra, 2006), p. 374. See also the succinct presentation of the use of the debt weapon by the World Bank to impose water privatization in Bolivia, in Éric Toussaint, *The World Bank, A Never-Ending Coup d'Etat: The Hidden Agenda of the Washington Consensus* (Mumbai: Vikas Adhyayan Kendra, 2006), p. 310. See also the work and proposals of the Assembly for a World Water Contract, www.acme-eau.org.

30. Mike Davis, *Planet of Slums* (New York: Verso Books, 2007).

31. Calculation made jointly by specialized UN agencies, namely, the World Bank, WHO, UNDP, UNESCO, UNFPA, UNICEF, and published in *Implementing the 20/20 Initiative: Achieving Universal Access to Basic Social Services*, 1998, www.unicef.org/ceecis/pub_implement2020_en.pdf. The organizations mentioned estimate that $80 billion is the additional sum to be devoted annually to the basic social services concerned, given that approximately $136 billion are currently devoted annually. The total annual amount to be guaranteed fluctuates between $206 billion and $216 billion.

32. Nevertheless, there are exceptions. In several countries, the internal debt, although expressed in national currency, is indexed on the dollar. Should the national currency be devalued, as was the case for Brazil in 2002, the internal debt automatically increases proportionately.

33. African Development Bank, Asian Development Bank, Inter-American Development Bank, European Investment Bank, and some twenty other international bodies.

34. Immediately after the Second World War, Washington implemented differentiated policies: giving to Western Europe (as well as to Turkey and South Korea) while lending to Africa, Latin America, and most Asian countries. See Éric Toussaint's explanation in *The World Bank*, chaps. 4 and 11.

35. Robert S. McNamara with Brian Vandemark, *In Retrospect: The Tragedy and Lessons of Vietnam* (New York: Random House, 1995).

36. Compare with the appointment of Paul Wolfowitz, mastermind of the wars in Iraq and Afghanistan in 2005, when Washington's political and military strategy proved a failure.

37. Paul Wolfowitz tried the same policy but failed dismally and was swept away by the 2007 scandal. See Damien Millet and Éric Toussaint, *Banque mondiale, du plomb dans l'aile*, www.cadtm.org/spip.php?article2660.

38. We cannot resist the urge to share some spicy gossip: on an official visit to Paris while still U.S. Secretary of Defense, McNamara had lunch with General de Gaulle's prime minister, Michel Debré. Afterward, the head-waiter found out that McNamara had taken the vermeil cutlery along. Madame Debré wrote to ask could he return it, which he did! After trade, war, and development—thieving! The incident was revealed by Bernard Debré, Michel Debré's son and French Minister for Cooperation from 1993 to 1995, in *Libération,* September 16, 2005.

39. See the *French National Assembly Finance Commission's Report on the Activities and Control of the IMF and the World Bank,* 2000.

40. Particularly regional development banks.

41. To become members of IBRD countries must first be members of the IMF.

42. See http://go.worldbank.org/J4OW7MGS80.

43. See World Bank, *Annual Report, 2007.*

44. Until November 1, 2008, this seat on the board was held by Belgium.

45. See, for instance, the threatened coalition between Belgium, the Netherlands, Switzerland, and Norway in June 2005, www.cadtm.org/spip.php?article1545 and www.cadtm.org/spip.php?article1546.

46. For a detailed analysis of U.S. influence within the World Bank, see Éric Toussaint, *The World Bank,* chaps. 5 to 9.

47. See http://go.worldbank.org/K40JW6O1P0.

48. John Perkins, *Confessions of an Economic Hit-Man* (San Francisco: Berrett-Koehler Publishers, 2004). See also his testimony in Philippe Diaz's documentary *The End of Poverty?,* www.cadtm.org/spip.php?article3175.

49. For a detailed analysis see Éric Toussaint, *Your Money or Your Life. The Tyranny of Global Finance,* (Chicago: Haymarket, 2005), chap. 16, "Argentina: The Tango of the Debt."

50. See Agir Ici-Survie, "Dossiers noirs de la politique africaine en France," *L'Harmattan* 13 (1999).

51. See *Jeune Afrique/L'Intelligent,* December 19, 2004.

52. *L'Humanité,* September 20, 2003.

53. See the CADTM pamphlet, "A qui profitent toutes les richesses du peuple congolais? Pour un audit de la dette congolaise," 2007, p. 15.

54. In constant dollars in 1985. See UNCTAD, *Commodity Yearbook,* 2003, http://r0.unctad.org/infocomm.

55. UNCTAD, *Economic Development in Africa. Commercial Results and Dependence on Commodities*, Geneva, 2003.

56. Ibid.

57. See chapter 12 of Toussaint, *The World Bank.*.

58. Two reasons for this halt: 1) Banks henceforth preferred to place their money in the United States and in the most industrialized countries that also increased interest rates; 2) banks began to fear that the money they were lending to the South would not be paid back due to the indebted countries' deteriorating situation in the Third World. But by stopping the loans, they actually provoked the crisis they had feared.

59. Nelson Rockefeller, *Report on the Americas* (Chicago: Quadrangle Books, 1969), p. 87, quoted in Cheryl Payer, *Lent and Lost. Foreign Credit and Third World Development* (London: Zed Books, 1991), p. 58.

60. *Banking,* November 1969, p. 45, quoted in Payer, *Lent and Lost,* p. 69.

61. See Task Force on International Development, "U.S. Foreign Assistance in the 1970s: A New Approach," Report to the President (Washington: Government Printing Office, 1970), p.10.

62. See Robert McNamara, *Cien países, dos mil millones de seres* (Madrid: Tecnos, 1973), p. 94.

63. Cited by Nicholas Stern and Francisco Ferreira, "The World Bank as 'Intellectual Actor,'" in D. Kapur, J. Lewis, R. Webb, eds., *The World Bank, Its First Half Century*, 1997, vol. 2 (1997) p. 558.

64. D. Kapur, J. Lewis, R. Webb, *The World Bank*, vol. 1. p. 598.

65. Ibid., p. 599.

66. This scenario, though closer to what actually happened, was still too optimistic.

67. Cited by Stern and Ferreira, "The World Bank as 'Intellectual Actor,'" p. 559.

68. José López Portillo was president from 1977 to 1982.

69. A. W. Clausen to His Excellency Jose López Portillo, president, United Mexican States, letter of March 19, 1982, in D. Kapur, J. Lewis, R. Webb, *The World Bank*, vol. 1, p. 603.

70. See www.house.gov/jec/imf/meltzer.pdf. The Meltzer Commission is a bipartite commission of the U.S. Congress, headed by Professor Allan Meltzer. Composed of 6 Republicans and 5 Democrats, it worked on the theme of international financial institutions and delivered a critical report in March 2000. After the serious Southeast Asian crisis in 1997–98, Congress was concerned by the frequency and cost of financial crises, pointing out the malfunctioning of certain multilateral institutions. The internal political context in the United States, with a Republican majority in Congress and a Democratic government led by Bill Clinton, played a role in Congress's decision to ask for a thorough reorganization of the Bretton Woods institutions, within which the U.S. Treasury has excessive influence.

71. Structural adjustment policies have their counterparts in the North, under

different appellations such as "austerity policies" or "financial stability criteria" as specified in the Maastricht Treaty. Also in the North, bailout plans for those organizations that made hazardous investments were very expensive for the populations: it took $200 billion to save the American saving and loans under the Reagan and Bush Sr. presidencies, and $18 billion to get the French Crédit Lyonnais back on its feet. Citizens of the North are not out of harm's way either. The private debt crisis that started in the United States in 2007, after the speculative bubble burst in the housing market, has already cost more public finances than the saving and loans bailout, and it's only the beginning. A similar crisis that shook Great Britain is the result of the fact that the public treasury fronted the bill for the nationalization of the Northern Rock bank. It's likely that similar events will take place in Ireland, Spain, and other countries. The struggle to erase the debt is thus not a battle between the North and the South, but an attempt to emancipate citizens, both North and South.

72. IMF, *Global Financial Stability Report,* April 2009, www.imf.org/external/pubs/ft/survey/so/2009/RES042109C.htm. For a detailed analysis of the subprime crisis, see Éric Toussaint, *Banque du Sud et nouvelle crise internationale* (CADTM-Syllepse, 2008), chap. 9.

73. World Bank, *Global Development Finance, 2008.*

74. AFP, "Rich Countries Criticize the IMF for Its Exaggerated Assessment of the Crisis," April 10, 2008.

75. See www.imf.org/external/np/exr/facts/finfac.htm.

76. The complete list of countries and their agreements can be found at: http://www.imf.org/external/np/exr/faq/contribution.htm.

77. See http://www.imf.org/external/np/tre/sdr/burden/2010/041210.htm.

78. Authors' emphasis.

79. See *Les Echos,* November 17, 2007, www.lesechos.fr/info/reperes/echosup20071117_05-les-subventions-agricoles.htm.

80. See, for instance, the excellent film by Stéphanie Black, *Life and Debt.*

81. Action of sowing land with cereals.

82. See *Libération,* June 24, 2006.

83. See World Bank, *Global Development Finance, 2008.*

84. See World Bank, *Migration and Development Brief,* July 5, 2008.

85. See Vincent Munié, "Bataille syndicale autour du rail sénégalais," *Le Monde diplomatique,* February 2007. See also www.cocidirail.info; and Survie, *Billets d'Afrique,* July–August 2007, www.survie-france.org.

86. See FAO, *Food Outlook, Global Market Analysis,* June 2008.

87. FAO, "FAO Director General responds to criticism by Senegalese President," May 15, 2008, www.fao.org/newsroom/en/news/2008/1000840/index.html.

88. See www.grain.org/articles/?id=39. GRAIN is a small international nonprofit organization that supports small farmers and social movements in their strug-

gles for community-controlled and biodiversity-based food systems.

89. The main institutional investors are the pension funds, insurance groups, and the banks; they have access to $60 trillion, which they place wherever they can get maximum remuneration. Also active are hedge funds, which can mobilize $1.5 trillion.

90. Note again the two-faced nature of this policy: the governments of the North do not shy away from subsidizing private industries and their agricultural producers, to ensure the development of the biofuel sector, whereas the World Bank, IMF, and WTO deny governments of the South the right to subsidize their local producers, whether it is in the sector of agriculture or industry.

91. See www.cadtm.org/spip.php?article3518.

92. "Secret Report: Biofuel Caused Food Crisis," *Guardian*, July 4, 2008, www.guardian.co.uk/environment/2008/jul/03/biofuels.renewableenergy.

93. OECD, "Economic Assessment of Biofuel Support Policies," July 16, 2008, www.oecd.org/dataoecd/20/14/41008804.pdf.

94. AFP, "OECD Issues Report Critical of Biofuels, Favors Moratorium," July 16, 2008.

95. IMF, press points for chap. 5 of *World Economic Outlook,* September 2006, www.imf.org/external/pubs/ft/weo/2006/02/pdf/c5sum.pdf.

96. AWP/AFX, press points for "Métaux de base/Revue hebdo: record du cuivre, aluminium en hausse," July 4, 2008.

97. Australia, Austria, Belgium, Canada, Denmark, Finland, France, Germany, Netherlands, Ireland, Italy, Japan, Norway, Russia, Spain, Sweden, Switzerland, United Kingdom, United States. Several other creditors can occasionally join them.

98. David Lawson, *Le Club de Paris. Sortir de l'engrenage de la dette* (L'Harmattan, 2004).

99. In principle; but more and more often these ODA credits are destined to support structural adjustment policies that prevent any real development. Quite the contrary, they generally maintain existing poverty, when they do not actually create it.

100. See www.clubdeparis.org/sections/principes-et-regles/principes/53-comparabilite-de.

101. He was only there a few months before becoming head of the French treasury at the end of 2005, and finally, after the election of Nicolas Sarkozy, a member of the French government as State Secretary for European Affairs.

102. For example, in August 1997, an IMF/World Bank report on Burkina Faso assumed a growth of export revenue of 8 percent per year for the period 2000 to 2019. In June 2000, after the disastrous cotton harvest, the IMF projections changed: the growth of export revenues was lowered to 7.6 percent per year from 2000 to 2007, then 5 percent from 2008 to 2018. After the price of cotton dropped by 35 percent in 2001, the IMF report published in 2003 showed that export revenue had actually gone down by

14 percent between 1998 and 2002. See Damien Millet, *L'Afrique sans dette* (CADTM/Syllepse), p. 175.

103. The corresponding technical term is "anatocism."

104. This text is based on the authors' article "Des créanciers unis, discrets et tout puissants," *Le Monde Diplomatique*, June 2006. See also the Paris Club website, www.clubdeparis.org.

105. The creditors were as wily as usual. Half of the $39 billion was in arrears since the first Gulf war. A financial embargo had prevented Saddam Hussein from making any payments on the debt and a large part of the canceled debt concerned these unpaid arrears.

106. See Damien Millet and Éric Toussaint, *Tsunami Aid or Debt Cancellation* (CADTM, 2005); www.cadtm.org/texte.php3?id_article=2306

107. Translation of email sent by Ramón Fernández, vice president of the Paris Club, April 7, 2006, to one of the authors. He is now one of Nicolas Sarkozy's advisors at Elysée Palace.

108. See www.guardian.co.uk/business/2005/apr/26/westafrica.debt; and *Courrier international*, April 27, 2005.

109. Survie, *Billets d'Afrique*, April 2007.

110. See Susan George, "Alternative Finances," *Le Monde diplomatique*, January 2007; http://mondediplo.com/2007/01/03economy.

111. See www.wto.org/english/docs_e/legal_e/legal_e.htm#finalact.

112. Its mandate concluded on September 1, 2009.

113. Argentina, Bolivia, Brazil, Chile, China, Cuba, Egypt, India, Indonesia, Mexico, Nigeria, Pakistan, Paraguay, Philippines, South Africa, Thailand, Tanzania, Venezuela, Zimbabwe.

114. The downside of China's success is an overexploitation of the Chinese workforce and a productivist model that destroys the environment and harms the population first and foremost.

115. The example of China does not contradict this argument: China holds a particular place in the world market because of its strong protections and considerable size of its internal market.

116. In June 2007, George W. Bush appointed him president of the World Bank.

117. See appendix for list of countries by region.

118. For China and Russia, the level of external debt compared to the economy is relatively low, especially since these two countries are overall creditors. For example, China holds more than $400 billion of the U.S. debt, having bought U.S. Treasury bonds.

119. It should be noted that the expression "long term" covers loans longer than one year and loans from the IMF, which are considered separately by the World Bank. Long-term debt is by far the greater part of the debt: $2.57 trillion of the $3.36 trillion of the total external debt of developing countries. It is the only type of debt for which the following data is available.

120. Mainly since the beginning of the 1980s.

121. For reasons of coherence we only report countries with a total population greater than 300,000.

122. See World Bank, *Global Development Finance, 2006*, p. 44.

123. See World Bank, *Global Development Finance, 2005*, p. 70.

124. See World Bank, *Global Development Finance, 2008*, chap. 3.

125. 1 USD = 1.61 Brazilian reals on August 10, 2008.

126. See Rodrigo Vieira de Ávila, " Brésil : La dette publique est toujours bien là," www.cadtm.org/spip.php?article3155; and "Brazilian public debt: who owes who," www.cadtm.org/spip.php?article3596.

127. In the 2005 debt reduction negotiations, the government mistakenly agreed to link the interest rate paid on the debt to inflation and to its GDP growth, with the result that the financial situation is becoming unsustainable again. See Eduardo Lucita, "Otra vez la deuda Argentina," www.cadtm.org/spip.php?article3517.

128. For an explanation of this type of operation, see Éric Toussaint, *Bank of the South: An Alternative to IMF-World Bank* (Mumbai: Vikas Adyayan Kendra, 2007), p. 23: www.cadtm.org/texte.php3?id_article=3293.

129. See World Bank, *Global Development Finance, 2006*, p. 154.

130. The ALBA treaty (the acronym means "dawn" in Spanish) signed by Venezuela, Cuba, Bolivia, and Nicaragua includes some barter agreements; for example, 20,000 Cuban doctors provide free health services to the Venezuelan population and 50,000 eye operations have been performed free of charge on Cuban soil in exchange for oil.

131. The date decided on when first brought before the Paris Club. In theory, loans granted after this date are not eligible for cancellation.

132. UNCTAD, *Economic Development in Africa. Debt Sustainability, Oasis or Mirage?*, 2004. In the rest of this chapter, UNCTAD quotations are from this publication.

133. Initially, there were forty-one countries, but Malawi has since replaced Nigeria. The Comoros were added shortly after.

134. See UNDP, *Human Development Report, 2002*.

135. Net present value (NPV) of debt is the total debt stock recalculated to take into account the fact that certain loans were contracted at a reduced rate. Lower than its face value, this NPV calculates the value the debt would have if all of it had been contracted at market rate while having the same impact on the finances of the country.

136. We should add that some very poor countries are very open and have a high level of annual exports. Despite considerable overindebtedness, their debt could be considered sustainable depending on the chosen criterion. To extend the initiative to these countries, another criterion was added: for countries having an export to GDP ratio over 30 percent and a fiscal revenues/GDP ratio over 15 percent (to ensure that the level of revenues mobi-

lized is satisfactory), the criterion selected for debt unsustainability is an NPV of debt to revenues ratio of over 250 percent. It was this criterion that allowed Mauritania, Senegal, and Ghana to be declared eligible for the HIPC initiative.

137. See www.clubdeparis.org.

138. This means that payments will be spread over twenty-four years, between the seventeenth and fortieth year. This suits governments who know that in sixteen years they will very likely no longer be in place.

139. It would top the $70 mark in August 2005 after Hurricane Katrina in the United States, reached $100 at the end of February 2008, and a record $145 in July 2008.

140. See *SIPRI Yearbook 2008*, http://yearbook2008.sipri.org.

141. See Joseph Stiglitz, *The Three Trillion Dollar War: The True Cost of the Iraq Conflict* (New York: W. W. Norton, 2008), p. 311. See also Stiglitz, "Le coût de la guerre en Irak," *La Croix*, March 18, 2008.

142. OECD press release, April 4, 2008.

143. See World Bank, *Global Development Finance, 2008*.

144. Authors' estimate based on World Bank, *Global Development Finance, 2008*.

145. Debt and Development, *Rapport 2003-2004: La dette face à la démocratie*, 2004; www.dette2000.org.

146. OECD, www.oecd.org/dataoecd/34/24/34732766.pdf.

147. UNCTAD, *Economic Development in Africa*.

148. *Financial Times*, title of editorial, April 12, 2005.

149. See Coordination Sud, "L'APD réelle de la France ou le gonflement statistique de l'aide française, Bilan 2001-2006," www.coordinationsud.org/IMG/pdf/Note_APD_francaise_-_Evolution_2001-2006.pdf.

150. See Assemblée nationale, *Rapport de la Commission des Finances, de l'Économie générale et du Plan sur le Projet de loi de finances pour 2008, Annexe n°4, Aide publique au développement et prêts à des États étrangers*, special rapporteur Henri Emmanuelli, October 11, 2007; www.assemblee-nationale.fr/13/budget/plf2008/b0276-a4.asp.

151. World Bank, *Global Development Finance, 2005*.

152. Robert McNamara, speech to the governors of the World Bank on September 30, 1968, quoted in Toussaint, *Your Money or Your Life. The Tyranny of Global Finance*.

153. See James Wolfensohn, "Help the poor by cutting red tape," *Daily Mirror* (Sri Lanka), February 26, 2003; www.dailymirror.lk/2003/02/26/opinion/3.html.

154. Assemblée nationale, *Rapport de la Commission des Finances*.

155. See OECD, Development Cooperation Directorate (DCD-DAC), Statistical Annex, *Development Cooperation Report, 2004*.

156. World Bank, *Global Development Finance, 2005*.

157. This position is based on the authors' article "Les faux-semblants de l'aide au développement," *Le Monde diplomatique*, July 2005.

158. See *Financial Times*, October 12, 2007.

159. The title of the French edition of the latest book of Muhammad Yunus, who also wrote *Creating a World Without Poverty. Social Business and the Future of Capitalism* (Public Affairs, 2007), is telling: *Towards a New Capitalism* (*Vers un nouveau capitalisme*). This book, from the publishing house Jean-Claude Lattès, begins with a tribute to Franck Riboud, the boss of Danone, with whom Muhammad Yunus has participated in business that he calls social business. On the back cover, we can read: "Can the power of capitalism contribute to the eradication of poverty and the reduction of inequalities? For many this seems impossible. But not for Muhammad Yunus."

160. Nicholas Stern, *Stern Review on the Economics of Climate Change*, October 2006. The following quotations are drawn from the conclusion of the Stern review; See www.hm-treasury.gov.uk/independent_reviews/stern_review_economics_climate_change/sternreview_index.cfm.

161. Lawrence Summers, Annual Assembly of the World Bank and the IMF, Bangkok, 1991; interview with Kirsten Garrett, "Background Briefing," Australian Broadcasting Company.

162. Lawrence Summers, "Summers on Sustainable Growth," letter in *The Economist*, May 30, 1992.

163. See Damien Millet and Éric Toussaint, *Tsunami Aid or Debt Cancellation* (Mumbai: Vikas Andyayan Kendra, 2005).

164. See interview in the magazine of Oxfam Solidarité, "Les changements climatiques, une injustice globale," *Globo*, 17 (March 2007). See also Cetri, "Changements climatiques: Impasses et perspectives," *Alternatives Sud* 13/2 (2006).

165. See Damien Millet and Olivier Ragueneau, "Dette écologique et dette financière," *L'Humanité*, January 19, 2008; www.humanite.fr/2008-01-19_Tribune-libre_Dette-ecologique-et-dette-financiere and www.cadtm.org/spip.php?article3035.

166. See "CO2 Emissions: A Piece of the Pie," *Science*, May 11, 2007.

167. See CDIAC, http://cdiac.ornl.gov.

168. UNCTAD, *Manual of Statistics 2006-7*, www.unctad.org.

169. Abraham Lincoln (1809–65), president of the United States from 1860, was an abolitionist against the slave trade.

170. Benito Juárez Garciá (1806–72) was a Mexican statesman of Amerindian origin. In 1861, elected to the presidency, he set up La Reforma, which was liberal and anticlerical. From 1863, he fought French intervention in Mexico and had the Emperor Maximilian shot in 1867.

171. Emiliano Zapata (1879–1919) was a Mexican revolutionary. This peasant leader led radical peasant struggles and in 1911, he helped to draw up a vast program of social changes, known as the Ayala Project. In 1914, as an

ally of Pancho Villa, he dominated the Mexican revolutionary scene and
occupied the Mexican capital. He was assassinated in 1919.

172. Pancho Villa (1878–1920) was a Mexican revolutionary who led the
Division del Norte (Northern Army). He was assassinated in 1920.

173. Lázaro Cárdenas (1895–1970), a general, was elected to the presidency in
December 1934.

174. See http://avalon.law.yale.edu/imt/partix.asp.

175. For a detailed analysis of the London Debt Agreement of 1953, see
Toussaint, *The World Bank*, chap. 4.

176. On December 27, 2006, the Argentine Supreme Court demanded that the
banks compensate those flouted savers.

177. See Eduardo Lucita, www.cadtm.org/spip.php?article3517.

178. See Hugo Ruiz Diaz, "La décision souveraine de déclarer la nullité de la
dette ou la décision de non paiement de la dette: un droit de l'État,"
www.cadtm.org/spip.php?article3520. See also Renaud Vivien's contribution at www.cadtm.org/spip.php?article3133.

179. As we explain further in Q53, we are not against all forms of borrowing, but
we support very stringent limits on borrowing.

180. See Michaël Roy, "S'enrichir sur le dos des plus pauvres !" *Le Courrier de
Genève*, December 23, 2000.

181. RFI, April 26, 2007, www.rfi.fr/actufr/articles/088/article_51334.asp.

182. Ashley Seager and James Lewis, "How 'vulture funds' are preying on the
globe's poorest countries," *Guardian,* October 22, 2007.

183. See "Le gouvernement congolais dénonce le harcèlement des 'fonds vau-
tours,'" *Panapress,* January 23, 2006.

184. See Voltaire.net, April 21, 2006, www.voltairenet.org/article138102.html.

185. In South Africa, migrants from neighboring countries were the target of real
pogroms in May 2008.

186. See the film *Memoria del Saqueo,* by Argentinean director Fernando
Solanas.

187. See Toussaint, *Your Money or Your Life.*

188. See Toussaint, *The World Bank,* chap. 3.

189. See ibid., chap. 2.

190. See CADTM, *Le droit international, un instrument de lutte?,*
CADTM/Syllepse, 2004; Frédéric Chauvreau, Damien Millet, *Dette
odieuse* (Odious debt), comic strip, CADTM/Syllepse, 2006.

191. This section is based on the CADTM document *L'Équateur à la croisée des
chemins* (Ecuador at the crossroads), www.cadtm.org/spip.php?arti-
cle2767.

192. See the full text in Spanish: www.cadtm.org/spip.php?article1398.

193. Summers was at the time chief economist and vice president of the World
Bank. He later became Secretary of the Treasury in Bill Clinton's government, before becoming the president of Harvard University, until June

2006. The extracts were published in *The Economist* (Februrary 8, 1992) and by *The Financial Times* (February 10, 1992) with the title "Save the Planet from Economists."

194. Millet and Toussaint, *Tsunami Aid or Debt Cancellation*.

195. See *Dimension 3*, bimonthly journal of the Belgian Cooperation, January–February 2008.

196. We consider in Q58 that measures should also be taken to deal with this public debt, which is mainly held by private financial institutions.

197. See www.banque-france.fr/fr/stat_conjoncture/zoneeuro/zoneeuro.htm.

198. They decided to sell 400 tons in April 2008 to help them get over the backlash from the crisis.

199. The states of the North know that the credits they hold for loans made mainly in the 1970s and 1980s would be worth a lot less than their nominal value were they to be sold on the money markets. That is why the public treasuries of the Paris Club member countries mark them down significantly. Thus the industrialized countries acknowledge that the value of the external debt is at most 25 percent of its nominal value. For example, the Belgian markdown is 75 percent for Vietnam, and over 90 percent for the Democratic Republic of Congo (formerly Zaire). The United States applies a 92 percent tax relief to those countries eligible for the HIPC initiative. France, for its part, does not apply any tax relief and contents itself on acting as if the debt will always be repaid—until the day when the debt is canceled once and for all! It should be noted that the private part contracted on the money markets is also significantly marked down, as we saw in regard to vulture funds.

200. See *SIPRI Yearbook 2008*, http://yearbook2008.sipri.org.

201. See www.infosud.org/spip/spip.php?article1256.

202. The principal of compound interest, that is, calculating interest on interest.

203. Authors' emphasis.

204. See the text of the final declaration: www.cadtm.org/spip.php?article3616. For a detailed argument in favor of the unilateral sovereign act from the international law viewpoint, see Hugo Ruiz Diaz Balbuena, "La décision souveraine de déclarer la nullité de la dette ou la décision de non paiement de la dette : un droit de l'État," www.cadtm.org/spip.php?article3520.

205. Referring to the investigations of special reporters, expert working groups, and the UN Secretary General.

206. Article 11, section 2. The declaration was adopted in September 2007. See http://iwgia.synkron.com/graphics/Synkron-Library/Documents/InternationalProcesses/DraftDeclaration/07-09-13Resolution textDeclaration.pdf.

207. Available at www.ml.com/media/100472.pdf.

208. *Étude sur le nouvel ordre économique international et la promotion des droits de l'Homme* (Study on the new international economic order and the promotion of human rights) E/CN.4/Sub.2/1983/24, par. 10.

209. Resolution 3281 (XXIX) of the GA of December 12, 1974.
210. See CETIM, *Quel développement? Quelle coopération internationale?* (What development? What international cooperation?), 2007.
211. Authors' emphasis.
212. For instance, Venezuela, a member of OPEC, signed agreements with some fifteen countries in South America and the Caribbean by which it can sell oil at a "friendly" price, much lower than that offered to the United States, Venezuela being one of its main suppliers.
213. Via Campesina, in Rafael Diaz-Salazar, *Justicia Global. Las alternativas de los movimientos del Foro de Porto Alegre* (Icaria editorial and Intermón Oxfam, 2002), pp. 87 and 90.
214. An offshore center or tax haven is a country or territory where certain taxes are levied at a low rate or not at all. A transaction taking place outside of such a territory can evade many of the ordinary controls and taxes since the transaction is considered, from a legal standpoint, to be taking place elsewhere.
215. See Article 322, quoted in Q53.
216. Article 8, section 1. The declaration was adopted by the UN General Assembly in resolution 41/128 on December 4, 1986. Authors' emphasis. The complete text is reproduced in Toussaint, *The World Bank*, pp. 286–92.
217. See the full declaration at www.unhchr.ch/html/menu3/b/74.htm.
218. See "Les Nations unies reconnaissent les droits des peuples indigènes,"*Le Monde*, September 14, 2007.
219. UN-CHR, E/CN.4/2001/56, January 18, 2001, p. 14.
220. For a detailed argument, see Toussaint, *The World Bank*, chaps. 22–24.
221. Quoted in *Les Echos*, November 28, 2007.
222. Ninth report on succession of states in respect of matters other than treaties, A/CN.4/301 and Add.l, p. 68.
223. CADTM, CETIM, AAJ, ATTAC Uruguay, COTMEC–AUDITORIA CIDADÃ DA DÍVIDA Brazil, Emmaüs International, Eurodad, Jubilee South and South Center have published a manual on how to organize audits, now translated into several languages. See *Let's Launch an Enquiry Into the Debt! A Manual on How to Organize Audits on Third World Debts*, www.cetim.ch/en/documents/dette-manuel-ang.pdf or www.cadtm.org/texte.php3?id_article=2296. See also Hugo Ruiz Diaz Balbuena and Éric Toussaint, in *Les Crimes de la dette* (CADTM-Syllepse, 2007), part 2, pp. 153–70.
224. Authors' emphasis.
225. For a presentation of the successive stages in the construction of the Bank of the South and the debates surrounding it, see Éric Toussaint, *Bank of the South. An Alternative to IMF-World Bank* (Mumbai: Vikas Adhyayan Kendra, 2007).

226. Susan George, *A Fate Worse than Debt* (Harmondsworth, UK: Penguin Books, 1988); *The Debt Boomerang: How Third World Debt Harms Us All* (Boulder, CO: Westview Press, 1992). Susan George is vice president of ATTAC France.

227. See Esther Vivas and CADTM, *En campagne contre la dette* (CADTM/Syllepse, 2008).

228. Only countries with at least 30,000 inhabitants are taken into account, which leaves out, for instance, the Tuvalu archipelago.

229. IMF, www.imf.org/external/np/exr/ib/2000/092300.htm.

Books from CADTM in English

ÉRIC TOUSSAINT

Globalisation: Reality, Resistance and Alternative,
Vikas Adhyayan Kendra, Mumbai, 2004

Your Money or Your life. The Tyranny of the Global Finance,
Haymarket, Chicago, 2005

Your Money or Our Life. The Tyranny of the Global Finance,
Vikas Adhyayan Kendra, Mumbai, 2005

The World Bank, a Never Ending Coup d'Etat,
Vikas Adhyayan Kendra, Mumbai, 2007

Bank of the South. An Alternative to IMF-World Bank,
Vikas Adhyayan Kendra, Mumbai, 2007

A Diagnosis of Emerging Global Crisis and Alternatives,
Vikas Adhyayan Kendra, Mumbai, 2007

DAMIEN MILLET AND ÉRIC TOUSSAINT

The Debt Scam. IMF, World Bank and Third World Debt,
Vikas Adhyayan Kendra, Mumbai, 2003

Who Owes Who ? 50 Questions about World Debt, 2004
University Press, Dhaka
White Lotus Co. Ltd, Bangkok
Fernwood Publishing Ltd, Nova Scotia
Books for Change, Bangalore
SIRD, Kuala Lumpur
David Philip, Cape Town
Zed Books, London

Tsunamis Aid or Debt Cancellation,
Vikas Adhyayan Kendra, Mumbai, 2005

CADTM

*Manifesto for Making Another World Possible. CADTM at the Heart
of Movements for Another World*,
Vikas Adhyayan Kendra, Mumbai, 2005